F# 4.0 Design Patterns

Learn how to apply functional F# design patterns to a huge
range of programming challenges, and discover a smart route
to building better applications

Gene Belitski

BIRMINGHAM - MUMBAI

F# 4.0 Design Patterns

Copyright © 2016 Packt Publishing

First published: November 2016

Production reference: 1251116

Published by Packt Publishing Ltd.
Livery Place
35 Livery Street
Birmingham
B3 2PB, UK.

ISBN 978-1-78588-472-6

www.packtpub.com

Credits

Author

Gene Belitski

Reviewers

Michael Newton

Commissioning Editor

Kunal Parikh

Acquisition Editor

Kirk D'costa

Content Development Editor

Priyanka Mehta

Technical Editors

Bhavin Savalia

Dhiraj Chandanshive

Copy Editor

Stuti Srivastava

Project Coordinator

Izzat Contractor

Proofreader

Safis Editing

Indexer

Rekha Nair

Graphics

Abhinash Sahu

Production Coordinator

Aparna Bhagat

About the Author

Gene Belitski is an accomplished professional software developer with a passion for functional programming. He is a proud representative of the fourth consecutive generation in a family of engineers.

In his professional career Gene was a member of the core development team at Multex.com, a start-up known for bringing Internet and PDF technologies to capital markets.

The author also spent a decade with Reuters, owning the application development for the collection and production of Reuters Consensus and Detail Estimates financial data consumed by quantitative hedge funds.

Currently with Jet.com Inc., Gene is enjoying hands-on development as a lead of the team building a line of business F# applications for their finance division.

He lives with his family on a rare tranquil backstreet of New York City between a park and a beach. In his spare time, Gene plays with code or reads books with his two feline sidekicks – the Turkish Angora siblings Cheri and Musya.

You can find Gene online on LinkedIn (`https://www.linkedin.com/in/genebelitski`) and StackOverflow (`http://stackoverflow.com/users/917053/gene-belitski`).

Gene occasionally blogs at `https://infsharpmajor.wordpress.com` and `https://tech.jet.com`. He is one of the founding members of F# Foundation (`http://fsharp.org/`)

Acknowledgements

This book wraps up a chain of events stretching along a period of almost two dozen years of my life. Behind all these events of various kinds and scopes were people whose valuable contributions and positive attitude allowed me to deliver. I want to use this opportunity and express my admiration for them.

Thanks to my Mom and Dad, who spotted my interest in math and computers early and provided a tremendous amount of love, understanding, and support needed for converting a kid's passion into a profession.

I am grateful to my closest friends, who caught me at the brink of an academic career failure and helped me make a fresh start as a computer software practitioner. Michael and Michael, I value your help and our friendship tremendously.

I am so thankful to my first U.S. employer for being there for me, for his empathy, generosity, and friendliness. Bill, you personify for me the best of the genuine American spirit. I'll never forget your helping hand.

Turning to the book's subject, I must admit that my fascination with F# was influenced to a great extent by the alliance with the amazing F# community. Folks, I admire your professional excellence, knowledge-sharing generosity, your brilliant OSS contributions, your vibrant attitude. You are the source of permanent inspiration.

Further, this book never would have happened without continuing support from Jet.com, the e-commerce company that I have the privilege to work for. I praise you, Purple People, for the engineering courage of putting F# at the cornerstone of Jet's technology, for the outstanding atmosphere of enthusiasm and thirst for knowledge, for the freedom to explore, for providing the necessary resources. Jet.com Technology is an exceptional workplace for software engineers to thrive. I hope that this book encourages more great folks to join us.

And finally, completing this book would never be possible without the support, sacrifice, patience and forgiveness that my family is continuously delivering my way. Thank you for everything, my dear, you are the best.

About the Reviewer

Michael Newton is a Developer, Architect, Trainer, and Consultant; Michael runs @mavnn Ltd. along with his wife, providing training and consultancy. If it relates to learning about or using anything that relates to .NET, functional programming, or build/infrastructure tooling, we can probably help you.

He blogs at `http://blog.mavnn.co.uk`, including tutorials, thoughts on software design, and write ups of many of the training sessions.

www.PacktPub.com

For support files and downloads related to your book, please visit www.PacktPub.com.

Did you know that Packt offers eBook versions of every book published, with PDF and ePub files available? You can upgrade to the eBook version at www.PacktPub.com and as a print book customer, you are entitled to a discount on the eBook copy. Get in touch with us at service@packtpub.com for more details.

At www.PacktPub.com, you can also read a collection of free technical articles, sign up for a range of free newsletters and receive exclusive discounts and offers on Packt books and eBooks.

https://www.packtpub.com/mapt

Get the most in-demand software skills with Mapt. Mapt gives you full access to all Packt books and video courses, as well as industry-leading tools to help you plan your personal development and advance your career.

Why subscribe?

- Fully searchable across every book published by Packt
- Copy and paste, print, and bookmark content
- On demand and accessible via a web browser

Table of Contents

Preface

Following design patterns is a well-known approach to writing better programs that captures and reuses the high-level abstractions that are common in many applications. This book will encourage you to develop an idiomatic F# coding skillset by fully embracing the functional-first F# paradigm. It will also help you harness this powerful instrument to write succinct, bug-free, and cross-platform code.

F# 4.0 Design Patterns will start off by helping you develop a functional way of thinking. We will show you how beneficial the functional-first paradigm is and how to use it to get the optimum results. The book will help you acquire the practical knowledge of the main functional design patterns, relationship of which with the traditional "Gang of Four" set is not straightforward.

We will take you through pattern matching, immutable data types, and sequences in F#. We will also uncover advanced functional patterns, look at polymorphic functions, see typical data crunching techniques, and learn adjusting code through augmentation and generalization. Lastly, we take a look at the advanced techniques to equip you with everything you may need to write flawless code. In addition, we will explore how the paradigm shift to functional-first affects the design principles and patterns of the object-oriented universe and wrap up the book with specifics of functional code troubleshooting.

By reading this book you will achieve the following goals:

- Acquire the practical knowledge to use the main functional design patterns
- Realign some imperative and object-oriented principles under the functional approach
- Develop your confidence in building and combining first-order and higher-order functions
- Learn how to use core language pattern matching effectively
- Learn how to use embedded algebraic data types in place of custom types for added effectiveness and code succinctness
- Navigate and use F# core libraries with ease by seeing patterns behind specific library functions
- Recognize and measure the difference in resource consumption between sequences and materialized data structures
- Master writing generic polymorphic code

What this book covers

Chapter 1, *Begin Thinking Functionally*, should help you in developing a manner of coding usually associated with the functional paradigm. It will equip you with the knowledge, the key concepts, and the target list of skills pertinent to the functional-first nature of F# programming language.

Chapter 2, *Dissecting F# Origins and Design*, will help you to find out the origins of F# contemporary design, how F# evolved, and what place it occupies in the .NET ecosystem.

Chapter 3, *Basic Functions*, helps you to acquire a firm foundation for idiomatic F# use. It gives you 360-degree review of the functional paradigm cornerstone, the notion of the function. You will be taught how to represent any solution as a assortment of functions plugged together with a handful of combinators. This chapter prepares you to absorb the main subject--the patterns of F# idiomatic use.

Chapter 4, *Basic Pattern Matching*, gives you a good grasp of the language mechanism that is put into at the core of the language to address any data transformations--F# pattern matching. The chapter covers basic pattern matching features leaving data decomposition and active patterns for the following chapters.

Chapter 5, *Algebraic Data Types*, shows you the patterns of using the F# standard algebraic data types (tuples, discriminated unions, and records) as a better alternative to developing custom types. It covers these types composition, equality, comparison, decomposition, and augmentation.

Chapter 6, *Sequences - The Core of Data Processing Patterns*, acquaints you with one of the most essential arrangements of functional programming, the sequences. Sequences lay in the foundation of few fundamental functional patterns, such as lazy evaluation, sequence generators, and sequences of indefinite lengths. This chapter also puts down a blueprint of data transformation patterns taxonomy.

Chapter 7, *Advanced Techniques: Functions Revisited*, builds upon already covered patterns of language use in functions, pattern matching, and sequences. It introduces readers to such F# patterns as recursion, folding, memoization, and continuation passing.

Chapter 8, *Data Crunching - Data Transformation Patterns*, continues to dig deeper into the data transformation patterns we began uncovering in relation to sequences. You are given a full taxonomy of polymorphic data transformation patterns captured by the F# 4.0 core library. Now you are fully prepared to blueprinting your designs with the help of highly optimized high quality library function compositions, mostly avoiding custom implementations.

Chapter 9, *More Data Crunching*, adds to the data transformation patterns defined by F# core library arrangement data queries with F# query expressions and data parsing with the help of type providers.

Chapter 10, *Type Augmentation and Generic Computations*, covers two F# usage patterns based on opposite type transformations--code generalization and code specialization. You will get a demonstration of the benefits that may be achieved through the application of these patterns.

Chapter 11, *F# Expert Techniques*, scratches the surface of really advanced F# patterns. We walk through the use of F# type providers, concurrent and reactive programming, and wrap up with metaprogramming.

Chapter 12, *F# and OOP Principles/Design Patterns*, correlates the book's vision of design patterns with those of the OOP paradigm. We will see that well-known OOP design principles and specific patterns may morph, diminish, or literally seize to be in the context of functional-first paradigm.

Chapter 13, *Troubleshooting Functional Code*, represents an important addendum to the main subject, showing how to develop following the explorative style, how the nature of problems with F# code development significantly shifts into compile-time from run-time, and how to address some typical issues.

What you need for this book

The most friendly development platform for the readers of this book is Visual Studio 2015 because some material, as the book's title indicate, is specific to F# v4.0 or above versions. If you already have Visual Studio 2015 Professional or above editions you are ready to go without any extra effort.

Otherwise you may install free Visual Studio 2015 Community edition from `https://www.visualstudio.com/vs/community/`.

For other options available for Windows platform please visit fsharp.org at: `http://fsharp.org/use/windows/`.

Somewhat limited set of book's code samples will also work under Linux and Mac. For correspondent installations instructions please visit `http://fsharp.org/use/linux/` and `http://fsharp.org/use/mac/`.

Requirements to the hardware are dictated by listed above versions of development environments.

Who this book is for

This book is for web programmers and .NET developers (C# developers and F# developers). So, if you have basic experience in F# programming and developing performance-critical applications, then this book is for you. For F# absolute beginners the comprehension curve would be rather steep, but preceding the book with one or more beginner courses from Learning F# (http://fsharp.org/learn.html) may make it more palatable.

Conventions

In this book, you will find a number of text styles that distinguish between different kinds of information. Here are some examples of these styles and an explanation of their meaning.

Elements of code such as language keywords, operators, expressions and value names are shown as follows: "In order to define recursive function `let` binding can be extended with modifier `rec`", "Literal "`$42`" is bound to value `total`"

A block of code is set as follows:

```
type OrderType = Sale | Refund
type Transaction = Transaction of OrderType * decimal
```

When we wish to draw your attention to a particular part of a code block, the relevant lines or items are set in bold:

```
// Imperative monolithic solution a-la C/C++
#load "HugeNumber.fs"
let number = hugeNumber.ToCharArray()
```

URLs are shown as https://jet.com.

Warnings or important notes appear in a box like this.

Tips and tricks appear like this.

New terms and **important words** are shown in bold. Words that you see on the screen, for example, in menus or dialog boxes, appear in the text like this: "Clicking the **Next** button moves you to the next screen."

Reader feedback

Feedback from our readers is always welcome. Let us know what you think about this book-what you liked or disliked. Reader feedback is important for us as it helps us develop titles that you will really get the most out of. To send us general feedback, simply e-mail `feedback@packtpub.com`, and mention the book's title in the subject of your message. If there is a topic that you have expertise in and you are interested in either writing or contributing to a book, see our author guide at `www.packtpub.com/authors`.

Customer support

Now that you are the proud owner of a Packt book, we have a number of things to help you to get the most from your purchase.

Downloading the example code

You can download the example code files for this book from your account at `http://www.packtpub.com`. If you purchased this book elsewhere, you can visit `http://www.packtpub.com/support` and register to have the files e-mailed directly to you.

You can download the code files by following these steps:

1. Log in or register to our website using your e-mail address and password.
2. Hover the mouse pointer on the **SUPPORT** tab at the top.
3. Click on **Code Downloads & Errata**.
4. Enter the name of the book in the **Search** box.
5. Select the book for which you're looking to download the code files.
6. Choose from the drop-down menu where you purchased this book from.
7. Click on **Code Download**.

Once the file is downloaded, please make sure that you unzip or extract the folder using the latest version of:

- WinRAR / 7-Zip for Windows
- Zipeg / iZip / UnRarX for Mac
- 7-Zip / PeaZip for Linux

The code bundle for the book is also hosted on GitHub at `https://github.com/PacktPubl ishing/Fsharp-4.0-Design-Patterns`. We also have other code bundles from our rich catalog of books and videos available at `https://github.com/PacktPublishing/`. Check them out!

Errata

Although we have taken every care to ensure the accuracy of our content, mistakes do happen. If you find a mistake in one of our books-maybe a mistake in the text or the code-we would be grateful if you could report this to us. By doing so, you can save other readers from frustration and help us improve subsequent versions of this book. If you find any errata, please report them by visiting `http://www.packtpub.com/submit-errata`, selecting your book, clicking on the **Errata Submission Form** link, and entering the details of your errata. Once your errata are verified, your submission will be accepted and the errata will be uploaded to our website or added to any list of existing errata under the **Errata** section of that title.

To view the previously submitted errata, go to `https://www.packtpub.com/books/conten t/support` and enter the name of the book in the search field. The required information will appear under the **Errata** section.

Piracy

Piracy of copyrighted material on the Internet is an ongoing problem across all media. At Packt, we take the protection of our copyright and licenses very seriously. If you come across any illegal copies of our works in any form on the Internet, please provide us with the location address or website name immediately so that we can pursue a remedy.

Please contact us at `copyright@packtpub.com` with a link to the suspected pirated material.

We appreciate your help in protecting our authors and our ability to bring you valuable content.

Questions

If you have a problem with any aspect of this book, you can contact us at `questions@packtpub.com`, and we will do our best to address the problem.

1
Begin Thinking Functionally

A man with a chainsaw enters a hardware shop and says to the assistant: "Two weeks ago, you told me this thing would allow me to chop down 30 trees in an hour. But I can only manage one tree. I want to return this for a refund". The assistant says "let me see" and starts the chainsaw. The visitor jumps back screaming "What's that noise?!"–An old joke

The joke opening my narrative is very relevant to the subject of this chapter: in order to achieve the benefits expected from the use of any tool, you should know how to use that tool the right way. Moreover, an advanced tool used in a wrong manner may be even less productive than the corresponding simple one used the right way. A hammer outperforms a microscope when it comes to nailing wooden boards together.

`Chapter 1`, *Begin Thinking Functionally*, should help you develop a manner of solving day-to-day software engineering problems that are usually associated with the functional paradigm. This means presenting the solution by verbs rather than nouns, avoiding the use of mutable entities to carry states, avoiding relying upon side-effects, and minimizing the amount of moving parts in the code.

In this chapter, we will cover the following topics:

- The multi-paradigm nature of F#
- A comparison of F# paradigms by solving the sample problem applying:
    - An imperative monolithic solution
    - An object-oriented solution
    - A functional solution
- Properties of the functional paradigm

I will wrap up this chapter with a list of key concepts to retain and recognize, as well as skills to reuse in your functional solutions.

Relationship between F# and programming paradigms

This chapter, as well as the other chapters, will teach you how to look at any given software problem from the functional paradigm angle. This view may differ significantly from paradigmatic views that you may have already developed while practising other programming approches. This assumption of the required paradigmatic shift is a much anticipated scenario, taking into consideration the factor of the programming language popularity of the so called **TIOBE Programming Community index** (http://www.tiobe.co m/tiobe_index?page=index), which can be considered an indicator of the popularity of programming languages.

At the time of this writing (February 2016):

- The winning Rank #1 of TIOBE index is held by the Java programming language, which is strongly associated with the object-oriented programming paradigm
- Rank #2 belongs to the C programming language, which can be considered representing as the traditional imperative procedural programming paradigm
- Programming languages associated with the functional programming paradigm make it into the TIOBE index ranks only for the rank range of 21 to 50, where F# carries modest Rank #36

Nevertheless, if you've managed to read upto this point, I can safely assume that your interest in F# is not driven by its mere popularity, which, in turn, is driven by factors that do not belong to the scope of this book. For me, the bearer of an advanced degree in applied math and computer science, engineering program code within the F# ecosystem carries these intangible aesthetic qualities similar to ones of exploring a beautiful solution of a math problem or from analyzing a great chess play.

Talking seriously, I personally value most of the functional paradigm benefits of the functional code readability and maintainability. The same qualities of a typical monolithic imperative C code might be quite poor. However, are these code qualities automatically granted for anyone who has grasped mere F# syntax? Certainly not.

In addition to learning the F# syntax, the preceding point means acquiring certain skills in order to use this programming language in an idiomatic manner. F# is a multi-paradigm programming language indeed. It allows programmers to entertain many programming paradigms. The functional manner of laying out the program code can be used side by side with the imperative monolithic programming manner, or an object-oriented approach may surface when interoperability with the environment is important . Nevertheless, F# makes a claim of being a functional-first programming language. This means that the congenial programming paradigm for F# is the functional one; the language will bring to the table most benefits if it's used in a functional manner, in which case:

> *"it empowers users and organizations to tackle complex computing problems with simple, maintainable and robust code"*–(http://fsharp.org/).

You may wonder what, exactly, idiomatic usage means and whether it will be possible to always use it. The best way of illustrating idiomatic F# use would be by performing a comparative study of correspondent coding examples. Let me take an arbitrary, simple problem and solve it by sticking to imperative, then to object-oriented, and finally, to functional paradigms. Then, I am going to compare solutions to highlight functional approach features. In order to make this comparison absolutely fair, the programming language of implementation in all three cases is going to be F#.

A sample problem to solve

I will use as a problem for the purpose the slightly amended version of Problem 8 of Project Euler (https://projecteuler.net/problem=8):

```
The four adjacent digits (9989) being highlighted in the 1000-digit numbers
that have the greatest product are as following:
9 x 9 x 8 x 9 = 5832.

73167176531330624919225119674426574742355349194934
96983520312774506326239578318016984801869478851843
85861560789112949495459501737958331952853208805511
12540698747158523863050715693290963295227443043557
66896648950445244523161731856403098711121722383113
62229893423380308135336276614282806444486645238749
30358907296290491560440772390713810515859307960866
70172427121883998797908792274921901699720888093776
65727333001053367881220235421809751254540594752243
52584907711670556013604839586446706324415722155397
53697817977846174064955149290862569321978468622482
83972241375657056057490261407972968652414535100474
82166370484403199890008895243450658541227588666881
16427171479924442928230863465674813919123162824586
17866458359124566529476545682848912883142607690042
24219022671055626321111093705442175069416589608408
07198403850962455444362981230987879972442842849909188
84580156166097919133875499200524063689912560717606
05886116467109405077541002256983155200055935729725
71636269561882670428252483600823257530420752963450
```

```
Find the five adjacent digits in the same 1000-digit number that has the
greatest product. What is the value of this product?
```

An imperative monolithic solution

Let me begin by approaching the solution in a straightforward monolithic imperative manner: convert the 1000-character string representing the number into a character array, and then convert it into a cycle across all 996 groups of the five adjacent digits, calculating the digit product of each group and maintaining the current maximum. The final value of the current maximum will be the solution; it's that simple.

In order to remove the input number from the way, let's put it into a separate source code file, HugeNumber.fs, pulled to the solution scripts with the F# #load directive. The F# source file HugeNumber.fs is shown as follows:

```
[<AutoOpen>]
module HugeNumber
let hugeNumber =
    "73167176531330624919225119674426574742355349194934\
    96983520312774506326239578318016984801869478851843\
    85861560789112949495459501737958331952853208805511\
    12540698747158523863050715693290963295227443043557\
    66896648950445244523161731856403098711121722383113\
    62229893423380308135336276614282806444486645238749\
    30358907296290491560440772390713810515859307960866\
    70172427121883998797908792274921901699720888093776\
    65727333001053367881220235421809751254540594752243\
    52584907711670556013604839586446706324415722155397\
    53697817977846174064955149290862569321978468622482\
    83972241375657056057490261407972968652414535100474\
    82166370484403199890008895243450658541227588666881\
    16427171479924442928230863465674813919123162824586\
    17866458359124566529476545682848912883142607690042\
    24219022671055626321111109370544217506941658960408\
    07198403850962455444362981230987879927244284909188\
    84580156166097919133875499200524063689912560717606\
    05886116467109405077541002256983155200055935729725\
    7136326956188267042825248360082325753042075296345 0"
```

This file is going to be used by all variants of the problem solutions.

Then, F# script `Ch1_1.fsx` implementing an imperative solution will look as follows:

```fsharp
// Imperative monolithic solution a-la C/C++
#load "HugeNumber.fs"
let number = hugeNumber.ToCharArray()
let mutable maxProduct = 0
let charZero = int('0')
for i in 0..995 do
  let mutable currentProduct = 1
  for j in 0..4 do
    currentProduct <- currentProduct * (int(number.[i + j]) -        charZero)
  if maxProduct < currentProduct then
    maxProduct <- currentProduct
printfn "%s %d" "Imperative solution:" maxProduct
```

The line `#load "HugeNumber.fs"` brings a `string` value `HugeNumber.hugeNumber` from the external code file `HugeNumber.fs` into the scope of this script.

The next line, `let number = hugeNumber.ToCharArray()` converts this `string` value into an array of 1000 individual characters, each representing a single digit.

The next line, `let mutable maxProduct = 0` introduces a mutable `int` value used to carry the running tally of a maximal product of five adjacent digits.

The following line `let charZero = int('0')` is just a helper value used for converting a character code of a digit into an actual `int` value in the range of 0 to 9. It represents integer 48 indeed, not 0 as some of you may expect. But given `char` values of decimal digits `'0'` to `'9'` all have adjacent values after being converted to `int`, the simple subtraction of `charZero` from the result of converting a `char` digit x into an `int` will yield exactly x as an integer. More details on this matter will be given as we proceed further in this chapter.

The following seven lines of F# code are the gist of implementation:

```fsharp
for i in 0..995 do
  let mutable currentProduct = 1
  for j in 0..4 do
    currentProduct <- currentProduct * (int(number.[i + j]) -        charZero)
  if maxProduct < currentProduct then
    maxProduct <- currentProduct
```

This part of the script performs the following actions:

- The outer numerical `for` loop traverses the number array from the leftmost to the rightmost chunk of the five adjacent character digits, keeping the sequential number of the chunk $(0, 1, 2, \ldots, 955)$ in the counter value `i`.
- The binding `let mutable currentProduct = 1` provides a mutable placeholder for the product of the current chunk's digits.
- The inner numerical `for` loop traverses a subarray of length 5, calculating `currentProduct` by multiplying the intermediary result by the `int` value of each digit having sequential number `j` using the expression `(int(number.[i + j]) - charZero)`. For example, if a current digit is 5, then `int('5') - int('0') = 5`.
- An `if` statement closing the outer loop ensures that `maxProduct` always contains the maximal product of already traversed chunks; hence, when the loop completes iterating, `maxProduct` contains the sought value.

Finally, the line `printfn "%s %d" "Imperative solution:" maxProduct` outputs the final result to the system console.

Running the script in its entirety with **F# Interactive (FSI)** yields the following solution:

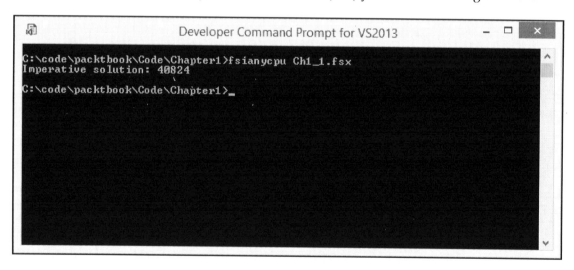

Running an imperative solution script in F# Interactive

There are a few points that I would like to accentuate prior to covering other approaches to solving the problem as follows:

- The solution represents detailed "how-to" instructions
- The solution has been expressed in terms of low-level computer notions, such as statements, loops, and global values
- Values change along the execution, representing the changing state
- The solution code does not look structured, it just flows

An object-oriented solution

Now let me turn to the object-oriented manner of solving the same problem. It is typical for this kind of approach to hide implementation details inside instances of custom classes and manipulate them with the help of their own methods. I will use for this purpose the F# `type` feature representing the concept of the .NET object type also known as **class** (https ://docs.microsoft.com/en-us/dotnet/articles/fsharp/language-reference/classe s). An object-oriented solution to the problem is present in the following code (script `Ch1_2.fsx`):

```
// Object-oriented solution a-la C# with Iterator pattern
#load "HugeNumber.fs"

open System
open System.Collections.Generic

type OfDigits(digits: char[]) =
    let mutable product = 1
    do
        if digits.Length > 9 then // (9 ** 10) > Int32.MaxValue
            raise <| ArgumentOutOfRangeException
              ("Constrained to max 9 digit numbers")
        let charZero = int '0' in
        for d in digits do
            product <- product * ((int d) - charZero)
        member this.Product
            with get() = product

type SequenceOfDigits(digits: string, itemLen: int) =
    let collection: OfDigits[] =
        Array.zeroCreate(digits.Length -itemLen + 1)
    do
      for i in 0 .. digits.Length - itemLen do
        collection.[i] <- OfDigits(digits.[i..
            (i+itemLen-1)].ToCharArray())
```

```
member this.GetEnumerator () =
    (collection :> IEnumerable<OfDigits>).GetEnumerator()

let mutable maxProduct = 1
for item in SequenceOfDigits(hugeNumber,5) do
    maxProduct <- max maxProduct item.Product

printfn "%s %d" "Object-oriented solution:" maxProduct
```

This solution is going to manipulate the objects of two classes. The first class named `OfDigits` represents the entity of the digit sequence, the product of which is the subject of our interest. An instance of `OfDigits` can be created from an array of a certain size of `char` elements carrying digits used as an argument to the `OfDigits` type constructor `OfDigits(digits: char[])`.

Upon its creation, each instance is associated with the `product` field representing the product of its digits. There is a reason for it not being possible to initialize `product` at once: in order to be representable as a positive integer value, the product can be constituted of nine digits or fewer (because the product of 10 or more 9 would exceed the maximum 32-bit `int` value 2147483647). In order to validate this, `product` is kept `mutable` and initially gets a value of 1 as given in the following line:

```
let mutable product = 1
```

Then, after the length validity check, the `OfDigits` constructor provides the genuine value to the field by performing the calculation:

```
let charZero = int '0' in
for d in digits do
  product <- product * ((int d) - charZero)
```

This value can be accessed via the instance property, `Product` as shown in the following line:

```
member this.Product with get() = product
```

The another class required to implement the object-oriented solution represents the entity taking a string of digits of arbitrary length and represents it as a generic collection of type `OfDigits`, allowing enumeration in order to traverse it and find a member with the maximum `Product` property.

For this purpose, the class named `SequenceOfDigits` has been equipped with a constructor parameterized by the digits string carrying the input number's digits and the `itemLen` length of individual `OfDigits` instance arguments. During the `SequenceOfDigits` instance construction, all `OfDigits` instances are created as elements of the collection field array. The `GetEnumerator()` instance method allows you to enumerate this array by upcasting to the `System.Collections.Generic.IEnumerable<OfDigits>` interface type and delegating the call to the `GetEnumerator()` method of the latter in the following instance method definition:

```
member this.GetEnumerator() =  (collection :>
IEnumerable<OfDigits>).GetEnumerator()
```

Having the preceding two classes at your disposal makes composing the solution of the original problem rather simple: you construct a `SequenceOfDigits` instance of five digit `OfDigits` elements off `hugeNumber` and traverse it with the help of the `for...in` cycle, maintaining the maximum product tally similarly to the imperative solution as shown in the following code:

```
let mutable maxProduct = 1
for item in SequenceOfDigits(hugeNumber,5)
   do  maxProduct <- max maxProduct item.Product
```

In the end, place the result on the system console. Running the script in its entirety with F# FSI yields the result of object-oriented solution as shown in the following screenshot:

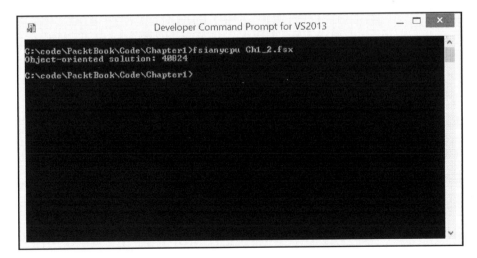

Running object-oriented solution script in F# Interactive

For those of you familiar with the object-oriented manner of approaching problem solutions, you may anticipate that the second solution rather differs from the first one:

- It is distinctively structured, with the segregation of definitions of pertinent classes from the usage of these classes
- Classes hide details of implementation, allowing usage only through exposed properties and methods
- The solution follows one of the well-known design patterns, namely the **iterator** pattern
- The amount of effort required for scaffolding substantially exceeds the effort required for the solution per se

A functional solution

Finally, let me turn to the solution manner that this book targets, namely, functional. Let's think of it as a series of data transformations. Let's look at it in a backward direction, from the sought solution back to the input string of digits as follows:

- The sought solution is the result of the `max` aggregate function application to the sequence of all products of five digit sequences.
- The sequence of all five digit sequences products is the result of the function application that maps each five digit sequence instance from the sequence of such sequences to the reduce of five digit sequence digits to their product.
- The sequence of all five digit sequences can be produced from the sequence of all initial digits by applying the F# core library windowing function `Seq.windowed<'T>` to the latter. In other words, this means taking a copy sequence of the first five digits from the left-hand side, placing this sequence in the output, shifting to the right of the source sequence by one digit, taking the first five digit copy and putting them after the first group in the output, shifting to the right by one digit of the source again, taking the first five digits, and so on, until there is no more possibility of taking the first five digits from the source. The output sequence of sequences is the sought function application result.
- Finally, the sequence of all initial digits is simply the initial string split by single digits, each converted into correspondent `int` from 0 to 9.

Each preceding step describes what transformation I want to apply to the single input argument in order to get the single result. Each next step takes the result of the previous step and treats it as its own input.

Let me show you how I usually derive the working code from the data transformation sketch similar to the preceding one with the help of the **Read-Evaluate-Print-Loop (REPL)** mode provided by FSI and the shrinking task dimension. The process of sequential progress toward the solution is shown in *Fig.1.3*, where I gradually start adding transformation steps to reproduce the data transformation process sketched earlier for a string consisting of just 10 digits `"0918273645"` by following these steps:

1. The input string is piped forward with the F# operator of the same name **pipe-forward** `|>` as the second argument of `Seq.map string`. The result is the sequence of 10 strings, each representing a single digit.
2. The result of step 1 is piped forward with `|>` as the second argument of `Seq.map int`. Now, the result is also the sequence, but it is a sequence of 10 `int` numbers, each representing the single digit.
3. The result of step 2 is piped forward with `|>` as the second argument of `Seq.windowed 5`. The result is the sequence of six arrays, each representing five sequentially taken digits of the result of step 2, each time shifting the beginning of the sequence to the right by one position.
4. The result of step 3 is piped forward with `|>` as the second argument of `Seq.map (Seq.reduce (*))`. The first argument is the higher-order function `Seq.reduce` converting its argument, which is an array of five numbers to the product of these numbers with the help of the multiplication operator (*). The result of this transformation step is just six numbers, each representing the product of the elements of the corresponding digit array.

5. The result of step 5 is piped into the `Seq.max` aggregate function, which produces the sought maximal product that equals 2520 ($7 * 3 * 6 * 4 * 5$) w:

The incremental process of getting to the smaller problem solution with REPL

Now, after becoming pretty confident that the thought-out solution is good, I can combine the preceding steps 1 to 5 with just another F# **function composition** operator >>, which just glues the result of the function to the left as an argument of the function to the right into a very compact F# script provided in the file `Ch1_3.fsx` as follows:

```
#load "HugeNumber.fs"
hugeNumber |> (Seq.map (string >> int) >> Seq.windowed 5
>> Seq.map (Seq.reduce (*)) >> Seq.max
>> printfn "%s %d" "Functional solution:")
```

The only difference between the preceding complete problem solution code and the smaller problem solution that I was running through a few REPL steps is the input value dimension. The final code uses the same 1000 digit `hugeNumber` taken from the source file `HugeNumber.fs` in the same manner as the imperative and object-oriented solutions did previously.

Running the script in its entirety with FSI yields the functional solution result shown in the following figure:

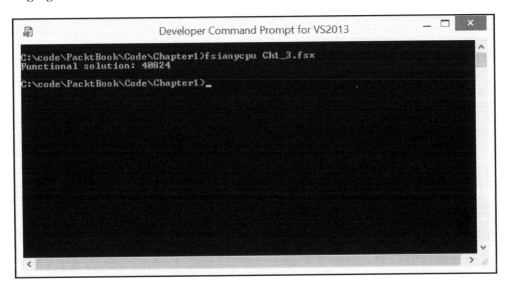

Running the functional solution script in F# Interactive

The code quality achieved by the functional solution, despite somewhat lengthy accompanying comments, is quite outstanding:

- It does not utilize even a single value carrying an intermediate state
- It contains just one arithmetic multiplication operator absolutely needed for product calculation
- It is extremely succinct
- It almost literally reflects the original "what to do" considerations
- It uses solely half a dozen core F# library functions combined in a certain way, and we may strongly believe that the implementations of these functions are error-free and performant

The preceding bullet points reflect pretty much all the properties typical for an idiomatic functional solution of a small-scale problem. Now I'm going to decipher these properties one by one.

Immutability of participating data entities

The positive qualities of the approach of not using mutable program entities are well known:

- Given the right state upon construction the immutable cannot be invalidated it during its whole lifetime
- Immutable entities are easy to test
- They do not require cloning or copy constructors
- Immutable entities are automatically thread-safe

I must note that F# is not 100% strict about using immutable entities. As you may have already noticed, I used values, changing the state in my imperative and object-oriented solutions earlier. But the language requires the programmer to make an extra effort to introduce a changeable state (with the `mutable` modifier to `let` binding or via `ref` cells, although F# 4.0 pretty much eliminates the need for the latter).

Also, the majority of data structures introduced by the language are also immutable, which means that a typical data transformation produces a new immutable instance of a data structure from the existing data structure. This consideration requires a certain caution from programmers when dealing with bulk in-memory instances, but as my experience has taught me, developers get used to this feature easily.

Thinking in verbs rather than nouns

Considering the process of data transformations in terms of verbs rather than nouns is very typical for a functional approach as functions are intuitively associated in our brains with actions, not objects. You may notice the single data item in the script `Ch1_3.fsx`, which is `hugeNumber`. The rest are few library functions combined in a certain manner, which transform the `hugeNumber` data item into a line of the console output. This manner of function combination allows persons reading this code to completely ignore intermediate results of the data transformations at each point where the operator >> occurs in the expression.

The less obvious corollary of this combination is the opportunity for the F# compiler to perform a so-called fusion or the manner of code optimization by merging together some adjacent data transformation steps. For example, when adjacent steps are fused together, the amount of data traversals may decrease.

"What" prevailing over "how"

This property of the functional solution mental process is easier to demonstrate with an example. I paraphrase here the great one from the early days of F# that's been used by several insiders previously. Imagine yourself in Starbucks for Caffè Americano.

The "how" approach would be to give detailed instructions such as:

1. Take a roasted coffee
2. Brew two espresso shots
3. Top them with hot water to produce a layer of crema
4. Put it into a cap of 12 oz size

The "what" approach would be to just ask "May I have a tall Caffè Americano?".

The second approach is evidently much more succinct and minimizes an opportunity of getting a result that deviates from the desired one. If you revisit now our three preceding solutions you should spot this property there.

Generalization over specialization

Another outstanding feature of the functional paradigm is generalization. By this, I mean preferring a general solution over a concrete one, when a concrete problem can be solved by applying a general solution that is accordingly parameterized. Let's turn to our sample problem for evidence of generalization. Adjusting the functional solution to a different length of digit sequences (for example, 8 instead of 5), another math operation on the group (for example, the sum instead of the product), another aggregation property (for example, minimum instead of maximum) are mere changes of parameter values for the correspondent functions. A comparison of how much the code changes will be required in case of the other approaches, which I leave for you as an exercise.

Minimizing moving parts over hiding them

This property is specifically related to a functional approach in comparison with an object-oriented one. Recall F# script file `Ch1_2.fsx`, which involved custom classes encapsulating details of implementation and exposing them outside the constructor, the iterator, and the aggregated property. In comparison with the object-oriented approach, the functional approach is flat and does not hide anything; it just combines some known parts.

Reduction to known parts over producing custom parts

One of the amazing properties of a functional paradigm differentiating it from the others is the limited need for producing custom parts at the level of manipulating data structures. Usually, functional programming newbies tend to implement their own functions for each case of data transformation. This infantile sickness normally ends with finding out from practice that pretty much any transformation upon typical data structures can be expressed as a combination of `filter`, `map`, and `fold` operations. I will devote a substantial amount of contents in relation to this phenomenon.

Lazy over eager data collections

Let me turn your attention to the comparison of memory consumption of the previously mentioned object-oriented and functional solutions. The object-oriented solution eagerly creates, materializes in computer memory the collection of 996 `OfDigits` objects; that is, its memory consumption is a linear function of the problem dimensions. In contrast to this approach, the functional solution does not require more than a single instance of `OfDigits` at any moment of the `max` aggregation, lazily producing the same 996 objects one by one according to the demand of the `max` aggregator function, hence having memory consumption that is constant and (almost) independent of the problem dimensions. This is a rather complex quality. If you imagine that the initial condition has suddenly changed and `hugeNumber` is really huge, then the object-oriented solution may become non-applicable due to the lack of required memory, while the functional solution, being agnostic to this factor, will continue to work. Generalizing this observation, the functional paradigm allows you to solve problems of a bigger scale, rather than taking other approaches by utilizing the lazy manner of data manipulation. The interesting corollary stemming from this approach is the technique of manipulating data sequences of unlimited length that do not require their complete materialization in the memory.

Summary

The following are the key concepts and the list of skills you should take away after finishing this chapter and strive for absorbing and mastering:

Avoid mutable state and achieve data transformations over immutable values and data structures. Think of programming solutions in terms of verbs rather than nouns. Avoid expressing a solution in highly detailed imperative "how" statements; use the "what to do" approach instead. Generalize: prefer a general parameterized solution to a concrete one. Strive to minimize the moving parts of your solution instead of hiding these moving parts into classes. Try expressing solutions by a few well-known facilities instead of delving into producing custom ones. When appropriate, prefer lazy data collections (sequences) over eager ones.

This process of mastering the functional manner of thinking may be framed around the following three Rs – **Retain, Recognize**, and **Reuse**. The sooner you learn to recognize idiomatic functional design patterns which I'm going to cover with a great amount of detail in this book and the sooner you reuse these patterns again and again in your day-to-day coding activities, the better functional programmer you will become.

In the upcoming chapters, I will walk you over the many idiomatic uses of F# in certain development situations. These repeated usages will represent genuine functional programming design patterns. Please keep in mind that many of these patterns only to a certain extent correlate with traditional **object-oriented design patterns** (https://en.wiki pedia.org/wiki/Design_Patterns), as well as other architecture design patterns of **software engineering** (http://www.amazon.com/Patterns-Enterprise-Application-Arc hitecture-Martin/dp/0321127420).

In the next chapter, I'll give you a 360-degree high-level view of the F# language features and parts with their origins and evolvement.

2

Dissecting F# Origins and Design

This chapter reviews F# features from the historical perspective tracking them back to origins where possible. The review covers:

- F# evolvement timeline
- Predecessor inherited language features
- .NET imposed language features
- Intrinsic F# language features

Although F# is a functional-first programming language, at the same time, you should not forget that it is a multi-paradigm tool that allows paradigms to be combined if required. Another important aspect you should keep in mind is that F# is designed for a .NET platform, so certain language facilities are shaped by underlying implementation mechanisms and interoperability requirements. The goal of this chapter is to dissect the language into components in a way that allows you to grasp the origins and the logic behind a contemporary F# design.

The evolvement of F#

Press began mentioning
(http://developers.slashdot.org/story/02/06/08/0324233/f—a-new-net-language) the
F# programming language in the Summer of 2002 as a research project at Microsoft
Research Cambridge (http://research.microsoft.com/en-us/labs/cambridge/) aiming
to create a dialect of **OCaml** language (https://ocaml.org/) running on top of the .NET
platform. Computer scientist Don Syme (http://research.microsoft.com/en-us/people
/dsyme/) was in charge of design and the first implementation.

Predecessors

The F# project of Microsoft Research Cambridge didn't come from scratch. F# belongs to ML
(https://en.wikipedia.org/wiki/ML_(programminglanguage)) programming language
family. It predecessors are Standard ML (https://en.wikipedia.org/wiki/Standard_ML)
and **OCaml**. Moreover, F# initially had a twin project at Microsoft Research Cambridge
named SML.NET, which aimed at bringing **Standard ML (SML)** to the .NET platform.

F# Version 1

The first release took place in December of 2004, labelled as a Microsoft Research project.
This means that at that time, it didn't have the status of a Microsoft product, although it was
providing integration with Visual Studio 2003 and Visual Studio 2005 Beta.

F# Version 1.1

Released in October 2005, this version is signified by bringing its object-oriented features to
the language. It represents the milestone where F# had turned into a genuinely multi-
paradigm language.

> *"The major addition to the F# language itself in this release is what we're calling the "F#
> Object and Encapsulation Extensions". This combines what I've found to be the best
> features of the .NET object oriented paradigm with the functional programming model that
> lies at the core of F#. This means that F# has become a mixed functional/imperative/object-
> oriented programming language."*
> *Don Syme* (http://blogs.msdn.com/b/dsyme/archive/2005/08/24/455403.aspx
>) *in his blog on August 23, 2005.*

Another feature that makes version 1.1 ponderous is introducing of F# Interactive, also known as FSI, the tool providing F# scripting capabilities and the manner of code development by frequenting REPL along the course. This release was suitable for use within the final version of Visual Studio 2005.

After the version 1.1 milestone, the language continued to have frequent releases and introduce new major features. On October 17, 2007, Microsoft Corp officially declared a transition of F# from research to product development organization, aiming to productize F# into another first class programming language on the .NET platform fully integrated into Visual Studio. Following another year of intensive work, in December 2008 came the announcement of F# to be shipped as the integral part of Visual Studio 2010.

F# Version 2

In February 2010, it was announced that the version of F# to be included into Visual Studio 2010 will be incremented to 2.0. Shortly afterwards, in April 2010, F# 2.0 was released, indeed, as part of Visual Studio 2010 and also as the matching installation for Visual Studio 2008 and standalone compiler for other platforms. The F# version 2.0 milestone reflects almost 5 years of F# 1.x evolvement, which has added to object-oriented facilities on top of its functional programming base such major language features as active patterns, sequence expressions, asynchronous and parallel computations, and significant library refinements. Also, it worth noting that integration with Visual Studio provided developers using F# on Microsoft platform with world class tooling such as, debugging, IntelliSense, and the project system. At this point, F# 2.0 is completely ready for enterprise software development.

Also, F# version 2.0 delineates the stage of language evolvement that is usually recognized as *full-fledged* F# in comparison with primordial versions that lack some core features.

F# Version 3

Another intensive year and a half of F# evolvement brought to life a preview version of F# 3.0 in the September of 2011. This version proclaimed targeting information-rich programming.

> *"A growing trend in both the theory and practice of programming is the interaction between programming and rich information spaces. From databases to web services to the semantic web to cloud-based data, the need to integrate programming with heterogeneous, connected, richly structured, streaming and evolving information sources is ever-increasing. Most modern applications incorporate one or more external information sources as integral components. Providing strongly typed access to these sources is a key*

consideration for strongly-typed programming languages, to insure low impedance mismatch in information access."Technical Report MSR-TR-2012-101 of Microsoft Research (http://research.microsoft.com/apps/pubs/?id=173076).

With this goal, the language acquires query expressions, an incredibly powerful mechanism of type providers along with numerous reference implementations of type providers for major enterprise information exchange technologies. It took another year for F# 3.0 to get released as part of Visual Studio 2012 in September 2012.

The following year, 2013, signified an explosive burst of activity around F#, indicating that the language reached some critical mass. Xamarin (https://xamarin.com) announced support for F#, reaching multiplatform mobile development, and multiple break-through developments took place in the fields of machine learning, cloud programming, finance time series, numeric libraries, and type providers.

This period also signifies strong cross-platform open engineering community effort, factually turning F# into an open source cross-platform shared implementation not fundamentally dependent on Microsoft anymore. The Microsoft affiliation with F# got limited to Visual F#, also known as *The F# Tools for Visual Studio*, and even in this space, Microsoft turned to enabling community contributions and open engineering.

F# Version 4

Announced in late 2014, F# 4.0 provided some new capabilities: type constructors were turned into first-class functions, mutable values could be captured by closures, and there were high-dimensional arrays, slicing syntax for lists, normalized collections in core run-time libraries, among others.

Getting you equipped with the vision of more than a dozen years of the language's exciting historical evolution, I now turn to the dissection of language features. In this chapter, these features are to be outlined only briefly, postponing the complete details of idiomatic usage to later chapters.

Predecessor inherited language features

F# inherits the core of the features associated with its functional-first nature from ML and OCaml. This means that its chief fashion of expressing computations is via the definition and application of functions.

F# functions are first-class entities

The ability to define and apply functions is a common feature of many programming languages. However, F# follows ML and other functional programming languages in treating functions similarly to, say, numeric values. The ways of treating functions in F# go well beyond the limits usually associated with stored-program computer concept:

- Functions can be used as arguments to other functions; the latter are higher-order functions in this case
- Functions can be returned from other functions
- Functions can be computed from other functions, for example, with the help of function composition operators
- Functions can be elements of structures usually associated with data

Functions are free of side effects

Computations with functions have the main form of *evaluating expressions* as opposed to *making assignments to variables*. Expressions do not carry the stigma of ever-changing values stored in rewritable memory. When the function `triple x` is applied to argument value 3, it evaluates some inner expression and returns 9. We are sure that this result is consistent, may be repeatedly reproduced, and may change from 9 only if the argument value changes from 3 to something else.

Functions can be curried and partially evaluated

Currying is a method of converting a function of many arguments evaluation into an equivalent evaluation of a sequence of functions of a single argument each. Partial evaluation binds one or more first arguments of a curried function, effectively producing a new function of fewer (non-bound) arguments.

Functions may be anonymous

Why bother giving a name to a function that is passed to a higher-order function or is returned from it? For the sake of succinctness F# allows using generic `fun` and `function` forms of function definitions that will not be invoked from elsewhere, hence the name is omitted.

Functions may be recursive

A frequently used example of recursive function (`https://en.wikipedia.org/wiki/Recursive_function`) implementation is a divide and conquer algorithm (`https://en.wikipedia.org/wiki/Divide_and_conquer_algorithms`) when a problem gets broken into a few of the same problems with less dimensions, so the same solving function can be applied. This breaking down continues until solutions get simple, and then smaller solutions are combined back to in the solution of the original size.

Functions may raise exceptions

Not every expression may always bring back a result value; the most beaten up example of such a situation is a number divided by zero. Another typical example would be invalid argument value that does not allow to return result. In such cases instead of returning the result an exception is to be thrown.

Functions may reference external values

The use of an external value freezes it in the function definition, creating a so called **closure**.

F# is a statically typed language

Expressions and their constituents carry unique types that can be inferred by the F# compiler. As a rule, no implicit type conversions have place ever. F# compiler type checks programs and catches errors that may otherwise occur at run-time for dynamically typed languages.

F# type inference provides type generalization

Type assignment algorithm performed by the compiler often allows the programmer to omit type declarations if the context unambiguously determines them. It finds most general type possible for value binding and expression evaluation.

F# supports parametric polymorphism

A function may allow a generic type of argument(s); for example, the implementation of a function calculating the sum of the list elements of `int`, or `int64`, or `bigint` may be the same.

F# inherits the variety of aggregate data structures from ML

Inherited data structures include the following:

- A tuple or values of the algebraic product type, allowing you to represent values of heterogeneous types
- A list or a finite sequence of zero or more values of the same type
- Discriminated union or a custom algebraic sum type defined via a mechanism similar to the ML data type, in particular, allows recursive type definition (for example, binary tree)
- The option to represent the absence or the presence of a value of a certain type
- A record that is like a tuple with components named rather than ordered
- An array, of course
- A sequence, which is implemented as extension of the data type with lazily evaluated value constructors in ML

F# supports pattern matching

Pattern matching is a powerful mechanism of data structure decomposition, allowing you to disassemble the data aggregate into components or define the processing depending on a particular structure/attributes of the data aggregate.

F# supports data references

Data references were introduced in ML in order to support mutable storage and, more broadly, imperative programming. F# inherits this feature for backward compatibility with ML without reservations. Values of the `ref` type allow you to achieve mutability, changing states and representing global variables.

Functions are non-recursive by default

F# follows OCaml in this respect, so recursive function binding should be labeled with the `rec` attribute. `let rec` immediately puts the name of the function into the scope shadowing the potential duplicate from the outer scope. In absence of `rec` attribute `let` puts the name of the function into the scope only after the body is fully defined, making the reference either unavailable within the function body, or in the worst case using an unintentionally shadowed outer one in place of the intended.

Modules

Following ML and OCaml, F# offers modules as a way of grouping together related values, functions, and types. Effectively modules resemble static classes of C# and provide developers with means of grouping together, maintaining, and extending related entities.

.NET-imposed language features

Along with the features inherited from the language predecessors, the multitude of F# features was brought into the language for the sake of interoperability with the .NET platform.

F# adheres to .NET Common Language Infrastructure

Run-time arrangement for the F# code has been defined by .NET **Common Language Infrastructure (CLI)** and does not anyhow differ from the same of C# or VB.NET. F# compiler ingests F# source code file(s) and produces the intermediate code in assembly language named MSIL packaged as binary .NET assembly(ies). During code execution stage MSIL is converted into machine code as needed, or **Just-in-time (JIT)**. Interoperability with other .NET languages is achieved as F#-produced assemblies do not anyhow differ from assemblies produced by C# or VB.NET. Similarly, the JIT compiler takes care of the target hardware platform providing portability. CLI also takes the burden of memory management on itself, making F# programs subject to .NET garbage collection.

F# has nominal type system

This is a significant deviation off OCaml and ML having a structural object system. Apparently, this design decision was dictated by the necessity to exist within and interact with the .NET object system, which is nominal.

F# fully embraces .NET object orientation

F# allows you to follow the object-oriented paradigm of .NET from both the direction of using the existing .NET frameworks and object-oriented libraries as well as the direction of contributing F# code in the form of .NET libraries, frameworks, and tools.

All F# entities are inherited from a single root type of `System.Object`, or `obj`. As such, they come with some common methods that are overridable and customizable. For custom F# entities such as discriminated unions, the compiler generates the implementation of these common `obj` methods.

In addition to the use of .NET classes, F# allows you to create your own custom classes consisting of *data* in the form of **fields** and *functions* manipulating these fields in the form of **methods** and **properties**. Special methods named **constructors** initialize instances of each class assigning certain values to fields. Classes may be further parameterized by type parameters getting generic this way. A class may inherit from the single **base class** and implement many **interfaces**. The subclass may modify the behavior of the base class by *overriding* its properties and methods. The custom classes are consumable from other tenants of .NET ecosystem.

F# requires calling the method of an explicit interface

F# differs from other .NET languages in this matter, so let me explain this with a short coding example as following (Ch2_2.fsx):

```
type IMyInterface =
    abstract member DoIt: unit -> unit
type MyImpl() =
    interface IMyInterface with
        member __.DoIt() = printfn "Did it!"
MyImpl().DoIt() // Error: member 'DoIt' is not defined

(MyImpl() :> IMyInterface).DoIt()

// ... but
let doit (doer: IMyInterface) =
    doer.DoIt()

doit (MyImpl())
```

The preceding MyImpl class implements the MyInterface interface. However, an attempt to use the implementation fails implicitly as if MyImpl does not have the method at all. Only after the explicit upcast of the MyImpl instance into MyInterface does the implementation get accessible.

The justification of this design decision that comes to my mind is this: it would disambiguate situations when there is a need for implementing more than one interface that has similarly named methods. Also, this matter gets less annoying if we consider typical interface use as in the preceding doit function that has the doer parameter of type IMyInterface. In this case, the compiler does the cast for using MyImpl in place of IMyInterface implicitly. The execution of the preceding script illustrates this subtlety in the following screenshot:

Object expressions

F# offers the way to implement an interface without bothering to create a custom type just for that purpose. The following code illustrates the implementation of IMyInterface from the preceding code with an object expression (https://msdn.microsoft.com/en-us/library/dd233237.aspx), followed by the implementation usage (Ch2_3.fsx):

```
// Define interface
type IMyInterface =
    abstract member DoIt: unit -> unit

// Implement interface...
let makeMyInterface() =
    {
        new IMyInterface with
```

```
            member ___.DoIt() = printfn "Did it!"
    }

//... and use it
makeMyInterface().DoIt()
makeMyInterface().DoIt()
```

Reflection

F# completely embraces .NET Reflection, allowing access to the metadata information of the program code at run-time. It is possible from F# as well as from other .NET languages to introspect the running application and get to type metadata and to attributes decorating the source code. The final goal of such exercises is usually to modify the run-time behavior of the already executing code. For example, the goal might be dynamically adding new components, or resolving dependencies.

F# core library contains the comprehensive tools for run-time analyzing and constructing F#-specific types and values within `Microsoft.FSharp.Reflection` namespace (`https://msdn.microsoft.com/en-us/visualfsharpdocs/conceptual/microsoft.fsharp.reflection-namespace-%5Bfsharp%5D`)

Extending classes and modules

F# allows a very unobtrusive way to extend classes and modules (`https://docs.microsoft.com/en-us/dotnet/articles/fsharp/language-reference/type-extensions`). The first form usually referred as **intrinsic extension** is similar to *partial classes* of C#. Unfortunately, in F#, this form of class augmentation cannot cross boundaries of the source file, namespace, or assembly.

The other form of extension, referred to as **optional extension**, goes through source files with ease. Its purpose clearly is augmenting any modules. Although much more widely applicable, this type of augmentation is not visible for reflection and cannot be utilized outside of F# from C# or VB.NET. We will take a close look at these augmentation methods later in the book.

Enumerations

Enumerations in F# (https://msdn.microsoft.com/en-us/library/dd233216.aspx) mimic C# enumerations, allowing you to create named numeric constants. As these are not discriminated unions, their use with pattern matching is limited. Also, they may be of use when manipulating combinations of binary flags.

Structures

Structures in F# (https://msdn.microsoft.com/en-us/library/dd233233.aspx) are lightweight classes represented with value types. As such, their instances can be put on the stack, they take less memory than reference types, and they may not be required to participate in garbage collection.

Events

F# events (https://msdn.microsoft.com/en-us/library/dd233189.aspx) allow interoperation with .NET events of CLI. However, F# goes further than CLI, providing powerful aggregation, filtering, and partitioning in observer-observable and publish-subscribe scenarios.

Nullable types

Nullable types (https://msdn.microsoft.com/en-us/library/dd233233.aspx) address null value related problems that normally do not exist in F# due to idiomatic option types usage. As a rule, in any internal scenario F# allows to cover absence of value with None case of correspondent option type. However, F# code interoperation with C# and VB.NET code as well as low-level database manipulations from F# when option types cannot be used may require using nullable types instead for expressing the absence of values.

Interoperation with the managed code

C# and VB.NET using F# code only can access public methods implemented in F#, leaving F#-specific data types or functions out of scope. Fortunately, the access in the opposite direction is easier as F# supersets C# and VB.NET features.

Interoperation with unmanaged code

When it comes to these infrequent cases of interoperation with legacy code or the use of libraries written in C/C++, F# follows C# using **P/Invoke** or **COM Interop**.

Intrinsic F# language features

Along with features inherited from F# predecessors, the F# language carries its own set of notable novel facilities. The outline of these facilities is discussed in the upcoming sections.

Indentation-aware syntax

Yes, this is correct; the F# compiler is sensitive to indentation in the source code (`https://msdn.microsoft.com/en-us/library/dd233191.aspx`), so correct code formatting is not just a matter of aesthetics. Why? Firstly, the improved code readability is enforced by the compiler, and secondly, this design choice dramatically decreases the amount of noise in the F# source code as block markers (such as curly brackets in C#) do not present, overall making the F# source code significantly shorter than the equivalent C# one.

Units of measure

This feature (`https://msdn.microsoft.com/en-us/library/dd233243.aspx`) allows you to decorate values with associated units and statically validate unit usage correctness by the compiler as well as infer units associated with the expression value based on units of operands. Let us look at the following example.

Here, I have defined two measures: <m> meters for distance and <s> seconds for time. Knowing how to find speed from acceleration and distance from physics, I defined a `fallSpeed` function to find the speed of objects falling from the given argument `height` at the time of hitting the ground as shown in the following code (`Ch2_1.fsx`):

```
[<Measure>] type <m> // meters
[<Measure>] type <s> // seconds
let fallSpeed (height: float<m>) =
  2.0 * height * 9.81<m/s^2> |> sqrt
```

Now using this function, it is easy to find that a water bottle that accidentally dropped from the top of the Empire State Building hit the pavement of 5th Avenue in New York City with a speed of 86.46 meters per second (`<m/s>`), hopefully not hurting a random bystander from the tourist crowd hanging out near the entrance. The following code represents the preceding example:

```
let empireStateBuilding = 381.0<m>
fallSpeed empireStateBuilding
```

Note that the compiler will not allow anything but float decorated with `<m>` as the argument for `fallSpeed`. Also, the function correctly infers that units of measure for the resulting speed are meters per second. Neat, right? But seriously, consider this CNN article back from 1999 titled *Metric mishap caused loss of NASA orbiter* (`http://www.cnn.com/TECH /space/9909/30/mars.metric.02/`). The $125 million loss of satellite would not occur if units of measure checks were in place. Unfortunately, NASA and Lockheed Martin software systems used for the satellite flight control were operating each in its own system of measures and integration tests failed to discover this defect prior to the actual flight beginning.

Overloaded operators

F# allows the overloading (`https://msdn.microsoft.com/en-us/library/dd233204.aspx`) of the existing operators as well as creating new unary and infix operators. It allows providing multiplicity of implementations for unary (prefix) and infix operations based on concrete types of operands. For example, an implementation of rational fractions arithmetic may use three versions of addition operation represented by infix operator + applicable to adding fraction to integer, integer to fraction, and fraction to fraction. Overloading has a positive side allowing to express semantic of manipulating objects of some domain tersely. But this feature is good in moderation as excessive overloading may be detrimental to code readability.

Inline Functions

Inline functions (`https://msdn.microsoft.com/en-us/library/dd548047.aspx`) represent a specific compilation technique. Normally a compiled function with non-generic type of arguments is associated with a single piece of MSIL and each function reference is compiled into invocation of this code and receiving back the evaluated result. However, it is impossible to have compiled MSIL for generic arguments within .NET type system. F# offers a smart workaround by statically evaluating arguments of each specific function invocation and creating MSIL adjusted for non-generic argument types of this particular function invocation. By following the outlined technique F# achieves function argument generalization under very limited support from .NET type system.

Type constraints and statically resolved type parameters

It is sufficient to have genuinely generic function type arguments in only very limited number of design and implementation situations . Usually, the addition of a custom combination of distinctive additional properties of the argument type is required in order to give the F# compiler a way of statically checking whether the type generalization is specific enough for the task. In most such cases, type inference is smart enough to derive such constraining from the static context, but sometimes, it may be desired that the developer provide some extra constraining. The process and further details of supplying the additional static constraints is described by the link: `https://msdn.microsoft.com/en-us/library/dd233203.aspx`. The book puts this matter under scrutiny in `Chapter 10`, *Type Augmentation and Generic Computations*.

Active Patterns

Active patterns (`https://msdn.microsoft.com/en-us/library/dd233248.aspx`) tremendously amplify the power of pattern matching by allowing the usage of custom functions within pattern matching rules. In other words, pattern matching can be specialized for any desired level of sophistication. Active patterns are absolutely essential for mastery over F#, and I will devote a lot of attention to them in the following chapters.

Computation Expressions

Computation expressions (`https://msdn.microsoft.com/en-us/library/dd233182.aspx`) represent quite an advanced topic. They provide tools for representation of complex nested computations sequenced and bound with simple looking syntax sugar. Some of F# language's very own features are implemented with the help of computation expressions, namely sequence expressions, query expressions, and asynchronous computations. F# also allows you to write custom computation expressions, providing tremendous extensibility power.

Query Expressions

Query expressions (`https://msdn.microsoft.com/en-us/library/hh225374.aspx`) represent the language-provided form of computation expressions addressing language integrated queries, also known as LINQ in F#. They are a part of mechanics addressing the information rich programming I've mentioned earlier, allowing data consumed from the multiplicity of sources and in the multiplicity of forms to be manipulated uniformly. For example, data obtained off OData service, web service defined with WSDL, or SQL server can be transformed to a certain extent without taking into consideration the specifics of their origin.

Asynchronous workflows

Asynchronous workflows (`https://msdn.microsoft.com/en-us/library/dd233250.aspx`) in F# are presented, in a manner similar to query expressions, by a language-provided form of computation expressions, and they demonstrate the mechanism's power and universal nature. They allow you to execute asynchronous code against implicitly provided thread pool at a high level of abstraction from asynchronous computations' arrangement details. As a corollary, writing F# asynchronous code is almost as simple as synchronous code.

Meta-programming

Meta-programming (`https://msdn.microsoft.com/en-us/library/dd233212.aspx`) is an extremely powerful and exciting technique that allows programs to write other programs. It may take different forms and occur at different levels: at native machine-level code, at MSIL level, or even at the source code level of F# or another programming language. A few years ago, I was quite excited about this feature and blogged a short series on this matter: **F# Metaprogramming part 1: JIT Some Native Code on the Fly** (`https://infsharpmajor.wordpress.com/2012/03/04/how-hard-is-to-jit-some-native-code-from-f/`), **F# Metaprogramming part 2: Dynamic synthesis of executable F# code** (`https://infsharpmajor.wordpress.com/2012/04/01/how-to-dynamically-synthesize-executable-f-code-from-text/`), and **F# Metaprogramming part 3: Creating MSIL on the Fly** (`https://infsharpmajor.wordpress.com/2012/04/12/creating-msil-from-f-on-the-fly/`).

However, usually, when developers consider F# meta-programming, a different program level is involved, namely F#, but in a partially compiled form associated with the language feature known as **quoted expressions**. When the F# compiler comes across specifically delimited F# code, then instead of making this code part of the program, it compiles it into a special object representing the F# expression. The great power of this feature is that when compiled in this manner, F# expressions can be further transformed into the form that's good for execution in a completely different environment, for example, inside a web browser in the form of JavaScript or in some **Graphic Processing Unit (GPU)**, reaching, in principle, a vast amount of diverse computational platforms.

Type providers

Type providers (`https://msdn.microsoft.com/en-us/library/hh156509.aspx`) represent the meta-programming feature as well. However, instead of transforming some form of source code into executable form type providers does something completely different. A typical type provider represents a data source of certain kind as an assortment of types with their methods and properties ready to be seamlessly used exactly the same way as human-written types or libraries. It's worth noting that the provided types carry the same qualities as the hand-written ones. They can be statically checked, introspected by Intellisense, inferred by F# compiler.

For example, the SqlClient type provider (`http://fsprojects.github.io/FSharp.Data.SqlClient/`) allows F# developers to get type-safe access to the complete set of features of the Microsoft SQL server.

Another fantastically powerful use case for type providers is the interoperability between F# and other programming languages. One of the big successes in this field is F# R Type Provider (`http://bluemountaincapital.github.io/FSharpRProvider/`), allowing access from F# to a vast amount of R programming language libraries for statistical computing. Using F# in tandem with **R Type Provider** gave a big boost to using F# in the fields of machine learning and data science.

Summary

This chapter familiarized you with F# features dissected according to origins and design motives. You now better understand where the each language feature comes from, what features come from the ML breed, what language design decisions are dictated by the hosting .NET platform, what features of F# are unique, and what the causes for their inclusion into the language were.

Equipped with this knowledge, you are now ready to absorb the main contents. In the next chapter, I'll turn to the feature at the core of F#: functions and their uses.

3

Basic Functions

In this chapter, I'll cover the core element of the program code built with the functional paradigm, that is, **function**. The notion of a function is ubiquitous indeed. In the world around us, it may mean plenty of things, from purpose of something to dependency and to work in a certain manner. But here, I will consider it through the prism of computer programming, where a function generally means a method of computing results based on inputs. This examination is going to include the following:

- The notion of a function, the function definition and type signature, pure functions, referential transparency, and side effects
- Function parameters and arguments: a special type `unit`, the parameter number and type, the return value and type, currying, partial function application
- Higher-order functions, functions as arguments and return values, anonymous functions, functions as data type constituents, and functions as interfaces
- Closures, mutable values, and reference cells
- Type inference and inferred versus explicit types of function components
- Recursive function basics
- Operators as functions
- Composing functions and combinators

As my ultimate goal is to make you embrace the REPL-based development style and spirit inherent to idiomatic F#, I'm going to run each and every mentioned feature through FSI in order to demonstrate the cause and effect.

The notion of function in F#

Let's begin with an intuitive definition of a function that many of us heard in school algebra class: function is a relationship that for each valid input yields a single consistent result. Such definition is a good enough to reflect both the commonality and the difference of functions and relations. In mathematics, a function is a relation, although not each relation is a function, as a relation may represent multiple results for the same single input. In the following figure, relation **Rij** on the left side is just fine for the representation of a function, as any item from set **I** maps to the one and only one item of set **J**. However, relation **Rxy** on the right side of the same figure cannot represent a function as at least one item of **X** exists, which maps to more than one item of **Y**, which is indicated by red mapping arrows.

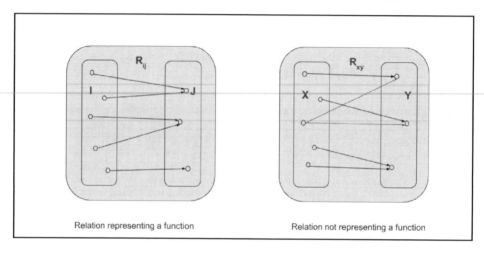

Relations and functions

Another very important matter is the mapping consistency. Any function, when being repeatedly given the same input must yield the same result.

Following our intuition, a function in programming languages, including F#, represents a computation where the result is determined by performing a transformation of a valid input. As with any concrete computation, it consumes some memory and certain time to complete and carries some kind of behavior. And the behavior, the way of the computation, and the manner of the transformation in turn is determined by the function definition.

The function definition

In general, the F# function carries a name, has a parameter(s), returns a result of some type, and has a body. The following figure illustrates the coupling of these components. A function resembles an opaque box performing some transformation of the input to the output. It hides the specific details of how the transformation is exactly performed, declaring only the purpose and the signature to the world, in other words, types of input and output. The function may be turned to a white transparent box if its definition is available, ripping the opaque box apart and revealing the details of implementation. However the definition may or may not be available; the latter case is typical for libraries and modules (remember the hiding of moving parts). I intentionally used input in place of parameter(s); I'll later show that functions of multiple parameters can be presented with functions of just a single parameter:

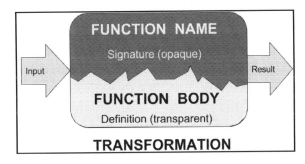

Function components and the purpose

These function components are fastened together in a language syntax by binding a function value as shown in the following pseudocode:

```
let function-name parameter-list [: return-type] = body-expression
```

The preceding binding is not the only way of defining functions in F#; it may carry a few additional elements for special cases. I'll cover these missing details later.

Using the preceding syntax, we may, for example, define the F# function for the computing of the area of a circle of the given radius, as shown in the following code (Ch3_1.fsx):

```
let circleArea radius = System.Math.PI * radius * radius
```

Here, `System.Math.PI` is a field of the .NET `System.Math` class representing the ratio of the circumference of a circle to its diameter.

Executing the function defined as such with the argument value `5.0` for the radius parameter in FSI yields the following result:

```
> circleArea 5.0;;
val it : float = 78.53981634
>
```

It is worth noting that F# does not introduce any keyword to return the function result. The result is just the value of the last expression calculated within the function.

The function type signature

Let's enter the sole name of the `circleArea` function into FSI, as shown in the following code:

```
> circleArea;;
val it : (float -> float) = <fun:it@7>
```

The FSI response represents the `circleArea` type signature, (`float -> float`), which means that it is a function that takes the argument of type `float` and returns the result of type `float`. This function type signature is very simple. As we dive deeper , we'll examine more complex examples of function signatures. I'll show you that reading and understanding them is an absolutely essential skill for a functional programmer.

Another detail that an attentive reader may have already spotted is this: how did the F# compiler jump to the conclusion that the type of `radius` is `float`? For now, just take my word that the compiler derived this following a deterministic procedure named `type inference`. It plays an outstanding role in decreasing the amount of bugs in the F# code and also attributes to code succinctness. F# implements a very specific manner of statically inferring types called **Hindley-Milner type inference algorithm** (https://en.wikipedia.org/wiki/Type_inference). I will devote substantial attention to the inferring of types later in the chapter.

Pure functions

A computer function implementation may or may not have this key property of the more abstract function notion: the consistency of repeatedly returning the same result when being given the same argument(s). The `circleArea` function defined previously, apparently carries this property. It does not depend on anything beyond its arguments and definition and does not change anything around beyond simply returning an idempotent result. Functions that have these useful properties are considered **pure**, or **referentially transparent** (`https://en.wikipedia.org/wiki/Referential_transparency`); otherwise, they depend on something or have side effects and are hence **impure**.

Let me demonstrate a simple impure function, in the following code (`Ch3_1.fsx`):

```
let opaque arg =
    System.DateTime.Now.Second * (if arg % 2 = 0 then 2 else 1)
```

Running the preceding code in FSI yields the following result:

```
> opaque 15;;
val it : int = 46
> opaque 15;;
val it : int = 49
> opaque 16;;
val it : int = 112
> opaque 16;;
val it : int = 6
```

So, the `opaque` impurity gets apparent from simply observing its subsequent calls with repeated arguments.

Function parameters and arguments

In our sample function definition given by the following code (`Ch3_1.fsx`):

```
let circleArea radius =
    System.Math.PI * radius * radius
```

The `radius` identifier represents the function **parameter**, that is, the name for a value that is expected to be transformed by the function. The value supplied for the parameter upon the function use represents the function **argument**, as shown when we apply our function in the following code line:

```
circleArea 15.0
```

`15.0` is the function's argument in the preceding line.

The tuples preview

At this point, in order to reveal the further details about function parameters, a certain notion would be required, which logically belongs to a completely different language facility, specifically to data types. I'm talking about **tuples**. As it doesn't seem feasible to build an ideally straight storyline, I will provide a necessary preview here and then revisit the subject of tuples in later chapters.

A **tuple** (`https://msdn.microsoft.com/en-us/library/dd233200.aspx`) is an immutable F# data type that represents a parenthesis enclosed, comma separated, ordered grouping of arbitrary values. That is, grouping assumes at least a pair of values. Types of these values are completely arbitrary, and it does not matter whether they are the same or not.

An example of a tuple is as follows:

```
let dateParts = (2016,"Feb",29)
```

The constituent value of a tuple can be represented by an expression as well, as shown in the following code:

```
let (perimeter,area) =
  (System.Math.PI * 2. * r, System.Math.PI * r * r)
```

I will wrap up this brief preview by covering what the tuple type signature looks like. It is built from types of constituents following the established order and separated by the `*` symbol. So following this arrangement, the type of tuple `dateParts` shown in the preceding code is `int*string*int`.

Special type unit

There is just another component of the functions realm, which comes from the distinction between computer programming functions and functions of mathematics. This is the special type with the sole purpose of denoting the absence of a parameter and/or result, namely `unit`. This type is the simplest imaginable and has just a single value, represented by just a pair of brackets that have nothing in between. The following is the representation:

```
()
```

Nevertheless, `unit` plays the important role of the absence indicator. This absence may manifest itself as shown in the following function definition, which can be a poor man's generator of random numbers between 0 and 1000 (`Ch3_1.fsx`):

```
let getNextRandom () = (%) System.DateTime.Now.Ticks 1000L
```

If you consider the preceding binding, then having `()` after `getNextRandom` is the only way to disambiguate the function binding that denotes the calculation process from just a value binding denoting the result of a single calculation.

Indeed, if I run both binding variants using FSI, the difference should be memorable: without a `unit` parameter, `getNextRandom` is bound to just an immutable `int64` value; otherwise, it is bound to a function that has the (`unit -> int64`) signature, and after being repeatedly called, it returns a different result each time. The following screenshot captures this distinction:

The argument unit differentiates between the value and function bindings

The similarly interesting case has place when unit is a value of expression returned from a function. Intuition should prompt you that if a function returns nothing, or rather (), then its purpose could be to induce a side effect. Let's slightly change the definition of getNextRandom as shown in the following code (Ch3_1.fsx):

```
let getNextRandom () =
  printfn "%d" ((%) System.DateTime.Now.Ticks 1000L)
```

Now, the function signature turns to (unit -> unit), and calling it, just outputs a random number between 0 and 999, returning the result of type unit.

Currying and partial function application

Let's define a simple function, myPrintFunC, which takes a string and an int as parameters and returns unit as shown in the following code:

```
let myPrintFunC header value = printfn "%s %d" header value
```

The type of myPrintFunC is (string -> int -> unit).

Another, almost similar, simple function is myPrintFunT, which also takes a string and an int as parameters and returns unit, but the parameters are tupled as shown in the following code:

```
let myPrintFunT (header,value) = printfn "%s %d" header value
```

The type of myPrintFunT is (string*int -> unit).

Applying myPrintFunC"The Answer is" 42 outputs The Answer is 42. Similarly, applying myPrintFunT ("The Answer is", 42) outputs The Answer is 42 too. So what's the fuss about?

The fundamental distinction is in the manner in which these functions accept their arguments: arguments of myPrintFunC are curried, but arguments of myPrintFunT are tupled.

Because of being familiar with tuples, you should not be surprised that let t = ("The Answer is", 42) in myPrintFunT outputs the same result: The Answer is 42. The signature of myPrintFunT prompted us of the single function parameter of the type string*int tuple.

The case of `myPrintFunC` is more interesting. The arrow `->` in its signature is the right associative operation, so I can rewrite its signature as (`string -> (int -> unit)`), correct? But wait a minute; isn't (`int -> unit`) representing a function that takes the `int` parameter and returns `unit`? Yes, it does. So, getting back to `myPrintFunC`, why can't I consider it as a function that takes the `string` parameter and returns a new interim function, in turn taking the `int` parameter and returning `unit`? In the end, functions are first-class entities in F#, so a returned value can be of the function type. Now let's turn back to the following code:

```
(myPrintFunC "The Answer is") 42
```

This still returns `The Answer is 42`. And in order to make the mechanics fully transparent, let's play the preceding transformation step by step in FSI:

Partial function application

As the preceding screenshot illustrates, the `myPrintFunC` function is originally defined as having two parameters. When it is applied just to the first argument, it returns another function, `interimFun`, which has just one parameter that, if in turn is applied to the second argument, returns exactly the same result as the original function applied to both arguments. As may be expected, the result is `The Answer is 42`; the fans of Douglas Adams already knew this.

My congratulations to you; you just grasped one of the utterly important techniques of functional programming, namely, **partial function application**. Partial application is achieved by simply omitting one or more trailing function arguments.

So, **currying** is built on the principle of partial function application. Any function definition of multiple parameters in a curried form is just a syntactic sugar for the process of currying, implicitly transforming the original definition to a composition of functions, each comprising one parameter. Currying is the default feature of F#; it makes partial function application available anytime.

The number and the type of function parameters and return values

I want to reiterate the earlier findings in relation to the F# functions parameters and return value in order to leave you with a very simple mental model, that is:

All F# functions have a single parameter and return a single result. Functions without parameters and/or without a return value fit this model using a `unit` value in place of the omitted entities.

Functions with multiple parameters and multiple return values may fit the preceding model by making the parameters and return values into a single tuple each.

Functions that have multiple parameters in a curried form fit the singular parameter model via a recurrent transformation into a function, taking the first argument and returning the new function that has this argument partially applied.

Further fine grain details to the preceding principle come from the .NET side, when we deal with not only pristine F# functions, but also with static and instance methods of .NET libraries and our custom types. These will be covered in later chapters.

Higher-order functions

I've mentioned on many occasions that functions are first-class entities in F# because they can be used as arguments for other functions or can be returned from other functions as results. This is exactly the indication of higher-order functions. A higher-order function may have another function as a parameter, it may return another function as a result, or it may perform both these things.

All functions are considered function values in F#; this treatment allows you to not make any distinction between functions and other kinds of values in any context where values are used. I will cover some such contexts here, namely an argument to another function, a value returned from a function, and a part of a data structure.

Anonymous functions

In some situations, it makes sense to have the ability of defining a function that does not carry the explicit name. Typically, such an ability is nice to have for functions that are the subject of manipulation by higher-order functions. A concise way to set arguments or results that does not involve a full blown function definition is required. Why is that? The first consideration that comes to my head is that the name may be needed for the future reference. If a function is defined by the name and then this name is referred multiple times from other locations of the program code, then this function that has a name makes perfect sense. On the contrary, if the function is defined as an argument of a higher-order function and is never used outside this single occurrence, then the name is redundant. Another consideration is the use of function values; for example, using a function as an argument to another function may not require any name for the former.

The syntax to define an anonymous function is as follows:

```
fun parameter-list -> expression
```

Here, `parameter-list` represents tupled or curried parameter names, optionally carrying explicit parameter types. Note that anonymous functions defined with the `fun` keyword represent a **lambda expression** (https://msdn.microsoft.com/en-us/library/dd233201.aspx). A lambda expression has the value represented by the anonymous function. Realizing this tidbit is important in order to understand the first-class treatment of functions in F#.

Functions as arguments

Functions as arguments is perhaps the most common use of functions in functional programs. Typical F# libraries are implemented as highly optimized sets of higher-order functions that can be tuned for any concrete task by providing specific functions as arguments. For example, a square scalar matrix 5 x 5 with main diagonal elements of 1s may be created using the `Array2D.init` library function. **Array2D.init** (https://msdn.microsoft.com/en-us/library/ee353720.aspx) is a higher-order function that has a signature of `(int->int->(int->int->'T)->'T[,])`, where the inner part of the signature represents the so-called **initializer** or the function that sets the individual elements of the matrix based on their indices. The following anonymous function for initializing the elements of a diagonal matrix according to their indices can be used:

```
fun x y -> if x = y then 1 else 0
```

The following screenshot demonstrates the achievement of this task in FSI by plugging the preceding function into the expression (Ch3_2.fsx) as follows:

```
Array2D.init 5 5 (fun x y -> if x = y then 1 else 0)
```

Observe the sought-for matrix being built and shown:

Using an anonymous function as an argument to a higher-order function

Functions as return values

As I mentioned in the function definition section, the function return value is just the value of the last expression. In order to return a function, we may use as the last expression of the host function: either an anonymous function definition, or a partial function application.

Let's look into this matter by performing a harder exercise. Quite frequently, it helps to have a function that allows you to accurately measure the duration of the execution of an arbitrary calculation wrapped into some other function. Furthermore, it is also helpful to have the information about the environment baked into measurement results.

So, I'm going to implement a higher-order function, stopWatchGenerator, which takes another function, f, with parameter, x, as its own arguments and returns a function value represented by an anonymous function with exactly the same signature. This anonymous function just wraps the calculation (f x) with this calculation duration measurement taken with millisecond precision. It communicates the measured duration to the output device, accompanying it with the name of the main executable file. So, for 32-bit FSI, it would be just [fsi]; for 64-bit FSI, it would be [fsiAnyCPU]; and for a custom executable, it would be the name of the executable file. Sometimes, such utility can be pretty helpful, right?

The implementation is given in the following code (Ch3_3.fsx):

```
let stopWatchGenerator (f:('a->'b)) (x: 'a) : (('a->'b)->'a->'b) =
  let whoRunsMe =
    System
    .Diagnostics
    .Process
    .GetCurrentProcess()
    .MainModule
    .FileName
    |> System.IO.Path.GetFileNameWithoutExtension
    |> sprintf "[%s]:" in
  fun f x ->
    let stopWatch = System.Diagnostics.Stopwatch() in
    try
      stopWatch.Start()
      f x
    finally
      printf "Took %dms in %s\n"
      stopWatch.ElapsedMilliseconds
      whoRunsMe

  let whatItTakes f x = (stopWatchGenerator f x) f x
```

Please note that I intentionally put explicit types for stopWatchGenerator arguments f, which is the function taking the argument of generic type 'a and returning the result of generic type 'b, and x, which is the value of type 'a, and for the stopWatchGenerator return type, which is the function taking two curried arguments of types ('a->'b) and 'a and returning the result of type 'b.

Does your head begin spinning yet? This is fine, please stay assured that you will get accustomed to these seemingly complicated manipulations and will soon find them as easy as apple pie.

The function `stopWatchGenerator` returns the sought anonymous function using the `fun` lambda expression, which creates the instance of .NET `System.Diagnostics.Stopwatch()` and wraps its start and take readings around the evaluation of the target expression (`f x`).

The function `whatItTakes` is just a convenient abbreviation for the arrangement with function evaluation shadow timing.

The following screenshot shows two examples of using the generated function:

A function returning another function in action

The first use case checks how much time is required in order to produce and add together the first 10 million positive numbers as shown in the following code:

```
> whatItTakes (fun x -> seq {1L .. x} |> Seq.sum) 10000000L;;
Took 242ms in [fsianycpu]:
val it : int64 = 50000005000000L
>
```

The second use case demonstrates a way of calculating the pi with certain precision by applying the **Gregory series** (`http://mathworld.wolfram.com/GregorySeries.html`) method, using an arbitrary series length as shown in the following code:

```
> whatItTakes (fun cutoff ->
  (Seq.initInfinite (fun k -> (if k%2 = 0 then - 1.0 else  1.0)/((float k)
* 2.0 - 1.0))
  |> Seq.skip 1
  |> Seq.take cutoff
  |> Seq.sum) * 4.0) 2000000;;
Took 361ms in [fsianycpu]:
val it : float = 3.141592154
>
```

As the results indicate, the Gregory series is not the greatest formula for the calculation of pi; nevertheless, it can serve the purpose of demonstrating the power of function values.

Functions as data type constituents

Now, you may come up with a crafty question: "Values of primitive types may be combined into more complex types; for example, a handful of `int` values can be stored in an `int` array. If functions are really first-class values, they should allow a similar kind of composition as well. How about constructing an array of functions?"

My answer is: "Sure, why not?" Let's consider the following function definition (`Ch3_4.fsx`):

```
let apply case arg =
  if case = 0 then
    sin arg
  elif case = 1 then
    cos arg
  elif case = 2 then
    asin arg
  elif case = 3 then
    acos arg
  else
    arg
```

The function `apply` takes two arguments, and if the first one, `case`, is in the range of 0 to 3, it applies the corresponding math library trigonometry function to the second argument, `arg`. Otherwise, it just returns the `arg` value unchanged, just a dull no-brainer implementation. Let's spice it up by arranging the functions into the array as shown in the following code:

```
let apply' case arg =
  try
    [|sin; cos; asin; acos|].[case] arg
  with
    | :?System.IndexOutOfRangeException -> arg
```

I've used the F# `try...with` construction in order to sift instances of case values that require the specific function application from those that return just the `arg` echo.

This is achieved with the `[|sin; cos; asin; acos|]` construction that has the (`float -> float`) `[]` signature. This means exactly what was expected, or an array of functions of the same type (taking the single argument of type `float` and returning a result of type `float`). Each array element position is tied with the specific function instance with the help of the `[case]` indexer, or `[|sin; cos; asin; acos|].[0]` yields `sin`, `[|sin; cos; asin; acos|].[1]` yields `cos`, and so on. The value of the `[|sin; cos; asin; acos|].[case]` expression is a function where the case value is in the valid range of 0 to 3. As such, it can be applied to `arg`, yielding the corresponding result. The `case` value out of the valid range entails the `System.IndexOutOfRangeException` exception and is caught and processed by simply returning the echoed value of `arg`. I must admit that abusing the exception mechanism the way it is done above is awful coding practice, but please forgive me for using it within the toy example while demonstrating some totally unrelated feature.

Functions are interfaces

In the light of the dual nature of F# being a functional-first language and at the same time supporting an object-oriented type system of .NET, it is worth taking a look at the relationship between functions and interfaces. The original **Gang of Four book** (http://www.informit.com/store/design-patterns-elements-of-reusable-object-oriented-9780201633610) points to the following principle of reusable object-oriented design in its introduction:

Program to an interface, not an implementation.

From this standpoint, a function is the quintessence of an interface. While in the object-oriented world, an interface must be explicitly declared prior to one of its implementations may be substituted by another, in the functional programming realm, this declaration is excessive. As long as two or more functions have the same signatures, they may be used interchangeably in the code. Function signature is the equivalent of the interface.

My previous example with the array of functions clearly demonstrates how the change of implementation can be achieved as simply as through changing the array element index value.

Closures

As I already mentioned, the function result depends on parameters. Is this dependency exhaustive? Certainly not. The function definition exists in a lexical context and is free to use some entities from this context in the course of the transformation of arguments into the result. Let's consider the following code example (Ch3_5.fsx):

```
let simpleClosure =
   let scope = "old lexical scope"
   let enclose () =
      sprintf "%s" scope
   let scope = "new lexical scope"
   sprintf "[%s][%s]" scope (enclose())
```

The preceding enclose() function does not have any parameters except unit. However, the result that's returned depends on the free value scope that was in the lexical scope at the time of the function definition. Let scope value be bound to the "old lexical scope" value. This value gets captured, "closed" by the enclose() definition. Together, the contextual part and the definition form the special entity named **closure**. This process is schematically presented in the following figure:

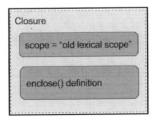

A sample of a closure

Because they're closed, the free values do not change. In the following sample, the value `scope` is later shadowed by the new value, `"new lexical scope"`. However, this does not change the value captured within the closure. This is reflected in the following figure, which shows the running of the last example in FSI, where both old and new scopes coexist:

A simple closure in action

Here, I provide another example of closure, demonstrating this time the capturing and updating of the state in the closure created by the anonymous function definition (`Ch3_5.fsx`):

```
let trackState seed =
  let state = ref seed in
  fun () -> incr state; (!state, seed)
```

In this snippet, the `trackState` function captures its own argument into a closure accompanied by the anonymous function, which increments the local counter hidden in this closure on each invocation. The upcoming figure illustrates two independent closures, `counter1()` and `counter2()`, created off separate `trackState` invocations with different seeds tracking their own state:

Closures representing objects

This sample highlights how closures can be used to represent inner fields even if the language does not really support objects. In this respect, as one of programming fables goes, **closures are a poor man's objects** (http://c2.com/cgi/wiki?ClosuresAndObjectsAreEquivalent) indeed.

Mutable values

In the spirit of the functional-first language, F# values are immutable by default. However, the language offers facilities for the use of mutable values.

Mutable variables can be created using the `let mutable` syntax of value binding and the `<-` assignment operator to mutate the earlier bound values. Mutable values bound with `let mutable` are stored on the stack.

Until F# v4.0, it was not allowed to write code capturing mutable values in closures, but beginning with the v4.0 version of the language, this limitation has been lifted.

Reference cells

An alternative facility for mutable values is reference cells inherited from OCaml. These values are allocated on the heap using the `let` binding with the special `ref` function. The underlying value of a reference cell is accessed with the help of dereference operator `!`. The referenced value can be mutated by the special assignment operator `:=`.

There is a subtle difference between mutable values and reference cells: mutable values are copied *by value* while reference cells are copied *by reference*. Let me offer you the code snippet illuminating this matter (`Ch3_6.fsx`):

```
let mutable x = "I'm x"
let mutable y = x
y <- "I'm y"
sprintf "%s|%s" x y

let rx = ref "I'm rx"
let ry = rx
ry := "I'm ry"
sprintf "%s|%s" !rx !ry
```

The following figure demonstrates by running the preceding code snippet in FSI how this difference manifests itself: mutable values x and y are independent, so changing y value from being identical to x value to something different does not anyhow affect x; their values stay different.

However, `rx` and `ry` reference the same object, so changing the underlying object via the `ry` reference simultaneously changes the previous object referenced by `rx` to the same one that `ry` references:

The difference between mutable and ref values

Type inference

I have already outlined type inference earlier in the chapter. It is a feature of F# (as well as many other languages: C#, to begin with) that stems from its property of being statically typed. By following the natural code flow direction from top to bottom and from left to right, the F# compiler is capable of deriving types of values present in the code, including function types. This ability, in turn, allows you to omit explicit type declarations from the F# code. In the end, the code can be written faster, is quite succinct, and if it compiles, is consistent type-wise.

Relying on type inference is not mandatory when writing the F# code. Adding an explicit declaration to the code may be especially meaningful in the following scenarios:

- When the types cannot be inferred and the compiler prompts for the explicit declaration
- If the code's author believes that providing explicit type declaration in some cases may simplify the code understanding and improve its readability

The most obvious way of inferring the value type is during binding based on the type of the expression to the right of the = sign as shown in the following code (Ch3_7.fsx):

```
let s = "I'm a string"
let dict =
  System.Collections.Generic.Dictionary<string, string list>()
```

For s, this is the type of literal on the right-hand side, or string. For dict, this is the Dictionary<string, string list> type of instance constructed on the right-hand side of the binding. In cases like the preceding one, adding explicit declarations of s and dict would just be adding unnecessary noise to the code.

Another rather obvious case is inferring a function signature based on its body definition in certain situations as shown in the following code (Ch3_7.fsx):

```
let gameOutcome isWin = "you " + if isWin then "win" else "loose"
```

Here, as isWin is used after if this fact allows the F# compiler to deduce its type as bool; the return type is apparently string, so the signature of the gameOutcome function can be inferred as (bool->string). Simple, right?

Not that simple case when type inference fails may be illustrated by the following (quite naive) snippet (Ch3_7.fsx):

```
let truncator limit s =
  if s.Length > limit then
    s.Substring(0, limit)
  else
    s
```

Here, the F# compiler complains about s.Length and s.Substring with the following message:

> *Lookup on object of indeterminate type based on information prior to this program point. A type annotation may be needed prior to this program point to constrain the type of the object. This may allow the lookup to be resolved.*

Changing the function definition to let truncator limit (s: string) = makes the F# compiler happy again.

Besides, if I would not be that naive and take at least some effort to check arguments for corner cases, as shown in the slightly enhanced definition in the following code (`Ch3_7.fsx`):

```
let truncator' limit s =
  if not (System.String.IsNullOrEmpty s) && s.Length > limit then
    s.Substring(0, limit)
  else
    s
```

Then, the compiler can infer a type of s as `string` from its use as the argument of the `System.String.IsNullOrEmpty` library function; the explicit type declaration is not required again.

Type inference gains more importance in the area of statically constrained generic types. Let's consider a slightly more loaded example of the `logAndTrash` function, which takes an ss disposable collection, scribbles each s item as a separate text line into .NET `StringBuilder`, disposes the collection, and returns the eventual `StringBuilder` value for later consumption elsewhere as shown in the following code (`Ch3_7.fsx`):

```
let logAndTrash ss =
  let log = System.Text.StringBuilder()
  for s in ss do
    sprintf "%A" s |> log.AppendLine |> ignore
  (ss :> System.IDisposable).Dispose()
  log
```

It is very nice of the F# compiler to infer a rather complicated signature of `logAndTrash` function that literally reads as follows:

```
'a -> System.Text.StringBuilder
  when 'a :> seq<'b> and 'a :> System.IDisposable
```

Or, in plain words, this is a function taking a value of generic type `'a` and returning an instance of `StringBuilder`, where `'a` must be a sequence of any generic type `'b` and at the same time be disposable.

Summing up the cases of type inference illustrated by the code examples given earlier I offer you the following take-away tip.

Types of values, functions, and generics with constraints in F# may be unambiguously inferred in many code contexts, including–but not limited to–literals, constructed instances, usage in certain expression parts, signatures of library or custom functions or methods.

Recursive function basics

In this chapter, I want to introduce you to the basics of recursive functions, leaving more detailed consideration for the more advanced contexts. At this point, I want to show how the F# default treatment of functions as non-recursive differs from a forced one when the function is explicitly declared recursive using the let binding modifier, rec.

Take a look at the following far-fetched snippet (Ch3_8.fsx):

```
let cutter s =
  let cut s =
    printfn "imitator cut: %s" s
  let cut (s: string) =
    if s.Length > 0 then
      printfn "real cut: %s" s
      cut s.[1..]
    else
      printfn "finished cutting"
  cut s
```

The cutter function here provides a non-empty string that's supposed to cut it from the left-hand side, symbol by symbol, until the argument is gone. Within the cutter body, there are two definitions of the cut internal function, of which the second definition apparently shadows the first. Also, it's important that within the second cut definition, it calls itself with the argument shortened from the left-hand side by one character, which is a clear case of **recursion** (https://en.wikipedia.org/wiki/Recursion).

The following screenshot shows the preceding code being fed to FSI and executed yielding some output:

Default non-recursive scoping of function definition

However, apparently, this code did not work as intended, as for the purpose of self-reference, the second instance of the `cut` definition is not lexically complete when `cut s.[1..]` occurs. The second `cut` definition did not shadow the first imitator instance of the `cut` definition, so the single output from the second (real) `cut` is followed by the single output from the imitator `cut`, and the computation is complete at this point. Oops, this is quite far from the intended output!

Things have changed dramatically in the following screenshot, where the second definition of cut is peppered with the rec modifier:

```
C:\VS2013>fsi

Microsoft (R) F# Interactive version 12.0.30815.0
Copyright (c) Microsoft Corporation. All Rights Reserved.

For help type #help;;

> let cutter s =
      let cut s =
          printfn "imitator cut: %s" s
      let rec cut (s: string) =
          if s.Length > 0 then
              printfn "real cut: %s" s
              cut s.[1..]
          else
              printfn "finished cutting"
      cut s
- cutter "wow!";;
real cut: wow!
real cut: ow!
real cut: w!
real cut: !
finished cutting

val cutter : s:string -> unit
val it : unit = ()

>
```

Forced recursive scoping of the function definition

Now, the second definition of cut immediately shadows the first one, allowing the second inner cut function to really call itself, which reflects the changed output; now, the implementation behaves as conceived: all performed cutting is real.

So, for now, you should be able to grasp that the rec modifier makes a function value available for referral immediately, without waiting until the function definition is lexically complete, thus enabling functions refer to themselves.

Operators as functions

What is an operator, thinking abstractly? It can be seen as a function of one or two arguments that just have a concise name represented by a single symbol or a very few symbols. F# heartily supports this abstraction. For example, take a look at the following expression:

```
(%) 10 3 = 10 % 3
```

Here, on the left-hand side of the equality sign (=), the (%) function is called with the arguments 10 and 3. On the right-hand side of the equality sign (=) just a 10 % 3 expression is present. Evaluating the whole expression in FSI shows its value as true because sub expressions on the left and right of the equality sign (=) are indeed identical.

Furthermore, the equality sign (=) itself is also an operator. Evaluating the equality sign (=) itself in FSI with the following expression (=);; will reveal the following function signature:

```
('a -> 'a -> bool) when 'a : equality
```

The preceding signature means that (=) is simply a function that takes two arguments of generic type 'a supporting equality and returns a bool value.

 For the description of F# core operators, refer to **Core.Operators Module (F#)** (https://msdn.microsoft.com/en-us/library/ee353754.aspx). Those of you who want to define your own operators, which is not a bad thing if done in moderation, I recommend **Operator Overloading (F#)** (https://msdn.microsoft.com/en-us/library/dd233204.aspx).

Function composition

Function composition is perhaps the most fundamental skill to be mastered by a functional programmer. However simple it may sound, this is about combining some functions into a more powerful combination. This may sound close to the higher-order functions I have covered earlier, and it is close indeed. Function composition is just concentrating upon building chains of function applications that allow more powerful data transformations from the bunch of less complicated ones.

Combinators

How exactly does the function composition take place if, by definition, the functions considered the basis for composition are just sort of black boxes that can only consume arguments and produce results? This is correct; functions, arguments, and the single operation of an application are all that's required for composition (remember minimizing the moving parts). Still, composition is performed by functions as well. The function that somehow applies just its parameters or values (some of them may be function values) in order to produce results without involving any external context is named **combinator**. There is an entire branch of applied math, that is, **Combinatory logic** (https://en.wikiped ia.org/wiki/Combinatory_logic) that is concerned, in particular, with the learning of combinators. This may take very capricious forms; those of you who want to delve deeper, I recommend that you Google the *idiot bird combinator* string and follow the links.

The id combinator

The simplest representative of combinators is id. Entering (id);; into FSI reveals this function signature ('a -> 'a). In other words, this combinator takes any value and simply returns it without any transformation.

Forward pipe |>

This combinator is the workhorse of idiomatic F#. Entering (|>);; into FSI reveals this function signature ('a -> ('a -> 'b) ->'b). In other words, this combinator applies its second argument, which is a function ('a -> 'b), to its first argument 'a, yielding the result 'b.

Also, it may seem that the order cannot be that important; however, it is important indeed. One of the factors involved is type inference, which works better for the piped function composition (remember left to right).

Backward pipe <|

Entering (<|);; into FSI reveals this function signature: (('a -> 'b) -> 'a -> 'b). In other words, this combinator applies its first argument ('a -> 'b) to the second 'a, yielding the result 'b. At first glance, this combinator may seem excessive. However, an important case when it becomes useful is in eliminating the need for parentheses around the argument and improving the readability of the code in the end.

Forward composition >>

This combinator composes functions together. Entering `(>>)` ; ; into FSI reveals this function signature `(('a -> 'b) -> ('b -> 'c) -> 'a -> 'c)`. In other words, having two functions and an argument, it applies the first function to the argument and the second function to the result of the first application.

Backward composition

This combinator composes functions together as well, but it does that differently. Entering `(<<)` ; ; into FSI reveals this function signature `(('a -> 'b) -> ('c -> 'a) -> 'c -> 'b)`. In other words, having two functions and an argument, it applies the second function to the argument and then the first function to the result of the first application. Sometimes, such an application order can be convenient for improved readability or other reasons.

Summary

I expect that this chapter moved your intuition in the direction of a handful of notions the functional-first nature of F# is based upon.

Recognizing and distilling these cornerstones from any relevant code context, you are now ready to absorb the main contents. In the next chapter, I'll turn to the cornerstone of F# programming techniques that is present in literally every data transformation, that is, *Pattern Matching*.

4

Basic Pattern Matching

This chapter continues the study of functional programming foundations that the previous chapter opened. It covers basic data pattern matching. Pattern matching is an essential feature-rich mechanism of powerful data processing that is embedded into the F# language's core.

A good grasp of the F# pattern matching features is an absolute must for an enterprise developer because most of the time, enterprise business is revolving around sophisticated data transformations in **Line Of Business (LOB) applications** (`https://blogs.msdn.micro soft.com/dragoman/2007/07/19/what-is-a-lob-application/`) and along **Extract Transform Load (ETL)** (`https://en.wikipedia.org/wiki/Extract,_transform,_load`) cycles in data warehousing and business analytics.

I intentionally narrowed down the subject of this chapter to basic pattern matching for a merely didactic reason. Usually, F# beginners first grasp pattern matching as an imperative switch on steroids or just a semantically equivalent way of coding lengthy `if...then...elif...elif... ...else...` expressions. Then, they begin to recognize the role of pattern matching in data structures decomposition. And finally, the pattern matching knowledge acquisition gets completed with embracing **active patterns**.

The goal of this chapter is to provide you with a thorough grasp of the pattern matching features associated with the F# `match` construction:

- The overall composition of this rather complicated language construction
- Tacit assumptions behind the parts of match (the ordering of matching rules and completeness of pattern cases, to name a few)
- Specific kinds of pattern cases and how to build composite cases

The decomposition abilities consideration is postponed until the coverage of the data structures in the upcoming chapters. Similarly, I will cope with **active patterns** when covering the advanced programming techniques of F#.

An explicit form of pattern matching with match construction

Explicit `match` construction in F# belongs to control flow elements, along with `if-then-else`, or `while-do`. Of other F# bits and pieces, a `match` is a relatively complicated combination of the following parts and governing rules:

```
match comparison-expression with
   | pattern-expression1 -> result-expression1
   .........................................
   | pattern-expressionN -> result-expressionN
```

It works in this manner, that is, `comparison-expression` is juxtaposed with each `pattern-expression` beginning with `pattern-expression1` and goes down the list until either the first match occurs, or passing `pattern-expressionN` still non-matched. If a match is found for `pattern-expressionX`, then the result of the entire construction is the result of `result-expressionX`. If no matches are found, then `MatchFailureException` is thrown, indicating that the match cases were incomplete.

The key points of pattern matching that are often missing by F# beginners on the first read are as follows:

- The `match` construction represents an expression, like any other F# construction excluding value binding. This means that the value of one and only one of `result-expressions` will be taken for the value of the entire construction (given that a certain matching has indeed taken place).
- Every `pattern-expression1` through `pattern-expressionN` must share the same type, which is also the same with the type of `comparison-expression` in order for the `match` construction to compile.
- Every `result-expression1` through `result-expressionN` must share the same type in order for the match construction to compile.

- Listed pattern to result cases are tried at run-time one after another in the top-down order. This arrangement prescribes a certain ordering of the cases from the standpoint of pattern commonality. More specific patterns must precede less specific ones; otherwise, more specific patterns will not have chances to be matched ever.
- The set of alternatives represented by all patterns must be exhaustive; otherwise, matching `comparison-expression` not covered by any of the patterns will cause `MatchFailureException`.
- More atomic pattern terms can be composed into broader pattern expressions using Boolean logic operators OR (`|`), AND (`&`), and a special `when` guard.

Now, I will walk you through the multiplicity of pattern kinds so that you get used to their broad repertoire and become comfortable with getting around `match` expressions.

Matching literals

One of the simplest cases of matching patterns is a pattern represented by a literal and assuming a simple `comparison-expression` value equality. Literals can be of any numeric, character, or string types. They can also be cases of a .NET enumeration (each such case is inherently a symbolic name alias of the integer value) or a value decorated with the `[<Literal>]` attribute.

In the following script, I can easily match `int` literals and the `int` value aliased as THREE, decorated with the `[<Literal>]` attribute (`Ch4_1.fsx`):

```
[<Literal>]
let THREE = 3

let transformA v =
  match v with
  | 1 ->"1"
  | 2 ->"2"
  | THREE ->"3"

transformA <| (1 + 2)
```

This yields string `"3"`, as expected. However, it wouldn't be possible to mix `int` literals with named `int` constant values from the following script (`Ch4_1.fsx`):

```
type Multiples =
  | Zero = 0
  | Five = 5

let transformB ``compare me`` =
  match ``compare me`` with
  | Multiples.Zero ->"0"
  | Multiples.Five ->"5"
Multiples.Five |> transformB
```

This yields string `"5"`, although being literals, `Multiples.Zero` and `Multiples.Five` are typed as members of the `Multiples` enumeration.

(Besides, if you did not grok this yet, placing almost any text between the doubled backticks, such as ` ``compare me`` ` above, makes this text a valid F# name and, when used in moderation, may add to improved code readability).

Wildcard matching

If I put the preceding scripts into Visual Studio, the F# source code editor will draw a blue warning squiggle line under the ` ``compare me`` ` comparison expression, indicating that the set of rules in this `match` construction is not exhaustive, as shown in the following screenshot:

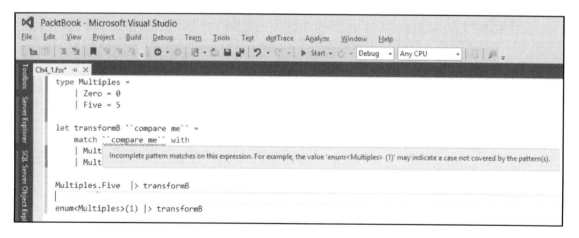

An example of an incomplete pattern matching

The compiler even gives a sample value of `` ``compare me`` ``, which is not going to match. Although this value is not present within the definition of type `Multiples`, if I synthetically create this value as `enum<Multiples>(1)` and feed it as an argument into `transformB`, the result would be the run-time exception of type `Microsoft.FSharp.Core.MatchFailureException`. This situation should raise the following question: how would it be possible to put a *match all* rule into the `match`, which means anything that was not specified in preceding rules?

For this purpose, F# offers the special **wildcard pattern** _ that matches anything that was not matched in the preceding rules. With its help and turning to the idiomatic F# way of processing undefined values by presenting the result as a value of type `option`, the function processing only legitimate `Multiples` values may be defined as shown in the following code (`Ch4_1.fsx`):

```
let transformB' m =
  match m with
  | Multiples.Zero -> Some "0"
  | Multiples.Five -> Some "5"
  | _ -> None
```

Now, the match within the `transformB'` definition carries the exhaustive set of match cases. Any legitimate value of `Multiples` given as `m` will be transformed into a correspondent `Somestring option` value, and any non-legitimate value of the `m` argument will be transformed into a `None` result.

Arranging matching rules

Wildcard pattern demonstrates the importance of arranging the match cases from more specific to less specific. For example, if I put the *match all* third rule with the wildcard pattern before the first two rules in the preceding script, then the F# compiler will put the blue squiggle line under explicit `Multiples` values, indicating that these rules will never be matched (check out `transformB''` definition in `Ch4_1.fsx`).

Named patterns

The F# compiler performs a certain analysis when a name (identifier) occurs in the position of a pattern case. Strictly speaking, there are some opportunities for the name to be as follows:

- A named literal (such as THREE in the earlier script)
- A case value of a discriminated union (such as None if matching an F# option)
- A type of an exception (such as System.ArgumentException if matching an exception type)
- A custom name of an active pattern (which will be covered in the upcoming chapters)

If the name occurrence does not fit any of the previously listed alternatives, the name is considered a **variable pattern** (https://msdn.microsoft.com/en-us/library/dd547125.aspx). It is treated similarly to the wildcard pattern, getting the value of comparison-expression parameter, which can be used in the corresponding result-expression. Sounds confusing, right? Then let's turn to a sample in order to make this matter clear.

I just took the definition of the transformA function from the matching literals section, changed the name of the function to transformA', and removed the definition of the THREE literal from the context (Ch4_2.fsx):

```
let transformA' v =
  match v with
  | 1 -> "1"
  | 2 -> "2"
  | THREE -> "3"
```

The results of experimenting with this function version are shown in the following screenshot.

```
                                        fsi                              _  □  ×

C:\VS2013>fsi

Microsoft (R) F# Interactive version 12.0.30815.0
Copyright (c) Microsoft Corporation. All Rights Reserved.

For help type #help;;

> let transformA' v =
-     match v with
-     | 1 -> "1"
-     | 2 -> "2"
-     | THREE -> "3";;

    | THREE -> "3";;
      ^^^^^
stdin(5,7): warning FS0049: Uppercase variable identifiers should not generally
be used in patterns, and may indicate a misspelt pattern name.

val transformA' : v:int -> string

> transformA' 50;;
val it : string = "3"
>
```

Turning of a literal pattern into a variable pattern

To begin with, the omission of the literal didn't blow up the script, producing just a benign warning that THREE might be a misspelled pattern name. Applying the function to the argument 50 that is completely off produces the same result as before for the legitimate argument value 3. What gives?

No magic here; in accordance with the description identifier, THREE was not recognized as a named literal, discriminated union case, exception type, or active pattern. This finding turned it into a variable pattern playing the role of a match-all pattern case, which result-expression just blindly outputs as string "3".

In my experience as an F# developer, I faced at least one occasion when this seemingly innocuous pattern type transformation typo turned into a nasty bug.

 The moral: handle with care, and do not disregard F# compiler warnings!

The as pattern

Interestingly, a pattern case may have the as clause appended to it. This clause binds the matched value to a name that may be used within the corresponding `result-expression` of the `match` construction or elsewhere within a local context of an outer `let` binding. The following script demonstrates how flexible the as pattern can be (`Ch4_3.fsx`):

```
let verifyGuid g =
  match System.Guid.TryParse g with
  | (true,_ as r) -> sprintf "%s is a genuine GUID %A" g (snd r)
  | (_,_ as r) -> sprintf "%s is a garbage GUID, defaults to %A"
                      g (snd r);;
```

In the first case, r is bound using as to the result of `TryParse`, which is the tuple, so the expression snd r yields the parsed GUID value.

In the second case, as bounds r to any tuple; however, it must be obvious from the match cases sequencing that this case matches the failed GUID parsing and the value of argument is a garbage.

The following screenshot reflects firing each of these using as binding match cases in FSI:

Pattern matching with as binding

Grouping patterns

Pattern match cases I've covered until this point can be composed together in a manner that resembles the terms of a Boolean expression with OR (|) and AND (&) operators. Let me demonstrate this technique by implementing a function that accepts two string arguments that represent keys and validates that both the given values are non-empty, providing a detailed diagnostics.

You should be able to grasp at this point why I should begin the matching with the most specific case when both the keys are empty. The next less specific match is represented by two symmetric cases when either the first or the second key is empty. Here, in order to demonstrate the flexibility provided by F# patterns grouping, I combine these two patterns with Boolean OR and at the same time capture key values into the local context with a variable pattern represented by the tuple (x,y). For the most generic leftover case, I know that both keys are not empty, so just a variable pattern is sufficient here. The sought function definition is as follows (Ch4_4.fsx):

```
open System

let validate keyA keyB =
  match (keyA,keyB) with
  | ("","") -> "both keys are empty"
  | (x,y) & (("",_) | (_,"")) ->
    sprintf "one key is empty: keyA = %s; keyB = %s" x y
  | _ & (x,y) ->
    sprintf "both keys aren't empty: keyA = %s; keyB = %s" x y
```

Although the boolean OR pattern combinator helps reach F# code succinctness by combining some cases that require the same transformation expression, boolean AND is not used that frequently for combining the pattern cases in regular pattern matching practice. However, it gets very relevant when grouping *active patterns*, which I will be covering in later chapters.

Guards

At this point, I believe you would agree that pattern matching is a powerful data transformation feature. Just to further amplify the facilities considered so far, F# offers enhancing pattern-expressions with additional matching logic. *Guard* is represented by an arbitrary boolean expression that is attached to pattern-expression using the when keyword. The guard kicks in only if its pattern-expression host has matched. Then, the guard expression is computed, and if true, it springs the transformation performed by the corresponding `result-expression` to the right. Otherwise, the entire rule is considered non matched, and the matching continues in an usual manner. The `when` guards can be mixed and matched within a `match` construction in a completely arbitrary manner.

To demonstrate `when` guards in action, let me slightly modify the previous example. In the case where both keys are not empty, there are two subcases: when the keys are equal to each other and when they are not. Furthermore, our function would be required to format the result for each of these cases differently.

All that is required for this modification is just one extra line of code preceding the last one (remember that I want to add a more specific match case, and then it must go in front of a more generic one). The code is as follows:

```
| (x,y) when x = y -> sprintf "both keys are not empty: keyA =    keyB =
%s" x
```

That's it for this modification. I encourage you to play with both scripts `Ch4_4.fsx` and `Ch4_5.fsx` in FSI by entering different arguments provided in the scripts and observing the changing function behavior.

The alternative syntax for anonymous function performing matching

F# offers a special syntax to define anonymous functions that perform matching, or **pattern matching functions** (`https://docs.microsoft.com/en-us/dotnet/articles/fsharp/language-reference/match-expressions`).

This syntax assumes that the anonymous function has a single parameter that is placed at the beginning of the function body in the invisible `match` construction. Having this alternative way of defining pattern matching anonymous functions just adds to the language succinctness and also better reflects the intent behind defining such kind of functions within the code.

Continuing with coding exercises, in the latest F# script I will rewrite the `validate` function using the alternative syntax. However, to achieve this, it is required that you address the following problem. The alternative syntax assumes that the pattern matching function has a single argument, while validate has a pair of arguments. The way out would be to apply skills acquired after reading the previous chapter and performing the currying. The following is the code (`Ch4_6.fsx`):

```
open System

let validate key1 key2 = (key1,key2) |> function
    | ("","") -> "both keys are empty"
    | (x,y) & (("",_) | (_,"")) ->
      sprintf "one key is empty: keyA = %s; keyB = %s" x y
    | (x,y) when x = y ->
      sprintf "both keys are not empty: keyA = keyB = %s" x
    | (x,y) ->
      sprintf "both keys aren't empty: keyA = %s; keyB = %s" x y
```

Summary

I hope that this chapter did not leave stones unturned in the matter of plain vanilla pattern matching. You should now be well prepared to overcome typical pattern matching challenges that F# beginner programmers experience. I remind you that further pattern matching features, namely data decomposition and active patterns, will be covered in later chapters in order to preserve the logical flow of the material.

In the next chapter, I will turn to the exciting subject of *Algebraic Data Types*. We will explore how data may be composed too and what are the benefits behind the data composition.

5

Algebraic Data Types

In this chapter, I turn to the F# features that are (almost) missing among mainstream programming languages, such as C#, that are collectively referred to in computer science as **algebraic data types** (https://en.wikipedia.org/wiki/Algebraic_data_type). They advance primitive data types to the higher type level with the help of the composition of other types (primitive or in-turn composite) which are as follows:

- **Tuples** and **records** that represent *product algebraic data types*
- **Discriminated unions** that represent *sum algebraic types*

I'll cover the same facets for each of these composite types as follows:

- Type composition
- Type equality and comparison
- Type decomposition
- Type augmentation

I will revisit the pattern matching as a type decomposition facility that can often be applied outside of the `match` construction.

Combining data with algebraic data types

Usually a conventional programmer considers the matter of data composition through the prism of the object-oriented paradigm.

Everyone usually intuitively understands that **primitive data types** are basic, built-in types supported by a compiler or library: `int64`, `string`, `bigint` (although if viewed with a rigor, `string` may be considered as `char` array, and `bigint` as a **record**).

The next thing programmers learn is that instances of primitive types can be aggregated into collections such as **arrays** or **lists**. However, these collections are monomorphic. That is, the type of all collection members must be the same. Pretty limiting, huh?

The object-oriented paradigm extends primitive types with **classes**. The class just represents a custom type that hides the details of the data composition with the help of encapsulation and offers visibility to just the public properties. Typically, .NET libraries offer plenty of such composite types, for example, `System.DateTime`.

F# certainly supports this way of constructing composite data types as well. However, following the cumbersome and error-prone venue of **Plain Old C Objects (POCO)** each time when a composite type is required is not in line with the F# promise of succinct and error-free code. What would be the way out? Welcome to algebraic data types!

Product algebraic data types

In the simplest case, consider that I use the analogy of *set product* to combine types A and B; the result would be a set of data pairs where the first pair constituent is of type A, the second constituent is of type B, and the whole combination is a Cartesian product of A and B.

F# offers two product algebraic data types, that is, **tuples** and **records**.

Tuples

I have already touched tuples in previous chapters; now I'll go deeper into this subject.

Tuple composition

A tuple is a combination of two or more values of any type. The tuple value element type can be of anything: primitive types, other tuples, custom classes, and functions. For example, take a look at the following code line (`Ch5_1.fsx`):

```
let tuple = (1,"2",fun() ->3)
```

This represents a tuple assembled from three elements of type `int* string * (unit -> int)`.

In order to belong to the same type of tuple, two tuple values must have the same number of elements with the similar types in the order of occurrence.

Tuple equality and comparison

F# automatically implements the structural equality for tuples if each element type supports the equality constraint. Tuples are equal if all their elements are equal pairwise as shown in the following code (Ch5_1.fsx):

```
let a = 1, "car"
a = (1, "car")
```

The preceding equality expression value is true. However, for the value of tuple bound above the following expression does not compile (Ch5_1.fsx):

```
tuple = (1,"2",fun() ->3)
```

The compiler complains that the (unit -> int) type, which is the function forming the third element of the tuple, does not support the 'equality' constraint. The equality relationship is not defined for the F# function values.

Structural comparison for tuples is similarly provided by F# out of the box and is based on pairwise comparisons of elements in a lexicographical order from left to right given that all element types fulfill the 'comparison' constraint as shown in the following code (Ch5_1.fsx):

```
a < (2,"jet")
```

The preceding expression value is true.

Tuple decomposition with pattern matching

This chapter is the perfect place to keep the promise I made in Chapter 4, *Basic Pattern Matching* regarding pattern matching in the capacity of the data structure disassembling tool. The following code snippet demonstrates how value binding can carry the functionality of pattern matching outside of the match construction (Ch5_1.fsx):

```
let (elem1, elem2) = a
printfn "(%i,%s)" elem1 elem2
```

Here, elem1 and elem2 effectively acquire values of the first and second elements of tuple a, which is reflected by the (1,car) output.

Elements of a tuple that are of no interest within a particular tuple disassemble pattern may be omitted using the familiar match-all _ template, as shown in the following code (Ch5_1.fsx):

```
let (_,_,f) = tuple in
f()
```

This snippet highlights how to obtain and invoke a function extracted from the third element of the tuple value; the first two tuple elements are simply ignored with the help of the _ template.

Tuple augmentation

The tuple type does not have an explicit name. This fact effectively makes normal F# type augmentation impossible. Nevertheless, there is still some space left for a good hack. This one exploits the need to have interop with other .NET languages.

Documentation (https://msdn.microsoft.com/en-us/library/dd233200.aspx) states that the compiled form of a tuple represents the corresponding overload of class **Tuple** (https://msdn.microsoft.com/en-us/library/system.tuple.aspx). Given this fact, I can augment the compiled presentation and apply the augmented method using the cast, as shown in the following code (Ch5_1.fsx):

```
let a = 1,"car"
type System.Tuple<'T1,'T2> with
  member t.AsString() =
    sprintf "[[%A]:[%A]]" t.Item1 t.Item2
(a |> box :?> System.Tuple<int,string>).AsString()
```

Here, I have augmented a tuple of two generic elements that have type System.Tuple<'T1,'T2> with the AsString instance method, which allows a very distinctive presentation of the tuple value. Then, given the instance of the int*string tuple, I have upcasted it to obj type with the box function and then immediately downcasted it with :?> operator to System.Tuple<int,string> type, followed by calling the AsString augmented method on the deceivingly constructed System.Tuple<int,string> class instance, getting the expected result, that is, [[1]:["car"]].

Wrapping it up, I can conclude that tuples represent a simple algebraic data type that fits simple designs well. Using tuples instead of custom types for data composition is archetypal for idiomatic F# usage.

Records

Records represent the other F# native product algebraic data type. It addresses the matter that exceptional simplicity of tuples causing some deficiencies. The most unfavorable feature of tuples is the lack of binding of a tuple to a concrete kind of otherwise structurally similar tuple type. For the F# compiler, there is no difference between (1, "car") and (10, "whiskey"), which puts the burden of distinguishing the instance type upon the programmer. Would it be nice to supply structurally similar but semantically different types with explicit names? Also it would be helpful to label tuple constituents with unique names in order to stop relying just on the element position? Sure, welcome to F# **records**!

Record composition

F# records may be considered as the tuples of explicitly named types with labeled elements. Referring to the tuple sample given in the preceding script Ch5_1.fsx, it can be rewritten as follows (Ch5_2.fsx):

```
type transport = { code: int; name: string }
let a = { code = 1; name = "car" }
```

After placing the preceding snippet into FSI, you get the result shown in the following screenshot:

```
C:\US2013>fsi

Microsoft (R) F# Interactive version 12.0.30815.0
Copyright (c) Microsoft Corporation. All Rights Reserved.

For help type #help;;

> type transport = { code: int; name: string }
- let a = { code = 1; name = "car" };;

type transport =
  {code: int;
   name: string;}
val a : transport = {code = 1;
                     name = "car";}

>
```

Defining the F# record type and instance

The preceding screenshot visually demonstrates the benefits of records over tuples when it comes to the unambiguous labeling of the whole and its parts.

Interestingly, the naming of record fields makes it unnecessary to stick to a certain order of field listing as shown in the following code (Ch5_2.fsx):

```
let b = { name = "jet"; code = 2 }
```

Without any problems, value b is recognized as a binding of type transport.

After being constructed, F# records are genuinely immutable, similar to tuples. The language provides just another form of record construction off the existing instance using the with modifier as shown in the following code (Ch5_2.fsx):

```
let c = { b with transport.name = "plane" }
```

This translates into an instance of transport { code = 2; name = "plane" }. Note the use of the "fully qualified" field name, transport.name. I put it this way in order to highlight how it can be possible to resolve ambiguity as different record types may have similarly named fields.

Record equality and comparison

No surprises here. F#, by default, provides structural equality and comparison for records in a manner similar to tuples. However, having an explicit type declaration allows more flexibility in this matter.

For example, if structural equality is not desired and reference equality is required for any reason, it is not a problem for records, which type definition may be decorated with [<ReferenceEquality>] attribute as shown in the following code snippet (Ch5_2.fsx):

```
[<ReferenceEquality>]
type Transport = { code: int; name: string }
let x = {Transport.code=5; name="boat" }
let y = { x with name = "boat"}
let noteq = x = y
let eq = x = x
```

The following screenshot illustrates what happens if running this code in FSI:

```
C:\VS2013>fsi

Microsoft (R) F# Interactive version 12.0.30815.0
Copyright (c) Microsoft Corporation. All Rights Reserved.

For help type #help;;

> type transport = { code: int; name: string }

- let a = { code = 1; name = "car" };;

type transport =
  {code: int;
   name: string;}
val a : transport = {code = 1;
                     name = "car";}

>
```

Referential equality for F# records

Note that after decorating the `Transport` type with the `ReferenceEquality` attribute, two structurally equal records, x and y, are not considered equal anymore.

 It is worth noting that decorating a record type with the `[<CLIMutable>]` attribute makes the underlying record a standard mutable .NET CLI type for interoperability scenarios; in particular providing additionally a default parameterless constructor and elements mutability. See **Core.CLIMutableAttribute Class (F#)** (`https://msdn.microsoft.com/en-us/visualfsharpdocs/conceptual/core.climutableattribute-class-%5Bfsharp%5D`) for further details.

Record decomposition with pattern matching

Disassembling records with pattern matching is similar to the disassembling tuples and may work with or without the `match` construction. The latter case is preferable from the standpoint of succinctness as shown in the following code (`Ch5_2.fsx`):

```
let  { transport.code = _; name = aName } = a
```

This discards the `code` field of `a` as not interesting and binds its `name` field with the `aName` value. The same effect can be achieved with even shorter code:

```
let { transport.name = aname} = a
```

If a single field value is required, then simple `let aName' = a.name` works too.

Record augmentation

Having an explicit type declaration for F# records allows a great deal of augmenting around. A nice example of augmenting a record type in order to implement a thread safe mutable **singleton** property can be found in the **SqlClient Type provider code** (https://gi thub.com/fsprojects/FSharp.Data.SqlClient/blob/c0de3afd43d1f2fc6c99f0adc605d 4fa73f2eb9f/src/SqlClient/Configuration.fs#L87). A distilled snippet is represented as follows (`Ch5_3.fsx`):

```
type Configuration = {
  Database: string
  RetryCount: int
}

[<CompilationRepresentation(CompilationRepresentationFlags.ModuleSuffix)>]
[<AutoOpen>]
module Configuration =
  let private singleton = ref { Database  = "(local)"; RetryCount = 3 }
  let private guard = obj()

  type Configuration with
    static member Current
    with get() = lock guard <| fun() -> !singleton
    and set value = lock guard <| fun() -> singleton := value

printfn "Default start-up config: %A" Configuration.Current

Configuration.Current <- { Configuration.Current with Database =
".\SQLExpress" }

printfn "Updated config: %A" Configuration.Current
```

Here, `Database` and `RetryCount` are kept as fields of the F# record that is placed as a thread safe static property backed by the `singleton` private reference. The beauty of the pattern is that at any moment, configuration can be changed programmatically at the same time keeping the singleton thread safe.

Sum algebraic data types

In contrast to the product algebraic data types covered earlier, sum algebraic data types use the *set sum* operation for the composition of new types. The easiest case for this type is an *enumeration* composed of just a bunch of individual values. A more generic case is a type that groups a bunch of different types called *variants*. Each variant contributes a set of its possible values, which are created with the help of the *variant constructor*. All possible values of all variants combined with a set sum (union) constitute the sum type.

Another contrast with product types is that of all possible variants, only a *single* one can be a value for an instance of the sum type, while *all* fields constitute the value of a product type.

This may sound complicated, but the concept is quite simple. Let's dive in.

Discriminated unions

Sum algebraic data types were introduced in F# by the native data type named *discriminated union* (**DU**). The utter flexibility of discriminated unions makes them handy to represent pretty much anything in the world. For this particular reason, F# programmers use discriminated unions to build the domain-specific languages they come up with when approaching solutions for miscellaneous problems. The ability of discriminated unions to provide meaningful naming to entities of arbitrary complexity, along with the benefits of static typing, is indispensable for clarity in representing problems of any scale.

Discriminated union composition

The manner of discriminated union composition follows its most natural presentation: it is a list of variant cases called *constructors*, separated from each other by the OR sign (|). Each case reflects the single variant (case). For example, take a look at the following definition (Ch5_4.fsx):

```
type ChargeAttempt =
  | Original
  | Retry of int
```

This can serve as a natural reflection of the payment processing domain part that is concerned with the performing charge of a credit card. `ChargeAttempt` can be represented by a discriminated union that has two cases: `Original`, reflecting that the credit card was successfully charged on the first attempt, and `Retry`, reflecting that the charge had some unsuccessful attempts first and then eventually passed through. `Retry` reflects the overall amount of charge attempts, for example, `Retry 4` as shown in the following code (`Ch5_4.fsx`):

```
let cco = Original
// equivalent let cco = ChargeAttempt.Original
let ccr = Retry 4
// equivalent let ccr = ChargeAttempt.Retry(4)
```

In the preceding snippet, `cco` is a value of type `ChargeAttempt` that has the `Original` case value; `ccr` is a value of type `ChargeAttempt` too, but it has the case value of `Retry 4`.

The empty constructor case

The *empty constructor* case variant represents the simplest case form. It is just a pure label without any kind of associated extra type. We already have used this case variant in the preceding code, it stands behind the solitary label `Original`.

The single constructor case

The *single constructor* case represents a discriminated union that has only one case. This is a very useful ubiquitous pattern that structures the underlying problem's domain and promotes type safety. For example, I need to represent an electric bulb that has characteristics such as electric voltage and optical brightness. Using single constructor cases, this can be achieved as follows (`Ch5_4.fsx`):

```
type Brightness = Brightness of int
type Voltage = Voltage of int
type Bulb = { voltage: Voltage; brightness: Brightness }

let myBulb = { voltage = Voltage(110); brightness= Brightness(2500) }
```

A person reading the preceding code instantaneously gets introduced to the key entities to operate with. Also, having the preceding numeric values wrapped into a discriminated union single constructor case creates an extra layer of type safety. That is, number 2500 wrapped into constructor `Brightness(2500)` can be used only for the `brightness` field of the `Brightness` type.

Discriminated union equality and comparison

Discriminated unions provide structural equality and comparison out of the box as shown in the following code (Ch5_4.fsx):

```
let lamp1br = Brightness(2500)
lamp1br = Brightness(2500) // true
lamp1br < Brightness(2100) // false
```

Discriminated union decomposition with pattern matching

Discriminated unions are aligned exceptionally well with pattern matching, so decomposing discriminated unions with the help of pattern matching is a breeze as shown in the following code (Ch5_4.fsx):

```
match myBulb.brightness with
| Brightness(v) -> v
// retrieves back 2500 wrapped upon construction
```

Discriminated union augmentation

Similarly to F# records, discriminated unions can be seriously augmented. Let's consider the following real-life augmentation example. In the electronic payments world, the payment amount may be discounted depending upon the chosen payment instrument. The quantity of the discount may be preset as follows (the whole setup and concrete numbers below are fictitious):

- For a credit card, the discount is zero
- For a debit card, the discount is $0.35
- For ACH, the discount is $0.75

Discounts are a part of the payment service configuration and may change from one marketing campaign to another.

Discount application depending upon the payment instrument can be achieved via the discriminated union augmentation as follows (Ch5_5.fsx):

```
type PaymentInstrumentDiscount =
  | CreditCard of decimal
  | DebitCard of decimal
  | ACH of decimal
```

```
member x.ApplyDiscount payment =
  match x with
  | CreditCard d -> payment - d
  | DebitCard d -> payment - d
  | ACH d -> payment - d
```

Here, the particular discount amount is tied to each payment instrument case via the discriminated union case constructor: `CreditCard`, `DebitCard`, or `ACH`. Along with the distinct cases, the type shares the `ApplyDiscount` single instance method, which calculates the discounted amount for an original payment amount based on the current discount for the selected payment instrument. The results of running the preceding script in FSI are shown in the following figure, where discounted payment amounts are shown for a payment of $20.23 for each of the covered payment instruments:

Augmenting F# discriminated union

Summary

In this chapter you get familiar with extremely important F# features that represent algebraic data types. For each of the types, the topics of composition, decomposition, standard and custom equality and comparison, and augmentation are covered. In the end, you are expected to understand the reasons behind the superiority of F# data composition with native algebraic data types over custom POCOs.

In the next chapter, I'll turn to the exciting subject of F# sequences that represent data and calculation dualism.

6

Sequences - The Core of Data Processing Patterns

In this chapter, we will take a deep dive into one of the most essential and utterly important arrangements of functional programming, that is, sequences. The ability to represent any data transformation as a composition of atomic functions applied to the elements of an arbitrary enumerable data container is a must for a functional programmer. The goal of this chapter is to help you acquire this mental skill. The way towards this goal is paved by the following topics covered here:

- Review the basic data transformations and partition the immense host of standard library data transformation functions by handful of underlying processing patterns
- Consider the duality of sequence data generators being at once a data and an on-demand calculation
- Cover how a sequence generalizes arbitrary collections by enumerating them, which represents the pull data transformation pattern
- Further consider just another pattern of using generated sequences for data drilling
- Wrap up by practically exploring how the usage of sequences affects the code performance

Basic sequence transformations

Let's revisit the functional solution of the sample problem from `Chapter 1`, *Begin Thinking Functionally*. It represents the common functional pattern of *finding a given property of the collection* as follows:

- From the given string literal representing 1000 consecutive single digit characters, make a collection of the collections represented by chunks of just five consecutive single digit characters of the original collection. Each chunk takes the inner characters of a five character-wide stencil aligned first with the left-hand side border of the string literal. The stencil then gets moved to the right by a single character before extracting the next sub collection. This sliding of the stencil to the right is continued until the right-hand side borders of both the stencil and the literal get aligned. To be exact, the main sequence consists of 996 such five character sub sequences.

- Note that the originally sought-for property of the maximal product of five consecutive digits at this point is substituted with a similar property of the sequence of elements, each representing a candidate group from which the sought-for property originates. It is worth pointing out that in order to solve the original problem, *all* elements of this secondary sequence must be taken into account (other patterns may differ in this respect, for example, *finding any sequence element with a given property*).

- Perform a complete scan of the substitute sequence, looking for the maximal value of the sought-for property, which is the product of the constituents of the inner sequence representing an element of the outer sequence that substitutes the original string literal.

Those of you who are attentive to detail may have already spotted the similarity of the preceding solution approach to the **MapReduce** (`https://en.wikipedia.org/wiki/MapReduce`) pattern, just without the possible partitioning and parallelization of the **map** phase for now. This similarity is not coincidental. After implementing a serious amount of F# **ETL** (`https://en.wikipedia.org/wiki/Extract,_transform,_load`) tasks, big and small for enterprise **Line of Business** (**LOB**) applications, I can conclude that the part of the F# core library covering basic operations upon enumerable sequences, namely the `Collections.seq` library module of the **Microsoft.FSharp.Collections** (`https://msdn.microsoft.com/en-us/library/ee353635.aspx`) namespace, has already distilled the typical functional patterns of data sequence processing. Any effective F# developer should be conversant in representing a sought-for data transformation solution at hand into a combination of these library functions from `Collections.seq`.

Based on my own experience, this set of 70 library functions (for version 4.0 of F#) is hard to grok when you consider it as a list that is just alphabetically ordered by the function name. It is hard to memorize what exactly this or that function is doing without distinguishing their commonalities and differences. This perception can be facilitated if we start seeing a certain data transformation pattern being implemented by each of these functions. These patterns stem from years of accumulated experience in applying functional programming to data processing and are coined into the selection of functions that the F# designers have slated for inclusion into the core library.

I believe that by observing the `Collection.seq` library constituents from this data processing pattern relationship angle, the following function groups can be distinguished:

- **Aggregates**: These functions traverse the sequence in its entirety, returning a single value calculated upon the sequence elements.
- **Generators**: These functions produce sequences "out of thin air", or seriously, sequences of special kinds (such as empty typed sequence) and sequences defined either by a quantitative relation between the element and its sequence order number or just by a recurrently defined function deriving the next element based on the previous element(s).
- **Wrappers and Type Converters**: These functions either wrap the entire sequence into a useful property (caching is a good example of a wrap) or just convert the sequence to other collection types (lists or arrays).
- **Appliers**: These functions just traverse the sequence, applying the given calculation to each element for the sake of a side effect, for example, to print out sequence elements as strings.
- **Recombinators**: These functions shuffle the sequence or extract its elements in a type-uniform manner; in other words, for a sequence of type `'T` dealing exclusively with `seq<'T>` or `'T` objects. For example, create a new sequence by skipping the first 100 elements of the original one.
- **Filters**: These functions are concerned with the selection of elements that conform to an arbitrary condition(s). For example, try to find the first element of a sequence for which a given predicate function returns true.
- **Mappers**: These functions change shape and/or the type of the original sequence(s) by producing a transformed sequence(s), for example, a zipping function that takes two input sequences and produces the single result sequence with each element being a tuple that combines elements from both input sequences sharing the same order number.

Equipped with this classification approach, I've partitioned the library functions by the following set of patterns. Under each pattern, all the relevant library functions are listed along with their signatures. I encourage you to explore the signatures in order to spot the commonalities responsible for each group formation.

Additional information for those of you who are eager to dig deeper is given in the `Ch6_1.fsx` script of this book's accompanying code, where the use of each of the library functions is illustrated by a brief code sample.

The aggregation pattern

```
average : seq<^T> -> ^T (requires member (+) and member     DivideByInt and
member get_Zero)averageBy : ('T -> ^U) -> seq<'T> -> ^U (requires ^U with
static     member (+) and ^U with static member DivideByInt and ^U with
static member Zero)
fold : ('State -> 'T -> 'State) -> 'State -> seq<'T> -> 'State
length : seq<'T> -> int
sum : seq<^T> -> ^T (requires member (+) and member get_Zero)
sumBy : ('T -> ^U) -> seq<'T> -> ^U (requires ^U with static  member (+)
and ^U with static member Zero)
max : seq<'T> -> 'T (requires comparison)
maxBy : ('T -> 'U) -> seq<'T> -> 'T (requires comparison)
min : seq<'T> -> 'T (requires comparison)
minBy : ('T -> 'U) -> seq<'T> -> 'T (requires comparison)
isEmpty : seq<'T> -> bool
reduce : ('T -> 'T -> 'T) -> seq<'T> -> 'T
exactlyOne : seq<'T> -> 'T
compareWith : ('T -> 'T -> int) -> seq<'T> -> seq<'T> -> int
```

The generation pattern

```
empty : seq<'T>
init : int -> (int -> 'T) -> seq<'T>
initInfinite : (int -> 'T) -> seq<'T>
singleton : 'T -> seq<'T>
unfold : ('State -> 'T * 'State option) -> 'State -> seq<'T>
```

The wrapping and type conversion pattern

```
cast : IEnumerable -> seq<'T>
cache : seq<'T> -> seq<'T>
delay : (unit -> seq<'T>) -> seq<'T>
```

```
readonly : seq<'T> -> seq<'T>
toArray : seq<'T> -> 'T []
toList : seq<'T> -> 'T
list ofArray : 'T array -> seq<'T>
ofList : 'T list -> seq<'T>
```

The application pattern

```
iter : ('T -> unit) -> seq<'T> -> unit
iter2 : ('T1 -> 'T2 -> unit) -> seq<'T1> -> seq<'T2> -> unit
iteri : (int -> 'T -> unit) -> seq<'T> -> unit
```

The recombination pattern

```
append : seq<'T> -> seq<'T> -> seq<'T>
collect : ('T -> 'Collection) -> seq<'T> -> seq<'U>
concat : seq<'Collection> -> seq<'T>
head : seq<'T> -> 'T
last : seq<'T> -> 'T
nth : int -> seq<'T> -> 'T
skip : int -> seq<'T> -> seq<'T>
take : int -> seq<'T> -> seq<'T>
sort : seq<'T> -> seq<'T>
sortBy : ('T -> 'Key) -> seq<'T> -> seq<'T>
truncate : int -> seq<'T> -> seq<'T>
distinct : seq<'T> -> seq<'T>
distinctBy : ('T -> 'Key) -> seq<'T> -> seq<'T>
```

The filtering pattern

```
choose : ('T -> 'U option) -> seq<'T> -> seq<'U>
exists : ('T -> bool) -> seq<'T> -> bool
exists2 : ('T1 -> 'T2 -> bool) -> seq<'T1> -> seq<'T2> -> bool
filter : ('T -> bool) -> seq<'T> -> seq<'T>
find : ('T -> bool) -> seq<'T> -> 'T
findIndex : ('T -> bool) -> seq<'T> -> int
forall : ('T -> bool) -> seq<'T> -> bool
forall2 : ('T1 -> 'T2 -> bool) -> seq<'T1> -> seq<'T2> -> bool
pick : ('T -> 'U option) -> seq<'T> -> 'U
skipWhile : ('T -> bool) -> seq<'T> -> seq<'T>
takeWhile : ('T -> bool) -> seq<'T> -> seq<'T>
tryFind : ('T -> bool) -> seq<'T> -> 'T option
tryFindIndex : ('T -> bool) -> seq<'T> -> int
```

```
option tryPick : ('T -> 'U option) -> seq<'T> -> 'U option
where : ('T -> bool) -> seq<'T> -> seq<'T>
```

The mapping pattern

```
countBy : ('T -> 'Key) -> seq<'T> -> seq<'Key * int>
groupBy : ('T -> 'Key) -> seq<'T> -> seq<'Key * seq<'T>>
pairwise : seq<'T> -> seq<'T * 'T>
map : ('T -> 'U) -> seq<'T> -> seq<'U>
map2 : ('T1 -> 'T2 -> 'U) -> seq<'T1> -> seq<'T2> -> seq<'U>
mapi : (int -> 'T -> 'U) -> seq<'T> -> seq<'U>
scan : ('State -> 'T -> 'State) -> 'State -> seq<'T> -> seq<'State>
windowed : int -> seq<'T> -> seq<'T []>
zip : seq<'T1> -> seq<'T2> -> seq<'T1 * 'T2>
zip3 : seq<'T1> -> seq<'T2> -> seq<'T3> -> seq<'T1 * 'T2 * 'T3>
```

The sequence: Duality of data and calculation

What makes the F# sequence so ambient and versatile is its dual nature. Being a strongly typed generic data collection, it exposes the contained data via two archetypal .NET interfaces of the System.Collections.Generic namespace, namely IEnumerable<T> (https://msdn.microsoft.com/en-us/library/9eekhta0(v=vs.110).aspx) and IEnumerator<T> (https://msdn.microsoft.com/en-us/library/78dfe2yb(v=vs.110).aspx).

These interfaces personify the classic data pull protocol, where a data consumer actively pulls data from the producer. Indeed, the type of seq<'T> in the F# is defined as the following abbreviation:

```
type seq<'T> = System.Collections.Generic.IEnumerable<'T>
```

The preceding line of code means in practice that each F# sequence is a data collection, which can be traversed by getting an *enumerator* that allows you to stir through the sequence from its head towards its tail, obtaining the values of its elements. The enumerator itself can be obtained using the GetEnumerator() method of the IEnumerable<'T> interface.

With the enumerator, which in turn implements the `IEnumerator<'T>` interface, the sequence can be traversed using the pair of members that constitute this interface: the `Current` property, which gets the value of the sequence element at the current position of the enumerator, and the `MoveNext()` method, which advances the position of the enumerator to the next element of the sequence.

Rather boring, right? Well, it might be boring when being applied to *materialized* data collections such as the F# list, where all elements exist in the physical memory space. However, nothing in the preceding scheme insists upon the element materialization! It doesn't require much mental effort to imagine `IEnumerator<'T>` being implemented by a calculation that returns the freshly constructed value of `'T` in response to getting the `Current` property, and for `MoveNext()`, it just advances the imaginable current position marker of the sequence. The whole arrangement is *immaterial* with regard to the memory space occupied by elements, as there is no need to keep more than just one materialized `Current` element, right? With that, you just rediscovered the inner workings of the F# sequences!

Sequence as a lazy data collection

The F# sequences do not eagerly materialize data elements in the memory. This feature aligns very well with the data pull protocol. That is, the current sequence element is not required unless the sequence enumerator has reached its position in the sequence after a series of `MoveNext()` method invocations and the element value has been demanded via getting the enumerator's `Current` property.

However, in order to really master the F# sequences, it is important that you understand its nuances. In particular, it is important to be aware of whether sequence elements are materialized or not. If a sequence has been calculated on the enumerator's demand and is not being converted from a materialized collection, such as a list or an array, or is not cached, then there is normally no backing memory where sequence element values are persisted. On the contrary, if a sequence has been produced from a concrete collection by a library function, for example, `Seq.ofList`, then at least one instance of the original list must be present for the entire lifespan of the derived collection, as this list can be completely arbitrary and no way exists to recreate it from scratch in a manner similar to a sequence being re-enumerated multiple times if the re-enumeration is cheap and performance considerations do not prompt for caching.

Sequence as a calculation

As I've just mentioned, a sequence can be an enumeration atop a concrete data collection where the enumerator is implemented on the collection's side. However, more interesting cases represent sequences that have an enumerator that programmatically generates sequence elements upon the traversal pull demand. These might be different, syntactically sugared forms as sequence comprehensions, sequence computation expressions, or standard library functions representing the *generator pattern* considered at the beginning of the chapter. As a last resort, a sequence can be brought to life in a fully de-sugared manner by implementing some required interfaces. The last approach is the most tedious and error-prone; however, it grants unprecedented flexibility in comparison to other methods. In a majority of development situations, the custom sequence enumerator implementation is unwarranted; however, there might be some situations where there is simply no alternative to the custom implementation. This topic will be my next subject.

Sequence as an enumerator interface wrapper

Although implementing a custom sequence is a tedious task, it's not rocket science. I'm going to walk you through the process and make you *understand* it. No matter how simple or complex the custom sequence is, the implementation process will be the same.

To begin with, what do you think defines the sequence behavior? Apparently, it is not syntactic constructions used for sequence traversing, and it does not matter whether it's sugared or not sugared. All implementation specifics are abstracted by the entity standing behind any sequence (and even more broadly, behind any .NET collection): the **enumerator**. Enumerator is a class that must implement the previously mentioned strongly typed interface IEnumerator<'T> (https://msdn.microsoft.com/en-us/library/78dfe2yb(v=vs.110).aspx) of the System.Collections.Generic namespace. In turn, IEnumerator<'T> inherits from two other interfaces: the routine System.IDisposable interface and the legacy untyped IEnumerator interface of the System.Collections namespace. (Pay attention to the difference between typed System.Collections.Generic and untyped System.Collections namespaces). IEnumerator<'T> overrides the Current property and inherits the MoveNext() and Reset() methods of the IEnumerator interface. As these relationships between involved components are quite intricate, I have provided a component relationship diagram in the following figure to facilitate comprehension:

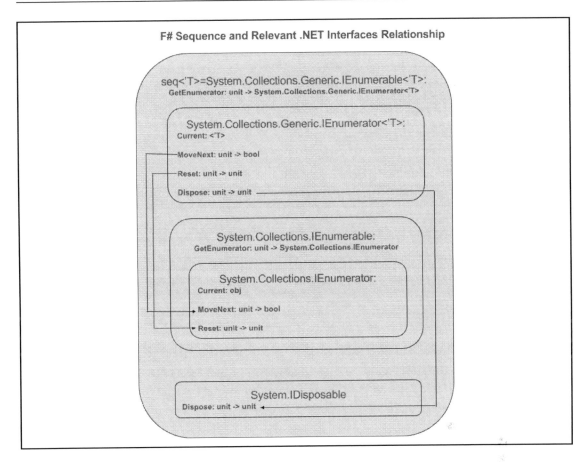

The relationship between components constituting the F# sequence implementation

Considering these intricacies, the implementation plan for any custom F# sequence is as following:

1. Provide a custom `Enumerator` class for the sequence that implements `System.Collections.Generic.IEnumerator<'T>`, `System.Collections.IEnumerator`, and `System.IDisposable` interfaces. For the first interface, just implement an override of the `Current` property, and the rest of the implementation goes into nongeneric `IEnumerator`.

2. Provide a factory function that is similar to the `GetEnumerator()` methods of generic .NET collections that have a `unit ->` `System.Collections.Generic.IEnumerator<'T>` signature. This function constructs the requested instance of the enumerator passing through its own arguments directly to the constructor, then it upcasts the constructed instance into `System.Collections.Generic.IEnumerator<'T>` and returns the result as a function of the previously listed signature.

3. Provide another factory function, this time to build a sought-for sequence out of the function built in Step 2.

As this may still sound a bit complicated, let's take a quick walk-through. I want us to implement the easiest thing: a strongly typed empty sequence, which is a sequence without elements, when its enumerator does not have anything to enumerate.

At the same time, apparently, it must be a normal sequence similar to any other native sequence from .NET libraries or a sugared one constructed with the F# language facilities or core libraries. Let's do this.

Step 1 – The custom enumerator implementation

The behavior of an empty sequence is pretty straightforward: both typed and untyped versions of the `Current` property never have a chance to work as any attempt to enumerate empty sequence must immediately terminate; `MoveNext()` always returns `false`, indicating that the end of the sequence has already been reached. Expressed in the F# code, these considerations are shown in the following snippet (`Ch6_2.fsx`):

```
type private DummyEnumerate<'T>() =
  interface System.Collections.Generic.IEnumerator<'T> with
    member x.Current = Unchecked.defaultof<'T>

  interface System.Collections.IEnumerator with
    member x.Current = box Unchecked.defaultof<'T>
    member x.MoveNext() = false
    member x.Reset() = ()

  interface System.IDisposable with
    member x.Dispose() = ()
```

As mentioned earlier, `System.Collections.Generic.IEnumerator<'T>` overrides `Current` and inherits `MoveNext()` and `Reset()` of `System.Collections.IEnumerator`. Both `Current` properties use the typed default value; the `Current` property of the untyped enumerator boxes this default value according to the specification. Step 1 is now complete.

Step 2 – The custom enumerator factory

Step 2 is quite simple, especially in our case, where the implemented sequence does not have any specifics to be communicated to the enumerator at the time of construction as shown in the following code (`Ch6_2.fsx`):

```
let makeDummyEnumerator<'T>() =
  fun() -> (new DummyEnumerate<'T>()
    :> System.Collections.Generic.IEnumerator<'T>)
```

Step 2 is now complete too.

Step 3 – The custom sequence factory

This one is a breeze, thanks to the great **object expressions** (`https://msdn.microsoft.com/en-us/library/dd233237.aspx`) feature of the F# as shown (`Ch6_2.fsx`):

```
let makeSeq enumerator =
{
  new System.Collections.Generic.IEnumerable<_> with
    member x.GetEnumerator() = enumerator()
  interface System.Collections.IEnumerable with
    member x.GetEnumerator() =
    (enumerator() :> System.Collections.IEnumerator)
}
```

Here we go; it is easy to spot that this particular piece does not in any way depend on the produced sequence and is a good candidate to be a member of a Helpers library. The implementation is complete.

Now is a perfect moment to give it a test drive to check whether everything is really OK and that I did not miss anything. The results of a concise testing are reflected in the following screenshot:

```
val it : unit = ()
> type private Enumerate<'T>() =
     interface System.Collections.Generic.IEnumerator<'T> with
        member x.Current = Unchecked.defaultof<'T>

     interface System.Collections.IEnumerator with
        member x.Current = box Unchecked.defaultof<'T>
        member x.MoveNext() = false
        member x.Reset() = ()

     interface System.IDisposable with
        member x.Dispose() = ()

  let makeEnumerator<'T>() = fun() -> (new Enumerate<'T>() :> System.Collections
.Generic.IEnumerator<'T>)

  let makeSeq enumerator =
     {
        new System.Collections.Generic.IEnumerable<_> with
           member x.GetEnumerator() = enumerator()
        interface System.Collections.IEnumerable with
           member x.GetEnumerator() =
              (enumerator() :> System.Collections.IEnumerator)
     };;
type private Enumerate<'T> =
  class
     interface System.IDisposable
     interface System.Collections.IEnumerator
     interface IEnumerator<'T>
     new : unit -> Enumerate<'T>
  end
val makeEnumerator : unit -> unit -> IEnumerator<'T>
val makeSeq : enumerator:(unit -> IEnumerator<'a>) -> IEnumerable<'a>

> let ss = makeSeq (makeEnumerator<int>());;

val ss : IEnumerable<int>

> ss |> Seq.isEmpty;;
val it : bool = true
> ss |> Seq.length;;
val it : int = 0
> ss |> Seq.skip 10;;
val it : seq<int> =
  Error: The input sequence has an insufficient number of elements.
>
```

Testing the implemented empty sequence

The empty sequence is created with the following code:

```
let ss = makeSeq (makeDummyEnumerator<int>())
```

Then some checks are performed as shown:

- `ss |> Seq.isEmpty`, as expected, returns `true`
- `ss |> Seq.length`, as expected, equals `0`
- An attempt to skip some elements with `ss |> Seq.skip 10` fails with the expected diagnostics

Before we switch to the next topic, I want to reiterate this: the de-sugared custom sequence implementation using bare .NET interfaces is not much fun. The good thing about it is that in most situations, you simply do not need to descend to this level. Syntactically sugared language constructions and core library functions will do the same job. However, once in a while, you will need to do something special, such as counting the number of times your code traverses a sequence, and this technique will be at your service.

Sequence of an indefinite length as a design pattern

The conventional engineering vision of data transformations is that they occur over finite collections materialized in the memory, hence allowing these collections to be enumerated with `Seq.length`, yielding a number of elements. However, the F# sequences (as well as .NET `IEnumerable<T>` per se) grant the following generalization: in some cases, a more math-centric vision might be useful, which suggests looking at sequences as countable but not necessarily finite.

A meticulous reader may immediately object that the *countable* entity, when applied to practical computing, is necessarily finite because eventually, it is limited by underlying physical hardware, which comes out in boundary values, for example:

```
System.Int32.MaxValue = 2147483647
System.Int64.MaxValue = 9223372036854775807L
```

However, I would oppose this objection by saying that this mere consideration does not in any way limit the length of the F# sequences that might be produced. As a proof, let's implement at the low level without using any F# syntactic sugar the **repeater**, or sequence that when being given an element of any type returns the endless repetition of the given element.

I will begin with a plain vanilla IEnumerator<'T> implementation as shown in the following code (Ch6_3.fsx):

```
type private Repeater<'T>(repeated) =
  let _repeated = repeated
    interface System.Collections.Generic.IEnumerator<'T> with
    member x.Current = _repeated

  interface System.Collections.IEnumerator with
    member x.Current = box _repeated
    member x.MoveNext() = true
    member x.Reset() = ()

  interface System.IDisposable with
    member x.Dispose() = ()
```

The preceding snippet is quite straightforward. The Repeater<'T> type defines a class with which the single default constructor obtains the element to be repeated as repeated and persists it within the class instance as _repeated.

Then, as a fulfillment of the System.Collections.Generic.IEnumerator<'T> contract, this interface is implemented with the single property Current returning the persisted _repeated value.

Then, the implementation of the nongeneric System.Collections.IEnumerator interface follows with its three contract methods. Here is the place where the desired sequence behavior is coined: the Current untyped property also returns a persisted _repeated value, but this time, it's boxed according to the contract, yielding obj. The MoveNext() method, as Energizer Bunny says, should keep going, going, going… so that it always returns true, which means that the next element is available no matter what. The Reset() legacy method is just a stub.

Finally, a bogus implementation of System.IDisposable that is required by the IEnumerator<'T> contract completes the implementation.

Now, for the usage convenience, I add a thin wrapper that upcasts the implemented interface of Repeater<'T> to the explicit System.Collections.Generic.IEnumerator<'T> as shown in the following code (Ch6_3.fsx):

```
let repeat<'T>(e) =
  (new Repeater<'T>(e)
  :> System.Collections.Generic.IEnumerator<'T>)
```

Finally, a generic `makeSeq` shim function provides the conversion of any `IEnumerator<'T>` into the corresponding `seq<'T>` sequence by implementing both generic and nongeneric flavors of `IEnumerable` as shown in the following code (`Ch6_3.fsx`):

```
let makeSeq enumerator =
{
  new System.Collections.Generic.IEnumerable<'U> with
    member x.GetEnumerator() = enumerator
  interface System.Collections.IEnumerable with
    member x.GetEnumerator() =
    (enumerator :> System.Collections.IEnumerator)
}
```

Here, the `enumerator` argument provides the underlying `IEnumerator<'T>` for both implementations of `IEnumerable` constituting an arbitrary F# `seq`.

It's time for field tests! Executing the freshly created `makeSeq` function with three different arguments that represent the `repeat '.'`, `repeat 42`, and `repeat"Hooray!"` enumerators in FSI yields sequences of indefinite length of the corresponding types, as demonstrated in the following screenshot:

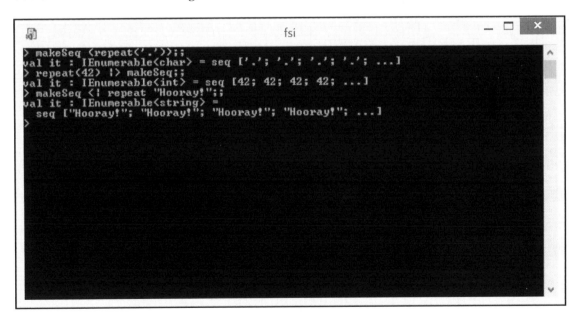

Generating sequences of indefinite length

However, how can we prove that these sequences are indeed of indefinite length? Ironically, only by counting elements: if for any indiscriminately big number, the sequence yields that many elements, then that is the proof that these sequences are of indefinite length. Unfortunately, this is exactly where we hit the already mentioned counting problem: counting might be effectively limited by the underlying hardware.

But wait a minute; .NET provides a numeric type that, for all practical purposes, represents an arbitrarily large countable **System.Numerics.BigInteger** (https://msdn.microsoft.com /en-us/library/system.numerics.biginteger(v=vs.110).aspx). So, it would be nice to base the counting on this type.

Assuming that you are not afraid of challenges, it would be a good exercise to implement a generic technique of counting not limited by standard int. For F#, this task is not very complicated. I would suggest the following idiomatic approach (Ch6_3.fsx):

```
let inline traverse n s =
  let counter =
    (Seq.zip
      (seq { LanguagePrimitives.GenericOne..n }) s)
     .GetEnumerator()
  let i = ref LanguagePrimitives.GenericOne
  let mutable last = Unchecked.defaultof<_>
  while counter.MoveNext() do
    if !i = n then last <- counter.Current
      i := !i + LanguagePrimitives.GenericOne
  last
```

The traverse counting function is inlined in order to allow the compiler to build the compiled code aligned with the type on argument n picked for the counting. The n argument of traverse represents the amount of elements expected to be generated. The second traverse argument s represents a generic unlimited sequence generator. makeSeq with a given generic repetitive element makes a perfect second argument for traverse.

The sequence counting enumerator can be elegantly expressed as Seq.zip zipping together the presumably unlimited length sequence of makeSeq and a limited length sequence that has exactly the expected arbitrarily large (within boundaries that the underlying type allows) number of elements. As zipping stops upon reaching the end of the shorter sequence, the counter value represents exactly the desired enumerator obtained from the zipper expression result.

Finally, I traverse the obtained enumerator until it stops yielding elements keeping track of the last traversed element. This `last` element, which is apparently a tuple of the last element number and the unbound sequence element, is returned as the evidence of arbitrary length. The following screenshot demonstrates how the field tests passed. The first test shows how `traverse` worked with the `BigInteger` counter; the second test just illustrates how to produce the sequence that is 10 elements longer than `System.Int32.MaxValue`:

Checking out unlimited sequence workings

Another interesting experiment would be to generate a sequence longer than `System.Int64.MaxValue`, which I leave to you as an exercise. My only concern is the time duration it may take to complete. My rough estimate shows that at the rate of 1,000,000 elements traversed per second, it would take no less than the next 29 centuries to complete; so, some serious revisions of the method and optimizations of the implementation may be due.

Generating the F# sequences

As you had a chance to notice recently, generating sequences with the de-sugared .NET way has a fair amount of moving parts and, frankly, is not the best *one fits all* use case. Fortunately, F# provides enough support through syntactic sugar as well as library functions, making the generation of sequences of finite and infinite lengths a breeze. Let's take a peek at them.

Sequence comprehensions

Sequence comprehensions allow you to represent a sequence as a special kind of expression, namely **sequence expression** (https://msdn.microsoft.com/en-us/library /dd233209.aspx). Or, the other way around, sequence expression, when being evaluated, yields a sequence.

Sequence comprehensions may take plenty of forms. We'll be discussing some that are typical.

Ranges

These are the simplest forms of comprehensions, producing sequences from ranges. Observe that ranges are not limited to just numeric ones; any type supporting the 'get_One' operator is fine too as shown here (Ch6_4.fsx):

```
// odd int64 between 1 and 1000
seq { 1L .. 2L .. 1000L }
// val it : seq<int64> = seq [1L; 3L; 5L; 7L; ...]

// range not necessarily must be numeric!
seq { 'A' .. 'Z' }
// val it : seq<char> = seq ['A'; 'B'; 'C'; 'D'; ...]
```

Maps

These expressions generalize ranges by allowing the projection of one or more enumerations into something of another type. Also, note that the enumeration definition can be very flexible: from a simple range to nested enumerations to just another sequence as shown here (Ch6_4.fsx):

```
// even int from 2 to 1000
seq { for i in 1..2..999 -> ((+) 1 i) }
// val it : seq<int> = seq [2; 4; 6; 8; ...]
```

```
// nested enumerations
seq { for i in 1..10 do for j in 1..10 -> if i = j then 1 else 0}
// val it : seq<int> = seq [1; 0; 0; 0; ...]

// cartesian product tuple projection
seq { for i in 1..10 do for j in 1..10 -> (i,j) }
// val it : seq<int * int> = seq [(1, 1); (1, 2); (1, 3); ...]

// cartesian product nested enumerations
seq { for i in seq {'a'..'b'} do for j in 1..2 -> (i,j) }
val it : seq<char * int> = seq [('a', 1); ('a', 2); ('b', 1); ('b', 2)]
```

Arbitrary sequence expressions

All sequence comprehensions represent the idiomatic F# syntax sugar related to the extremely powerful mechanism of **computation expressions** (`https://msdn.microsoft.co m/en-us/library/dd233182.aspx`), in particular, providing a convenient syntax for dreaded *M-word things*, also known as **monads. Computation expressions** represent the extremely powerful F# pattern of sequencing and combining computations. They may be custom built; however, F# also offers some built-in computation expressions: along with **sequence expressions**, there are **asynchronous workflows** and **query expressions** as well. I will be covering built-in computation expressions in the upcoming chapters of this book.

Arbitrary sequence expressions are just computations wrapped by `seq { and }` tokens, although in contrast to the **ranges** and **maps** covered earlier, computations can be pretty much anything. Two constructs within sequence expression tokens play a special role as shown here:

- `yield <expression>` makes the expression value the next element of the final sequence
- `yield! <sequence expression>` (reads *yield-bang*) appends the sequence expression operand to the end of the final sequence

The presence of `yield!` turns arbitrary sequence expressions into extremely powerful data transformations. In particular, as `seq {...}` is still an expression, being used as a return value of recursive functions, this pattern allows you to extremely succinctly and elegantly implement sequences of finite and infinite length, in particular, easily turn any finite sequence into an infinite circular one, which is often very convenient for the partitioning of other sequences through the element markup.

Enough words; let's look at some code!

I begin with a sample demonstrating how the entire pattern match construct can be nested into a sequence expression in order to detect when the sequence should halt. The following snippet produces a descending sequence of an integer from any non-negative number down to zero (`Ch6_4.fsx`):

```
let rec descend top =
  seq {
    match top with
      | _ when top < 0 -> ()
      | _ ->
      yield top
      yield! descend (top - 1)
  }

// descend 3;;
// val it : seq<int> = seq [3; 2; 1; 0]
// descend -3;;
// val it : seq<int> = seq []
```

Note how generation halting is achieved by returning `unit` instead of yielding the next element.

So far, so good. Now let's generate just an endless sequence of alternating strings as shown (`Ch6_4.fsx`):

```
let rec fizzbuzz = seq {
  yield "Fizz"
  yield "Buzz"
  yield! fizzbuzz
}
in fizzbuzz

// val it : seq<string> = seq ["Fizz"; "Buzz"; "Fizz"; "Buzz";  ...]
```

To wrap up the theme, look at how elegantly the circularization of any arbitrary sequence can be achieved as shown here (`Ch6_4.fsx`):

```
let rec circular ss =
  seq { yield! ss; yield! circular ss }

circular (seq { yield '+'; yield '-' })
// val it : seq<char> = seq ['+'; '-'; '+'; '-'; ...]
```

Deserves two bangs that are required in the definition above to arrange the circularization indeed.

Library functions generating sequences

Now I turn to the support for sequence generation that the F# core libraries provide.

Seq.init

This method is for sequences of predefined length as the length sits right in the function signature. This is quite a simple function that assumes but does not prescribe a projection of the current element number. Here goes a sample with a projection of the sequence number in a string performed in the **tacit** (https://en.wikipedia.org/wiki/Tacit_programming) manner (Ch6_4.fsx):

```
Seq.init 10 (sprintf "%s%d""I'm element #")
//val it : seq<string> =
//   seq
//      ["I'm element #0"; "I'm element #1"; "I'm element #2";
//       "I'm element #3"; ...]
```

Seq.initInfinite

This function is very similar to the previous one, but it is missing the first argument indeed, as shown here (Ch6_4.fsx):

```
Seq.initInfinite (sprintf "%s%d""I'm element #")
//val it : seq<string> =
//   seq
//      ["I'm element #0"; "I'm element #1"; "I'm element #2";
//       "I'm element #3"; ...]
```

Pretty much nothing has changed, but the underlying abstraction is more powerful than the finite variant. Unfortunately, the power of abstraction can be easily hurt by the implementation limitation that shrewd F# programmers may guess: it has only as many element sequence numbers as the hardware architecture allows. This is easy to check with the following little hack (Ch6_4.fsx):

```
Seq.initInfinite (fun _ -> ())
|> Seq.skip (System.Int32.MaxValue)
//>
//val it : seq<unit> =
// Error: Enumeration based on System.Int32 exceeded
System.Int32.MaxValue.
```

Ouch, it hurts!

Seq.unfold

The `Seq.unfold` library function, which concludes the matter of sequence generation, is my favorite. Instead of bothering with sequence numbers, its projection function unwraps the recurrent relationship between the current and the next element. It also demonstrates a very smart manner of addressing the halt problem by prescribing the projection result as `option` when returning `None` signals to stop generating further elements. Let's look at this library function in action using rather worn down by bloggers and Academia **Fibonacci numbers** (`https://en.wikipedia.org/wiki/Fibonacci_number`) as an example shown here (`Ch6_4.fsx`):

```
// Oh NO! Not Fibonacci again!
let fibnums = Seq.unfold (fun (current, next) ->
  Some(current, (next, current+next)))(1,1)

fibnums |> Seq.take 10 |> Seq.toList
// val it : int list = [1; 1; 2; 3; 5; 8; 13; 21; 34; 55]
```

After some years of using F#, I'm still excited what clarity of intent it allows! The projection function literally explains itself, so I do not have anything to add.

Sequence and the code performance

Sequences are, without doubt, extremely powerful members of the functional programmer tool belt. However, they are not free of *gotchas* that may hurt the performance badly. It is best that they are known and avoided. A few of them are as follows:

- Unfortunate materialization, which may be either unnecessary/premature elements materialization or the other way around, missing elements materialization.
- Data laziness, in concert with the non-preserving once current element values, can severely hurt the performance in a situation where the algorithm requires multiple traversals or where calculating elements is expensive. The developer should be able to compensate for these detrimental factors by applying patterns such as **caching** and/or **memoization**.

- Often, when composing data processing pipelines, the developer may carelessly use a library function that unexpectedly requires them to enumerate the entire sequence. This is not necessarily a bad thing, but it should be used sparingly.
- With all the aesthetic beauty of sequences of indefinite length, if misdemeanors mentioned in the previous bullet point just hurt the performance of finite length sequences, the first such negligence upon an indefinite length sequence simply *kills!* Beware and proceed with due caution when dealing with unlimited length sequences!

Sequence caching

F# language creators were nice enough to provide an out-of-the-box tool for caching, namely the `Seq.cache` library function. It should be used in a situation where lazy materialization is not a killer, but element generation is not cheap and repetitive enumerations are really required. Let me demonstrate how easy putting caching to work would be.

To begin with, I need an indicator of the enumerator consumption. This is not complicated for those who already have experience working with sequence guts. Let's slightly modify our good old `makeSeq` function as following (`Ch6_5.fsx`):

```
let makeSeq f =
{
  new System.Collections.Generic.IEnumerable<'U> with
    member x.GetEnumerator() = printfn "Fresh enumerator given"; f()
  interface System.Collections.IEnumerable with
    member x.GetEnumerator() =
    (f() :> System.Collections.IEnumerator)
}
```

Now we are ready to see how the caching works as shown here (`Ch6_5.fsx`):

```
//caching
let nums = (seq {1..100}).GetEnumerator |> makeSeq
// non-cached - double enumeration
((nums |> Seq.sum),(nums |> Seq.length))
//Fresh enumerator given
//Fresh enumerator given
//val it : int * int = (5050, 100)

let cache = nums |> Seq.cache
// cached - single enumeration
((cache |> Seq.sum),(cache |> Seq.length))
//Fresh enumerator given
```

```
//val it : int * int = (5050, 100)
// just another time - no enumerations at all
((cache |> Seq.sum),(cache |> Seq.length))
//val it : int * int = (5050, 100)
```

First, in the absence of any caching, Seq.sum and Seq.length each imposed an independent sequence traversal, which the presence of two enumerator alerts confirms.

Then, after wrapping the working sequence with Seq.cache, I repeat the calculation using the wrapper sequence. As expected, we notice only a single enumerator alert to populate the cache; the second traversal did not leave any traces as it went through the cache.

To be sure, just reissue the calculation. Now, all the data come from the cache, and no traversals of the original sequence take place at all.

The fusion of sequence transformations

I want to wrap up this chapter by demonstrating a pattern known as **fusion**. It is not conceptually difficult: imagine that you have a composition of functions that collectively transform a data sequence. At some point, your implementation requires multiple traversals of the sequence. However, the compiler in principle, or the human in practice, may optimize the transformation, so multiple traversals have now fused into just the single one.

Let's perform fusion in practice, reusing our makeSeq implementation as the indicator of obtaining enumerators as shown in the following code (Ch6_5.fsx):

```
let series = (seq {1..100}).GetEnumerator |> makeSeq
let average dd = (Seq.sum dd) / (Seq.length dd)
average series
//Fresh enumerator given
//Fresh enumerator given
//val it : int = 50
```

The preceding naive implementation of average traverses the sequence twice, of which the enumeration alerts give the evidence.

However, rewriting the implementation of `average` less naively as `averageFused` ends up in the fusion of these traversals as shown in the following code (`Ch6_5.fsx`):

```
let averageFused dd =
  dd
  |> Seq.fold (fun acc x -> (fst acc + x, snd acc + 1)) (0,0)
  |> fun x -> fst x / snd x
averageFused series
//Fresh enumerator given
//val it : int = 50
```

The single enumeration alert confirms my statement completely.

Summary

This chapter covers one of the cornerstones of the F# data processing, namely sequences. The existing F# core sequence library allows you to apply all typical patterns of functional data processing.

When you feel an urge to implement just another custom function for sequence processing, the first thing you need to do is determine which known pattern groups it would belong to and then check twice whether this function is really not implemented already or whether it can be simply composed from the remaining library functions. Recollect the *Minimizing moving parts over hiding them* section from `Chapter 1`, *Begin Thinking Functionally*. Core libraries are minimalistic sets of such high-quality parts, so sticking to them eventually positively influences the quality and readability of your code.

You obtained plenty of details about the inner workings of the F# sequences and should now be able to produce sequences by a variety of means by dealing, when appropriate, with conceptually clean sequences of indefinite length.

Finally, I provided some sequence performance clues and considerations accompanied by some practical optimization coding, leaving you in a good position for further mastery.

In the next chapter, I will revisit the subject of functions as you should now be ready to pick up some advanced techniques on top of the already acquired skills.

7

Advanced Techniques: Functions Revisited

This chapter builds upon the basic F# idioms in functions, pattern matching, and data sequences that we have observed in the previous chapters. Here, I turn to the advanced patterns of data transformations, in other words, the repeated use of functions over data. The goal of this chapter is to familiarize you with the major patterns where combined basic F# idioms work in synergy. This chapter covers the following topics:

- Advanced **recursion** patterns, including tail recursion and the mutual recursion of functions and sequences
- **Folding** as a universal pattern of aggregation
- **Memoization** and **lazy evaluation** as complementary patterns of the **just-in-time principle** applied to data
- The **continuation passing** pattern extending the core **call-return** principle of function interaction
- Advanced pattern matching by generalizing matching with **active patterns**

These synergies often manifest themselves in clean, concise, and efficient F# code.

A deep dive into recursion

I've already scratched the surface of **recursion** in Chapter 3, *Basic Functions*, showing how the `rec` modifier changes the scoping of the function definition. This explicit indication allows the function to reference itself before the function body is fully defined. Now I'll show you how recursion can be employed in the right or wrong way so that you can learn to follow the right recursion pattern.

Tail recursion

I would not be breaking new ground by pointing out that a function, recursive or not, as it is implemented these days, consumes a certain amount of resources for local values, argument values, and so forth. A non-recursive function consumes these resources upon being called and releases them upon returning the result. So far, so good.

But what happens when the function calls itself? Each nested call can stash local resources to be released when this particular level of recursion is done. Hence, a deep recursion may temporarily increase resource consumption. Quite frequently, run-time implementations of the function call and return semantics (including the F# one) use the application *stack space* of a limited volume to temporarily stash the local resources. If a recursive function aggressively consumes this space by deeply nesting self-calls without unwinding the stack, this reserved volume can be exhausted, ending the chain of nested self-calls with the notorious .NET `StackOverflowException`. Even when stack overflow is not the case, the stack space hungry implementation puts a strain on resources and the performance, as the allocations and releases of stack frames keeping the function call local context take time.

A classic (although severely worn out) example of a poorly arranged recursion aiming at the calculation of the **factorial** (`https://en.wikipedia.org/wiki/Factorial`) function is as follows (`Ch7_1.fsx`):

```
let rec ``naive factorial`` = function
| n when n = 0I -> 1I
| _ as n -> n * ``naive factorial`` (n - 1I)
```

(I retreat to the `BigInteger` type here, as in order to cause the stack overflow the argument should be in such a range that the result of the factorial function may easily consist of thousands of digits). Now, with the help of FSI, let's look at what would be the values of ``naive factorial`` 1000 and ``naive factorial`` 10000. The following screenshot shows a number of quite a high magnitude for the first call, but the second call fails exactly as was predicted with `StackOverflowException`:

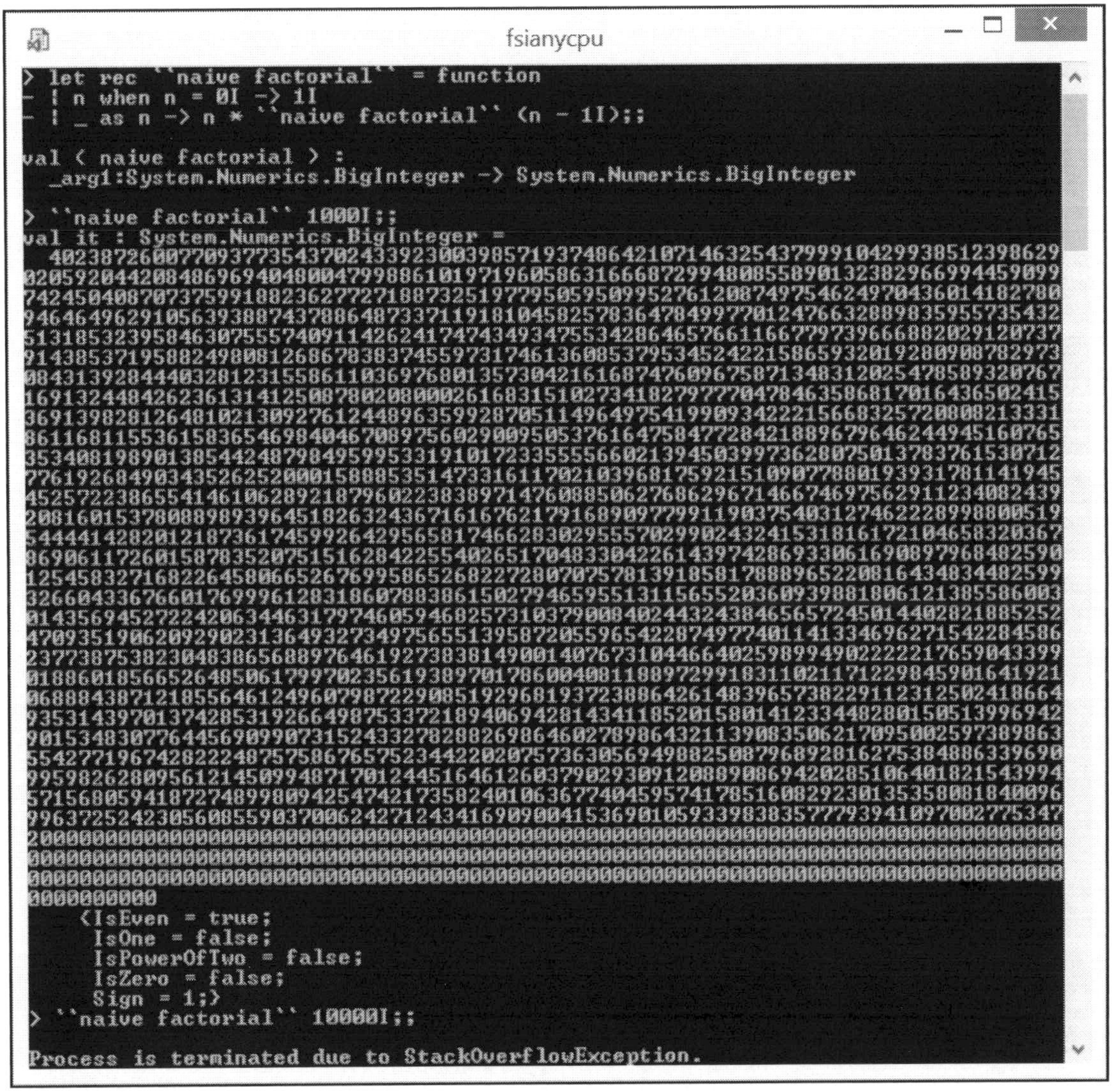

The failure of a non-tail recursive function call

What happens here is that this implementation continuously nests calls to ``naive factorial``, with the decreasing argument value piling stack frames until it reaches ``naive factorial`` 0. Then, it begins to unwind the stack performing deferred multiplications, ending up with an empty stack and sought function value. It is easy to notice that the amount of consumed stack frames coincides with the function argument value. It is enough stack space to accommodate 1000 frames, but 10 times more than overwhelms the application.

What can be done here? We may grasp that all partial multiplications can be done immediately as the recursion unwinds and the interim result may be passed as an extra argument. Such a wise twist to the previous naive approach is shown in the following snippet (Ch7_1.fsx):

```
let ``wise factorial`` n =
  let rec factorial_tail_call acc = function  | n when n = 0I -> acc
  | _ as n -> factorial_tail_call (acc * n) (n - 1I)
  factorial_tail_call 1I n
```

In the preceding ``wise factorial`` definition, recursion is delegated to the inner factorial_tail_call function, which has two arguments instead of one:

- One is the **factorial** argument for any calculation step (it is hidden by the use of function in place of more descriptive match construction)
- The other is **accumulator** acc, carrying the interim product for the already performed recursion steps

It is easy to spot now that the recursive call to factorial_tail_call does not constitute any sort of subexpression of any other expression involving other values from the context; also, evaluating this self-contained expression is the last action the self-calling function performs. That's why it is called a **tail call**, and thereafter, the function having all the recursive calls as tail calls is called **tail recursive**.

Let's take a look at how the ``wise factorial`` implementation will do after being exercised with arguments of a substantial magnitude. In order to save space, let's output the number of digits in the function's result string presentation with an elegant let howLong = (string >> String.length) combinator instead of the actual result factorial number as the following screenshot shows:

Pushing factorial limits with the tail-recursive implementation

After tail recursion's invigorating refactoring, our ``wise factorial`` implementation does not have any problem calculating even the factorial of 100,000, or in traditional math notation, *100,000!*. It's time to get excited indeed, as this number requires almost half a million digits to be recorded, 456574 to be exact!

Careful readers may observe that the implementation of ``wise factorial`` that's free of subexpressions and context-carried values very closely resembles the good old imperative cycle. Surprisingly, this is exactly what the F# optimizing compiler does in such cases. I refer those of you interested in the inner workings of the tail recursion compilation to this blog from the Microsoft Visual F# team: **Tail calls in F#** (https://blogs.msdn.micro soft.com/fsharpteam/2011/07/08/tail-calls-in-f/).

Mutual recursion

So far, all the considered use cases related to recursion were dealing with **self-recursion**, where the recursive function calls itself. However, it is not hard to extrapolate that recursive function abstraction allows a natural generalization, where the group of two or more functions dispatch to each other in definitions, allowing circular dependencies. This generalization brings the **mutual recursion** pattern to the table.

To express this kind of mutual dependency, F# introduces a special kind of `let rec` binding, where definitions of two or more constituent functions are grouped together with the `and` keyword as shown here:

```
let rec fname_a arguments =
  < fname_a definition>
and fname _b arguments =
  < fname_b definition>
. . . . . . . . . . . . . . . . . . . . . . . . . . .
```

As outlined in **recursive functions** (`https://msdn.microsoft.com/en-us/library/dd 233232.aspx`), I have already covered the inner workings of the single function binding that has the `rec` modifier in `Chapter 3`, *Basic Functions*. Mutual recursion binding simply extends the same principle: one or more `and` parts just throw in additional bindings, making the bound function names available for forward referral immediately.

Conceptually, the mutual recursion is quite a simple generalization. However, the growing number of moving parts may make the reasoning about mutually recursive function behavior quite complicated, allowing bugs to sneak in. A good illustration of the above observation can be the example definition of the mutually recursive functions pair `Even` and `Odd` provided on MSDN at the reference given above. The following code shows the following two mutually recursive functions definition taken from there (`Ch7_2.fsx`):

```
// Beware, does not work as expected!
let rec Even x = if x = 0 then true else Odd (x - 1)
and Odd x = if x = 1 then true else Even (x - 1)
```

The definition looks very succinct and elegant, right? Unfortunately, this impression is superficial, and the preceding definition does not work as expected in certain cases, allowing recursion to run away without stopping. Just check for yourself how the preceding code works for the `Even(1)` test case: it runs away! I refer those of you interested in the fixing of this mutually recursive definition to my blog post **A Tale of Two Functions** (`https://infsharpmajor.wordpress.com/2013/04/21/a-tale-of-two-functions/`) published in April 2013, where I covered the bases of the issue, its history, and the suggested fix.

It seems to me that a certain similarity exists between the definition of mutually recursive functions and the piece of imperative code peppered with many `goto.` operators. In both cases it is similarly hard to mentally track the flow of control, which in turn creates the opportunity for bugs to sneak in.

Let me now turn to a sample of a good application of a mutual recursion pattern, demonstrating the bits and pieces of reasoning behind taming its power. I'm going to use my own **Stack Overflow answer** (http://stackoverflow.com/a/9772027/917053) to the question there **Using Functional Programming to compute prime numbers efficiently** (htt p://stackoverflow.com/questions/9766613/using-functional-programming-to-compu te-prime-numbers-efficiently). I approach this challenge with the arsenal of patterns already uncovered until this point in the narrative as shown here (Ch7_2.fsx):

```
let rec primes =
    Seq.cache <| seq { yield 2; yield! Seq.unfold nextPrime 3 }
and nextPrime n =
    let next = n + if n%6 = 1 then 4 else 2 in
    if isPrime n then Some(n, next) else nextPrime next
and isPrime n =
    f n >= 2 then
        primes
        |> Seq.tryFind (fun x -> n % x = 0 || x * x > n)
        |> fun x -> x.Value * x.Value > n
    else false
```

The first piece is the definition of the `primes` sequence of an indefinite length (in fact, limited by the manner of the preceding implementation to `int` prime numbers only but this matter can be easily generalized). The surprising part here is that a sequence binding `seq {...}` can be a part of mutually recursive function bindings. Nevertheless, the `primes` binding uses the `seq { yield 2; yield! Seq.unfold nextPrime 3 }` sequence expression, which yields the first prime number 2, followed by `yield!` of the `Seq.unfold` generator function relying on the assumption that there is a `nextPrime` function around that, being given a prime number argument can generate the next prime number of the greater value. Please take into account how I use a forward reference to `nextPrime` granted by the `rec` modifier of the `let` binding. It's very convenient and it allows you to postpone the definition of `nextPrime`, concentrating only on the sequence generation at the moment.

So far, so good. Now, I turn directly to the definition of `nextPrime`. I do that with an assumption that there is a function `isPrime` around that, being given an `int` argument, can find out whether it's a prime number or not. Again, as discussed earlier, I will make a forward reference to `isPrime` without bothering about its implementation at the moment thanks to the `let rec ...and...` binding that allows me such freedom.

The `nextPrime` function is built by the rules of the `Seq.unfold` higher-order function. The first thing it calculates is the next candidate for primeness regardless of the primeness of the argument at the moment with a slightly obscure binding, `let next = n + if n%6 = 1 then 4 else 2`. In fact, there is nothing exciting here, apparently, potential candidates are odd numbers and I begin unfolding with the smallest odd prime, 3. For each candidate of value n, if n is greater by 1 than a multiple of 6, then the next candidate would be `n + 4` (as `n + 2` is apparently; the multiple of 3); otherwise, it's just `n + 2`, you know, just a small optimization. Next, having a prime candidate n and the following n prime candidate `next` at hand, I check whether value n is prime with the help of the (not yet defined) `isPrime` function. If affirmative, it returns the `Some(n, next)` option; otherwise, it recursively calls itself with `next` as the argument.

Great! The last piece of the puzzle is to define `isPrime`. The first thing is that it sifts out integers of less than 2 (an additional useful property of `isPrime` is that it can be used just as a primeness detector to be called from elsewhere). Now pay attention: for argument values greater than or equal to 2, it actively uses the members of the already generated `primes` sequence of lesser than or equal to the square root of the argument values with the help of the `Seq.tryFind` higher-order function for the checking! That's why I cached the output of the sequence expression with `Seq.cache` in the definition of `primes`; otherwise, `isPrime` would be slow. We trade here the memory space for the execution speed. So, `Seq.tryFind` traverses the cache until it either finds the factor of the argument value or it reaches the point where the `primes` member multiplied by itself gets greater than the argument. The first outcome means that the argument is not a prime number, and the second means that it is a prime number. This statement wraps up the lengthy and slightly annoying comments about the implementation of `primes`.

I wrap up this section by checking how performant the `primes` implementation is. For this purpose, let me turn to the familiar **Project Euler** (`https://projecteuler.net/`), particularly to the **Problem 10 – Summation of Primes** (`https://projecteuler.net/probl em=10`):

```
let problem010 () =
  primes
  |> Seq.takeWhile ((>) 2000000)
  |> (Seq.map int64 >> Seq.sum)
```

Applying the `primes` definition to the summation of prime numbers not exceeding 2,000,000 is shown in the upcoming figure. It takes just less than 1.5 seconds on my computer. Also, consider that the repeated run yields the result in just 10 milliseconds, thanks to the sequence caching:

Using mutual recursion for primes generation

Personally, I find a lot of aesthetic value in the `primes` code, in how it uses forward references twice, finally closing in on the self-computed data. And each of three circularly dependent parts of the definition is a pure function (well, kind of, as caching definitely represents a hidden state but in a very clean form). This is the power of functional programming!

Folding

Now is the perfect time to revisit the `factorial` function that I used at the beginning of this chapter when covering tail recursion. Let's take a sequence of `bigint` numbers from 1I to a value n represented by the following expression:

```
Seq.init (n + 1) bigint.op_Implicit |> Seq.skip 1
```

Does the `factorial(n)` function represent nothing else but a product of the factors, each being a member of the preceding sequence? Sure, it can be seen (and implemented) as such. Let me create this implementation in the best traditions of the imperative programming style as shown here (`Ch7_3.fsx`):

```
let ``folding factorial (seq)`` n =
  let fs = Seq.init (n + 1) bigint.op_Implicit |> Seq.skip 1
  use er = fs.GetEnumerator()
  let mutable acc = 1I
  while er.MoveNext() do
    acc <- acc * er.Current
  acc
```

Expressed in plain words, this implementation can be laid out in the following manner:

- Take a mutable value that will serve as a result accumulator
- Enumerate the sequence of factors
- For each factor in the sequence, get a new value of the accumulator by multiplying the current accumulator value by the current factor
- Return the final accumulator value as a function result

Some of you with experience in object-oriented design may perhaps have already spotted the signs of the **visitor** (`https://en.wikipedia.org/wiki/Visitor_pattern`) pattern in the preceding implementation. Indeed, the operation (multiplication in this case) is applied to the sequence data without in any way changing this data, eventually deriving the result as the aggregate of these repeated operations.

Generalizing this in the form of a higher-order function signature, the following can be derived:

```
fold: ('State -> 'T -> 'State) -> 'State -> 'T seq -> 'State
```

Here, the function of type (`'State -> 'T -> 'State`) named `folder` applies to the pair of arguments:

- The first of type `'State` representing the accumulator
- The second of type `seq 'T` representing the sequence of elements that have the type `'T`

The `folder` function returns the final value of the accumulator. This function, named `fold`, represents the ubiquitous pattern of data processing by name `folding`.

As can be expected, the generic folding of the preceding form is indeed a member of the F# core library: **Seq.fold<'T,'State> function** (https://msdn.microsoft.com/en-us/library /ee353471.aspx). Rewriting ``folding factorial (seq)`` with the help of the Seq.fold library function, which hides all these pesky moving parts involved (the enumerator, state holder, and traversing enumeration), gives the following, much more terse version (Ch7_3.fsx):

```
let ``folding factorial (lib)`` n =
  Seq.init (n + 1) bigint.op_Implicit
  |> Seq.skip 1
  |> Seq.fold (*) 1I
```

Let's compare both implementations from a performance standpoint. The results of running both versions side by side are given in the following screenshot:

Hand-coded folding versus the library fold function performance

---

It should not be surprising to observe that the `library` function shows slightly better performance than the hand coded imperative version. The `library` function implementation is highly optimized. For those who are curious, the current library implementation of the `fold` function taken from GitHub looks like what is shown in the following snippet (`Ch3_7.fsx`):

```
// Excerpt from seq.fs of FSharp.Core.Collections:
[<CompiledName("Fold")>]
let fold<'T,'State> f (x:'State) (source : seq<'T>)  =
  checkNonNull "source" source
  use e = source.GetEnumerator()
  let f = OptimizedClosures.FSharpFunc<_,_,_>.Adapt(f)
  let mutable state = x
  while e.MoveNext() do
    state <- f.Invoke(state, e.Current)
  state
```

You may have already noticed how closely folding resembles tail recursion with the accumulator. This resemblance is not accidental. Both thread the state through the sequence of function calls, although the `recursive` function materializes these calls when it is executed, while the `fold` function applies the `folder` function to the explicit to-be-folded data sequence.

 It can be formally proven that in a language with first-order tuples and functions, which F# is, any function can be expressed as `fold`. I refer those of you who are interested to the classic paper on this subject: Graham Hutton's **A Tutorial on the Expressiveness and Universality of Fold** (`www.cs.nott.ac.uk/~pszgmh/fold.pdf`).

Memoization

The next two relatively advanced topics I will cover somehow resemble the **Just in Time** approach taken outside of the compilation context. With **Just in Time** (`https://en.wikipedia.org/wiki/Just_in_Time`), Wikipedia comes up first with a production strategy in manufacturing, where components are delivered immediately before being utilized as a way of being *lean* on inventory costs.

As a matter of fact, **memoization** and **lazy evaluation** complement each other in this *lean* calculation sense. While laziness allows you not to perform calculations until the result is absolutely required, memoization makes the results of the already performed *fat* resource expensive calculations reusable by not allowing them to be wasted.

I have already used memoization somewhat when implementing prime number generation earlier in this chapter for covering mutual recursion. An expensively generated sequence was cached there in order to use the already generated elements to find the next ones, which are not generated yet. Now, I want to concentrate on memoization in general, allowing any function to be memoized. Prior to doing this, it is important that you realize the following:

- Memoization may work for *pure functions only*. This is almost obvious; if a function is not referentially transparent, it cannot be memoized as memoization captures solely arguments, not arguments, *and* state
- Memoization exploits a precalculated state

With this in mind, let's mimic implementations presented elsewhere on the Internet (https://blogs.msdn.microsoft.com/dsyme/2007/05/31/a-sample-of-the-memoization-pattern-in-f/ and http://www.fssnip.net/8P) in order to investigate related limitations and gotchas as shown here (Ch7_4.fsx):

```
// Memoization (F# 4.0 is required)
let memoize f =
  let mutable cache = Map.empty
  fun x ->
    match cache.TryFind(x) with
    | Some res -> printfn "returned memoized";res
    | None -> let res = f x in
    cache <- cache.Add(x,res)
    printfn "memoized, then returned"; res
```

The type inferred for memoization by the F# compiler is shown here:

```
memoize : f:('a -> 'b) -> ('a -> 'b) when 'a : comparison
```

Here, f represents a function to be memoized, cache serves as a state repository using the immutable **Map F# collection** (https://msdn.microsoft.com/en-us/library/ee353880.aspx) under the hood. memoize itself represents a full-fledged high-order function that takes a function as an argument and also returns a function. This closes over mutable cache (an F# 4.0 feature) and does the following:

- If its argument x, which is used as a key against the closed Mapcache can be found, then it logs the indication that the precached value is to be used and returns this res value.
- Otherwise, it mutates the closed cache to a new Map that has, in addition to the existed entries, the entry represented by the newly calculated tuple (x, f(x)), then it logs the fact that memoization took place and returns f(x).

Let's see for now how this works in FSI, which the following screenshot captures:

Memoization with F# Map

First, I memoized the `funx -> x*x` function, which is supposed to represent a "fat" resource hungry calculation into the `fm: (int -> int)` function. Then, I used `fm` a couple of times with different arguments as shown here:

- `fm 10`: The result `100` was memoized for argument 10 and then returned
- `fm 42`: The result `1764` was also memoized and then returned
- `fm 10`: As this argument value has already occurred, the result `100` is returned without any recalculation

This pattern seems quite straightforward; however, it carries a few gotchas.

For example, the signature of `memoize` indicates that `'a` is required in order to represent comparison; what gives? Digging down the `memoize` implementation allows you to conclude that this constraint is a mere corollary of using F# `Map` to back the state persistence.

As the implementation behind Map is likely to be a **balanced tree**, it requires its keys to be *comparable* for rebalancing. Oops! Sounds like a **leaky abstraction** (https://en.wikipedia.org/wiki/Leaky_abstraction) takes place here. Also, this may be a limiting factor for the application of memoization generically, as comparability is not a universal property of a generic type 'a.

Let's change the persistence implementation mechanism to a generic **Dictionary** (https://msdn.microsoft.com/en-us/library/xfhwa508(v=vs.100).aspx), as shown in the following code (Ch7_4.fsx):

```
let memoize' f =
  let cache = System.Collections.Generic.Dictionary()
  fun x ->
    match cache.TryGetValue(x) with
    | true,res -> printfn "returned memoized";res
    | _ -> let res = f x
    cache.Add(x,res)
    printfn "memoized, then returned"
    res
```

This changes the memoized argument constraint from comparison to equality as shown here:

```
memoize' : f:('a -> 'b) -> ('a -> 'b) when 'a : equality
```

This can be considered more universal, only until some innocuous usage like this occurs:

```
let disaster = memoize' (fun () -> 5)
......
disaster()
```

Executing this code will end up with the following exception:

```
System.ArgumentNullException: Value cannot be null
```

What the heck? Turns out nothing special happened, just another leaky abstraction has taken place, and consequently, the gotcha occurred. This time, the gotcha stems from the underlying persistence mechanism that does not allow you to have the null value as a Dictionary key (on the contrary, Map happily allows this)!

Finally, I want to touch the matter of combining memoization with recursion, as quite frequently, recursion is the tool to solve problems with the **divide and conquer** strategy, where memoization fits naturally and may really shine.

Let's take some use case more appropriate for the purpose, for example, the simple calculation of *binomial coefficients* with the help of **Pascal's triangle** (https://en.wikipedia .org/wiki/Pascal%27s_triangle) as shown here (Ch7_4.fsx):

```
let rec binomial n k =
  if k = 0 || k = n then 1
  else
    binomial (n - 1) k + binomial (n - 1) (k - 1)
```

The easily noticeable recurrent relationship between elements of Pascal's triangle rows allows you to expect a serious benefit from memoization.

The memoized implementation of binomial is also straightforward; memoize is turned into an internal function in order to strip the logging introduced within its initial version. The only other problem left is that the memoized function has one argument. However, applying uncurrying helps with this trouble nicely as shown here (Ch7_4.fsx):

```
let rec memoizedBinomial =
  let memoize f =
    let cache = System.Collections.Generic.Dictionary()
    fun x ->
    match cache.TryGetValue(x) with
    | true,res -> res
    | _ -> let res = f x
    cache.Add(x,res)
    res
  memoize
  (fun (n,k) ->
    if k = 0 || k = n then 1
    else
      memoizedBinomial (n - 1, k) +
      memoizedBinomial (n - 1, k - 1))
```

Now it's time to measure the gain achieved from the memoization. The code in the upcoming figure measures the duration of repeating binomial 500 2 10,000 times compared to the duration of repeating it 10,000 times as memoizedBinomial (500,2):

```
> #nowarn "40"
- let rec binomial n k =
-     if k = 0 || k = n then 1
-     else
-         binomial (n - 1) k + binomial (n - 1) (k - 1)

- let rec memoizedBinomial =
-     let memoize f =
-         let cache = System.Collections.Generic.Dictionary()
-         fun x ->
-             match cache.TryGetValue(x) with
-             | true,res -> res
-             | _ -> let res = f x
-                    cache.Add(x,res)
-                    res
-     memoize
-         (fun (n,k) ->
-             if k = 0 || k = n then 1
-             else
-                 memoizedBinomial (n - 1, k) + memoizedBinomial (n - 1,k - 1));
- ;
val binomial : n:int -> k:int -> int
val memoizedBinomial : (int * int -> int)

> #time;;

--> Timing now on

> for i in [0..10000] do ignore <| binomial 500 2;;
Real: 00:00:23.806, CPU: 00:00:23.781, GC gen0: 0, gen1: 0, gen2: 0
val it : unit = ()
> for i in [0..10000] do ignore <| memoizedBinomial (500,2);;
Real: 00:00:00.009, CPU: 00:00:00.015, GC gen0: 0, gen1: 0, gen2: 0
val it : unit = ()
>
```

Memoizing of the "divide and conquer" solution

The results of the comparison are absolutely stunning, that is, 23781 / 15 = 1585, which means that memoization has improved the performance by 1585 times!

Lazy evaluation

This concept is very simple. By default, F# follows the **eager evaluation** (https://en.wikip edia.org/wiki/Eager_evaluation) strategy, or an expression is evaluated as soon as it is bound. The alternative strategy available in other functional programming languages is to postpone the calculations until their result is absolutely necessary. F# can be explicitly told where to use lazy evaluation; by default, it uses lazy evaluations only for sequences. Expressing lazy evaluation if F# is not complicated syntactically, the following binding serves the purpose as shown:

```
let name = lazy ( expression )
```

Here, `name` is bound to the result of calculating `expression`, but the calculation itself is postponed. The type of value `name` is a special one, that is, `Lazy<'T>`; it represents a wrapper over `'T`, which is the type of the expression per se. The computation gets performed by calling the `Force` method of type `Lazy<'T>`, like this `name.Force()`. This action also unwraps the underlying type of `Lazy`, so the type of the `name.Force()` expression is `'T`.

Take into account that this feature is not specific to F#; the `Lazy<T>` class is a part of the .NET framework class library of the System namespace.

It is important to understand that the expression is calculated only once, so if the expression wrapped into the `lazy` method has a side effect, it is performed only once on the expression calculation. Even if the calculation is forced another time, nothing will happen on the side; only the cached result will be returned.

Let's demonstrate this with the following snippet (`Ch7_5.fsx`):

```
let twoByTwo  = lazy (let r = 2*2 in
  printfn "Everybody knows that 2*2=%d" r; r)
twoByTwo.Force()
twoByTwo.Force()
```

The following screenshot shows how this code behaves in FSI:

Lazy evaluation and side-effects

Note that the binding for `twoByTwo` did not bring any calculations to life, but it wrapped the future calculation into the `Lazy` type. Then, the first `twoByTwo.Force()` function performed the wrapped calculation, so the side-effect popped up. Finally, any consequent `twoByTwo.Force()` function will just repeatedly bring the result of the very first calculation without any side-effects.

The lazy evaluation pattern has its own niche in enterprise F# development. I often use it when in need of a resource that's probably being initialized; if this need really materializes, I want it to happen only once. For example, we can consider reading the Production environment configuration settings from Azure `KeyVault` when a service runs in the Production environment while using some other configuration information carrier in other environments, for example, environment variables pointing to data stubs.

Continuation passing style

This sophisticated technique of arranging recursion allows you to avoid stack consumption by putting all function calls into the tail position with **continuation**, that is, a function that performs the remaining computations instead of returning result to the caller. Let me demonstrate this technique by refactoring the *factorial* implementation one more time as shown in the following snippet (`Ch7_6.fsx`):

```
let rec ``factorial (cps)`` cont = function
  | z when z = 0I -> cont 1I
  | n -> ``factorial (cps)`` (fun x -> cont(n * x)) (n - 1I)
```

Although slightly mind-bending, the code consists of all tail calls:

- A recursive call to itself ``factorial (cps)`` is a tail call
- A new continuation anonymous function also makes a tail call to the old continuation, `cont`

The `cont` function has inferred signature of (`BigInteger -> 'a`); so, in order to perform the sought-for calculations, using the `id` identity function for the `cont` as the first argument of `` `factorial (cps)` `` would be just fine. Testing the continuation passing style implementation of `` `factorial (cps)` `` function in FSI is presented in the following screenshot:

Implementing a factorial function with the help of continuation passing style

This works perfectly, although those of you not already familiar with continuation passing style may develop a headache when dealing with this code for the first time.

Active patterns

I promised in Chapter 4, *Basic Pattern Matching*, that I would add to the subject by covering **active patterns**; now is a perfect time. Remember matching with **guards?** Guards provide a way to drill down into the matched `pattern-expression` function by attaching an arbitrary calculation having the `bool` result.

Guard mechanism adds a certain customization potential to the vanilla pattern matching, but it is kind of detached: regardless of how much data decomposition is required in order to complete the guard calculation, all this effort is discarded for both matching and non-matching possible calculation results. Wouldn't it be nice to have a fully customizable transition between the recognition and transformation phases of pattern matching? Active patterns aim exactly at this matter. Broadly speaking, active patterns represent a special kind of function allowed to be used inside `pattern-expression`.

They allow you to implement some typical patterns of data transformations in a very terse and elegant manner as following:

- Advanced transformations between types
- Partitioning data into groups by relevant and irrelevant categories
- Performing full categorization, in other words, taking any data and processing it according to this piece of data belonging to a specific category out of the couple given

Let's look at how active patterns play with each case of these data processing patterns.

Type transformations with active patterns

Active patterns use a special naming convention when being defined within a `let` binding:

- The name of the active pattern function must begin with a capital letter even if it is a double-ticked like this: `` ``I'm active pattern`` ``
- The name of the active pattern function must be wrapped into *banana clips* (`|` and `|`) as in ``(|``Another active pattern``|)``

The data in which an active pattern works always comes as the last argument in the definition and at the time of its use being taken from the context (`match`, `function`, or any other F# construction where pattern matching occurs); all but the last arguments in a multi-argument definition are parameters that generalize the active pattern workings.

Finally, when a literal is used at the place of the last argument, the `pattern-expression` is considered matched when the result of the active pattern calculation matches the literal. If a name is used instead of the literal, then this name gets bound to the result of the active pattern calculation to be used in the corresponding `result-expression` transformation.

Does this sound confusing? In fact, it is easier than it may sound. Let me turn to some illustrative samples that might help.

The first one represents a dummy sample as shown in the following code (`Ch7_7.fsx`):

```
let (|Echo|) x = x
let checkEcho p =
  match p with
  | Echo 42 -> "42!"
  | Echo x -> sprintf "%O is not good" x
```

The `Echo` active pattern is very minimalistic; it just echoes the input into the result. Then, the `checkEcho` function puts this definition to use. In the first `pattern-expression`, it simply checks whether the result of the `Echo p` calculation (p is implicitly taken from the head of the `match` construction) equals `42`. If it does, then the corresponding result expression returns string `"42!"`. Otherwise, the next `result-expression` is evaluated by unconditionally binding the result of the `Echo p` calculation to variable x, which in turn is used in `result-expression` to produce a `"... is not good"` string.

So, when using the preceding sample in FSI, `checkEcho 0` produces `"0 is not good"`, while `checkEcho 42` produces `"42!"`.

Is it getting clearer? Another simple sample reinforcing this understanding would be an active pattern:

```
let (|``I'm active pattern``|) x = x + 2
```

While keeping the same type for the argument and result, this performs just a simple value transformation. The usage of the above active pattern is shown in the following screenshot:

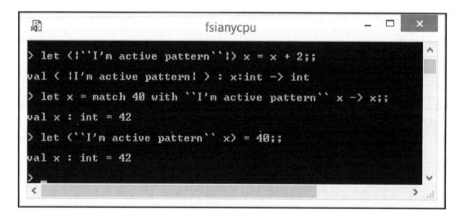

A simple type transformation with an active pattern

The binding `let (|``I'm active pattern``|) x = x + 2` that defines the active pattern does not match anything; instead, it takes the matched value and returns it, adding 2.

The binding `let x = match 40 with ``I'm active pattern`` x -> x` is used as a part of the match construct and given the input argument `40`, it returns `x` bound to a sum value of `42`.

The binding `let (``I'm active pattern`` x) = 40` is a slightly mind boggling example that becomes clear if you remember that the `let` binding of a value is a corner case of pattern matching based data disassembling, so ``` ``I'm active pattern`` ``` gets applied to input argument `40` and binds the result `42` to `x`.

At this point, this specific use case of applying active patterns for data transformations should be clear enough; I want to apply it in a more practically sound use case.

It is a rather widespread technique to use **globally unique identifiers, or GUIDs** (`https://en.wikipedia.org/wiki/Globally_unique_identifier`) to label unique entities popping up in the course of running a business. For example, in Jet.com, GUIDs are used to label customer orders, merchant orders, merchant order items, shipping, fulfillment centers, SKUs...the complete list would be too long. These codes are mostly exchanged and displayed as strings of 32 hexadecimal digits. In some nodes of the system, it is required that you validate that a given string is a legitimate representation of a GUID. This task can be easily performed with the help of active patterns as shown here (`Ch7_7.fsx`):

```
let hexCharSet = ['0'..'9'] @ ['a'..'f'] |> set in
let (|IsValidGuidCode|) (guidstr: string) =
  let (|HasRightSize|) _ = guidstr.Length = 32
  let (|IsHex|) _ = (guidstr.ToLower() |> set) = hexCharSet
  match () with (HasRightSize rightsize & IsHex hex)-> rightsize && hex
```

The preceding code has many interesting bits and pieces, such as the set of allowable `hexCharSet` hexadecimal characters that are calculated only once and are local to the active pattern `IsValidGuidCode` definition; the pair of internal active patterns `HasRightSize` and `IsHex`, each responsible only for the single verified property and disregarding its own input argument using one from the outer active pattern instead; and finally, the way two `pattern-expressions` are combined with `&`, again omitting the argument as it is already delivered to their bodies and combining the final result within `result-expression` based upon entities distilled in the complementary `pattern-expression`. Those of you who fully understand how the preceding snippet works can claim yourselves to be experts on the subject of active patterns.

To ensure that this code really works, let me perform a quick test drive. The upcoming figure reflects the results of this test, showing that the `IsValidGuidCode` active pattern correctly identifies the `"abc"` string as an invalid GUID and `"0123456789AbCdEfFFEEDDCCbbAA9988  "` as a valid one:

Verifying a GUID string using active patterns

By the way, active patterns of the (`|active pattern name|`) form that I have covered so far are named **single total active patterns**, as they deal with a single data type, transforming it into the same or a different data type by the enclosed calculation. Another peculiarity of considered samples is that all of them were working on a single argument. I will cover **active patterns with parameters** later in this chapter.

Data partitioning with active patterns

My next foray into F# active patterns use as processing patterns is concerned with the typical practice of having data that may constitute one or more cases suitable for the processing and "just the rest" unsuitable. In the spirit of F#'s ubiquitous use of options active patterns capable of performing the above manner of partitioning transform the input data type into an `Option` type, where the `None` case represents unsuitable data and `Some` wraps one or more types of suitable data.

The definition of such active patterns is unambiguously distinguishable by having |_ characters prepended to the right-hand side banana clip |) of the active pattern definition. The active patterns of this type are called **partial active patterns** and their name groups look like this: (|name 1[|name 2...]|_|). Let's consider a pretty sizeable piece of real code from one of the Jet.com production systems to demonstrate this technique.

The task at hand is to process the invoices from Jet.com vendors (shipping carriers, payment processors, and others) that package their data in the form of comma-separated files. I use "comma-separated" broadly here, as separators can be any characters. Files may or may not have headers and can carry just a gazillion other irregularities. Uploading these invoices for processing followed by archiving is a problem that carries a certain complexity.

For the purposes of this chapter, I will take only a partially related problem, namely recognizing whether the last uploaded file is of a known Processable type and should be processed or whether it is not and should be rejected.

In order to keep the code implementing the preceding task reasonably short for the purposes of the book, I'll limit the number of vendors to just three, that is, **FedEx** and **OnTrac** shipping carriers and the **Braintree** payment processor.

I begin with the Processable here that lists known vendor files as following (Ch7_8.fsx):

```
type Processable =
| FedexFile
| OnTracFile
| BrainTreeFile
with
    override this.ToString() = match this with
        | FedexFile -> "Fedex"
        | OnTracFile -> "OnTrac"
        | BrainTreeFile -> "BrainTree"
```

Nothing fancy here; just a common practice of representing domain entities with discriminated unions, perhaps slightly augmented.

Next, file headers are hardcoded here and also significantly stripped from the right-hand side as the complete contents do not matter much as shown here (Ch7_8.fsx):

```
let BraintreeHdr = "Transaction ID,Subscription ID,..."
let FedexHdr = ""Bill to Account Number";"Invoice Date";..."
let OntracHdr = "AccountNum,InvoiceNum,Reference,ShipDate,TotalCharge,..."
```

And finally, the active pattern definition is as follows (Ch7_8.fsx):

```
let (|IsProcessable|_|) (stream: Stream) =
    use streamReader = new StreamReader(stream)
```

```
let hdr = streamReader.ReadLine()
[(Processable.BrainTreeFile,BraintreeHdr);
(Processable.FedexFile,FedexHdr);
(Processable.OnTracFile,OntracHdr)]
|> List.tryFind (fun x -> (snd x) = hdr)
|> function
| None -> (if hdr.StartsWith(""1",") then
  Some (Processable.OnTracFile) else None)
| _ as zx -> Some (fst zx.Value)
```

The active pattern name, as expected, points to the partial active pattern, the argument is of type `System.IO.Stream` carrying the file contents, and its return is of type `Processable` option.

The function first creates `StreamReader` and reads the first line from there into the `hdr` value.

Then, it takes a list of tuples, which members perform pairing of `Processable` cases with the string literals denoting the corresponding comma-separated file headers and tries to find the element that has the second part of the tuple that is equal to the `hdr`. If such exists, then the file can be processed and the function returns option value `Some`, wrapping the first part of the found tuple.

If the element is not found (option value `None` case), consider at this point that often `OnTrac` files may not carry headers. To exploit this knowledge, I examine a bit more into the already taken stream contents and whether the file begins with some symbols pointing to the `OnTrac` origin the active pattern returns `Some (Processable.OnTracFile)`; otherwise, the file is considered non-processable.

In my opinion, the `IsProcessable` active pattern represents quite a terse and clean implementation of the business feature.

Data categorization with active patterns

I wrap up our journey into the exciting world of F# active patterns with the active pattern type that applies to the processing pattern of **categorization**, or partitioning the data into the entirety of subcategories that completely cover the domain entity, not leaving any space for non-applicable outliers.

As some of you may have already deducted, the name associated with this active pattern is **multicase active pattern**. Its syntactic definition is also very distinguishable from the already considered cases. It has contained between the banana clips just few case names separated from each other by | pipe symbols.

Let's delve into the illustrative sample. An e-commerce domain operating with payments considers different payment terms and policies. In particular, if the payment terms are not immediate, it make sense to introduce a certain policy or policies concerned with determining when each particular payment is due. Hence, given the date on which a service or merchandise was supplied, the corresponding payment is due or not due depends on the amount of time passed from that date to now.

The implementation using active patterns is very straightforward; just for simplicity, let's assume that the business has adopted a single policy of postponing the payments for no more than three days (certainly, the policy can be a subject of parameterization in a more sophisticated design) as shown here (Ch7_9.fsx):

```
open System

let (|Recent|Due|) (dt: DateTimeOffset) =
  if DateTimeOffset.Now.AddDays(-3.0) <= dt then Recent
  else Due

let isDue = function
| Recent -> printfn "don't do anything"
| Due    -> printfn "time to pay this one"
```

The function using the active pattern is also pretty simple, but this is OK for the purpose of illustration. The preceding code is presented in the following figure:

Multi-case active patterns for data categorization

I forgot to mention that the maximal number of cases in F# 4.0 multicase active patterns as of today is limited to 7, which may be the limiting factor in using active patterns in some cases.

Summary

This chapter was quite a long field trip into relatively advanced F# idioms that an average F# developer uses in the course of a work day quite frequently.

The next chapter will cover even more widely used language patterns playing the central role in data crunching, with F# demonstrating polymorphic behavior for multiple data collection types.

8
Data Crunching – Data Transformation Patterns

After dealing with advanced patterns of the function definition and application in the previous chapter, I want to revisit the topic that was just slightly scratched in `Chapter 6`, *Sequences – The Core of Data Processing Patterns* in connection with sequences. There, I claimed that the quite bulky `Collection.seq` library absorbs and implements just a handful of universal data processing patterns. Then I regrouped the library members by assigning to one of these patterns.

This chapter digs deeper into these patterns of data transformation that are applicable not only to sequences, but also to other data collections. The goal of this chapter is to help you develop the skill to convey your data processing needs with functions belonging to a handful of typical polymorphic transformation categories composed of a handful of combinators, and by operating upon data collection types that are best suitable for the task at hand. This approach allows you to uniformly cover the widest assortment of specific data transformations. Sticking to the above approach is essential for F# programmer practitioners as it effectively curbs the development of lengthy custom solutions without compelling reasons and overall adds to the positive properties of F# programs, such as succinctness, correctness, and performance.

In this chapter, we will inspect:

- How normalization of data transformation libraries in F# 4.0 reflects upon underlying transformation patterns commonalities. These commonalities have a polymorphic nature being applicable to the various data collections that the libraries aim.
- How the transformation patterns scoped in `Chapter 6`, *Sequences – The Core of Data Processing Patterns* reveal themselves over various data collections.

It will be a long trip, so please stay with me, cool and hydrated.

Core data transformation libraries in F# 4.0

One of the enhancements to the FSharp.Core run-time brought by F# 4.0 is **normalized data collection modules** (`https://blogs.msdn.microsoft.com/fsharpteam/2014/11/12/anno uncing-a-preview-of-f-4-0-and-the-visual-f-tools-in-vs-2015/`). It is quite interesting that this development:

- Confirms the commonality of data processing patterns across data processing platforms. Functions such as `map` or `filter` can be found in functional programming languages such as F#, query tools such as **LINQ**, and scripting engines such as **PowerShell**, to name a few.
- Recognizes that concrete functions belonging to these patterns are polymorphic and may be uniformly apply across different data collection types. F# 4.0 successfully delivers this polymorphism over the most frequently used data collection types, namely for `Array`, `List`, and `Seq` modules.

Overall, this library normalization added 95 new optimized per collection type function implementations to F# 4.0 data crunching offering. This addition bumps the overall amount of individual functions in the previously mentioned three collection modules to 309 (as of April 2016), which is definitely a sizable result. However, it would be really challenging for a random developer to memorize and recall this arrangement by heart without recognizing some formative principles.

Considering that most of the functions apply uniformly to three base collection types (some of them naturally do not apply to some concrete collections; for example, `toList` does not apply to `List`), this still leaves 117 (as of April 2016) *different function names* just for the base data collections. And do not forget about a certain number of functions related to less widely used data collections, such as `set`, `IDictionary`, or `Array2D`. How should you approach this variety?

Fortunately, the number of data transformation patterns is just a handful. Recognizing the underlying pattern most often imposes an order on associated library functions, leaving just a dozen or so functions associated with each pattern. Such categorized amounts are much easier to recall.

In the rest of the chapter, we will examine these concealed patterns and their correspondent cohesive function groups. The provided idiomatic code examples facilitate the pattern retention, recognition, and reuse.

Data transformation patterns

A good question about data transformation libraries richness would be: Where does such an overwhelming variety come from in the first place? Why do designers of F# include as many as hundred-something functions over base data collections into the *core* library?

I believe a single "right" answer to this question simply does not exist. However, some clues may come from considering a typical **ETL – Extract, Transform, Load** (https://en.wikipe dia.org/wiki/Extract,_transform,_load) enterprise data crunching process. In the world of mutable collections and arbitrarily changing states, this operation can be expressed as follows:

```
void PerformETL()
{
    ExtractData();
    TransformData();
    LoadData();
}
```

This C#-like pseudocode demonstrates how literally gazillions of possible data transformations can be hidden behind the same few opaque lines of code. We cannot say anything about the details until we meticulously delve into the implementation of each of the above pieces, find out what it does, how it gets to the data, and how it shares the mutating state with other involved pieces.

Now let's express the semantically similar chain of activities in a more functional manner as following:

```
let performETL params : unit =
    let inputCollection = extractData params
    let outputCollection = transformData inputCollection
    loadData outputCollection
```

The preceding snippet tells a better story than its imperative sibling. We can see right away that `extractData` is a collection generator function that is based on certain input parameters `params` that produce the initial `inputCollection` function out of some sort of persistent store. This collection is given as an input parameter to the transformation function `transformData` that produces as a result the output collection `outputCollection`. Finally, this collection is given to the data loader function `loadData`, and it ends up being stored back into the persistent store. Given that the communication with the persistent store is implemented in an *idempotent* manner and the involved functions are referentially transparent, this chain of transformations can be replayed an arbitrary number of times with the same results.

We can even take another step toward idiomatic use and rewrite the last snippet as follows:

```
let performETL params : unit =
  params
    |> extractData
    |> transformData
    |> loadData
```

Now we really deal with the code, transforming immutable data. This code does not dependent on the side effects of an internal state. Its components are better composable and it can be easily extended, if necessary. Finally, this code is simply more elegant now, it is easier to read and comprehend.

You may ask how this rather simplistic passage relates to significant library members' variety?

First of all, there are a few dozen of typical transformations that exist in correspondence with the widely accepted ways in which data processing algorithms are captured in computer science. For example, if we are going to provide a library function to split a collection into a pair of partitions, we cannot make it much differently than with a higher-order function of the following pseudo-signature:

```
partition: predicate:('T -> bool) -> source:'T collection
        -> ('T collection * 'T collection)
```

Here, `predicate` is a function that takes a single collection member of type `'T` and returns `bool`, where `true` signifies that the input element will go to the first collection of the result tuple, and `false` means it will go to the second collection. The `source` parameter represents the input collection to be split. I intentionally put "generic" `collection` into the preceding signature, and I will explain the reason in a bit. The result is a tuple carrying `source` elements being partitioned into two collections by the `predicate` values.

Many known algorithms of computer science can be succinctly implemented almost barely using the above `partition` function. For example, the famous **QuickSort** (https://en.wik ipedia.org/wiki/Quicksort) representing the broad **Divide and Conquer** (https://en.w ikipedia.org/wiki/Divide_and_conquer_algorithms) class of algorithms. Let's look at how **QuickSort** may be elegantly implemented using `partition` as shown by the following snippet (Ch8_1.fsx):

```
let rec qsort : int list -> _ = function
  | [] -> []
  | x::xs ->
      let less, greater = List.partition ((>) x) xs
      qsort less @ x :: qsort greater
```

The `qsort` function (somewhat simplistically) partitions a non-empty input list argument into two groups: one containing only elements that are less than one `x` in the head of the list, and the other containing the rest. The result would be to append the list that has `x` prepended to `qsortgreater` to the list `qsortless`. Beautiful! Let's look at how this plays out in FSI in the following screenshot:

Implementing quicksort with the partition function

Now let me return to the reason I used `collection` in the signature of the preceding `partition` function. Coincidentally, this is another piece of the consideration prompting the variety of library members, which is *performance*. You can bet the farm on the assertion that in order to be effective, `partition` should be implemented separately for `array` and `list` collections, yielding the pair of functions, each belonging to their respective module as shown:

```
List.partition: predicate:('T -> bool) -> list:'T list
        -> ('T list * 'T list)
Array.partition : predicate:('T -> bool) -> array:'T[]
        -> 'T[] * 'T[]
```

Along these lines, an interesting point is the lack of the `Seq.partition` function in F# 4.0 core libraries. The root cause for this artifact comes down to the performance. I refer those of you who are curious to to **pertinent piece of F# design specs** (`https://github.com/fsh arp/FSharpLangDesign/blob/5cec1d3f524240f063b6f9dad2f23ca5a9d7b158/FSharp-4. 0/ListSeqArrayAdditions.md#regular-functional-operators-producing-two-or-mor e-output-collections`) and a more mundane **explanation on StackOverflow Q&A website** (`http://stackoverflow.com/a/31750808/917053`) that gives of the exact reason.

Summing up, F# language designers, when defining and implementing the F# core library of data transformation functions, are continually looking for equilibrium between the following factors:

- Good coverage of typical use cases distilled by many years of functional programming practice
- Not bloating the size of the library above reasonable limits
- Making each library-provided function optimized to the extent that makes nonsensical any custom implementation of the same

Equipped with this holistic view, let me turn to covering patterns per se. In cases where the demonstration of a function representing a pattern can fit a one-liner I'll provide the result of the evaluation in the upcoming line as a comment for the sake of saving space.

The generation pattern

This pattern is very easy to recognize: it represents a transition from the state without any collection to the state where a collection has been created. Generation pattern is represented by library functions that have a generic signature structure as shown here:

```
name: <zero or more input parameters> -> collection<'T>
```

This generalized signature leads to some concrete use cases depending on the specific shape of the result collection.

Generating an empty collection

To generate an empty collection of a generic type, the core library function, `empty`, exists, allowing you to produce a strongly typed empty collection for any of the base collection types as shown here (`Ch8_2.fsx`):

```
let el = List.empty<string>
// val el : string list = []
let ea = Array.empty<float>
// val ea : float [] = [||]
let es = Seq.empty<int -> string>
// val es : seq<(int -> string)>
// es;;
// val it : seq<(int -> string)> = seq []
```

The same can be also achieved using corresponding constant expressions for each base collection type (Ch8_2.fsx):

```
let ell: string list = []
// val ell : string list = []
let eal: float[] = [||]
// val eal : float [] = [||]
let esl: seq<int -> string> = seq []
// val esl : seq<(int -> string)> = []
// esl;;
// val it : seq<(int -> string)> = []
```

Generating a single element collection

This simple task belonging to a generation pattern can be achieved by the core library function singleton that exists for each of the base collection types. It does not need explicit declaration of collection elements type as it can be easily inferred from the typed literal given for the single collection element as shown in the following code (Ch8.fsx):

```
let sl = List.singleton "I'm alone"
// val sl : string list = ["I'm alone"]
let sa = Array.singleton 42.0
// val sa : float [] = [|42.0|]
let ss = Seq.singleton (fun (x:int) -> x.ToString())
// val ss : seq<(int -> string)>
// ss;;
// val it : seq<(int -> string)> = seq [<fun:ss@24>]
```

Again, this can be also achieved using corresponding constant expressions for each base collection type as shown here (Ch8_2.fsx):

```
let sll = ["I'm alone"]
// val sll : string list = ["I'm alone"]
let sal = [| 42.0 |]
// val sal : float [] = [|42.0|]
let ssl = seq [fun (x:int) -> x.ToString()]
// val ssl : seq<(int -> string)> = [<fun:ssl@24>]
```

Generating a collection of a known size

This task of the generation pattern is represented by two different cases: the case where all elements in the collection are of the same value and the case where they can be of different values.

Generating a collection of a known size – all elements of the same value

The F# 4.0 core library provides functions to replicate each base collection type that has the following signatures:

```
List.replicate: count:int -> initial:'T -> 'T list
Array.replicate: count:int -> initial:'T -> 'T[]
Seq.replicate: count:int -> initial:'T -> seq<'T>
```

Examples of this usage are as following (Ch8_2.fsx):

```
let fl = List.replicate 3 "blah"
// val fl : string list = ["blah"; "blah"; "blah"]
let fa = Array.replicate 3 42
// val fa : int [] = [|42; 42; 42|]
let fs = Seq.replicate 3 42.0
// val fs : seq<float>
// fs;;
// val it : seq<float> = seq [42.0; 42.0; 42.0]
```

As I discussed earlier, this can be achieved using literals and comprehension expressions as shown here (Ch8_2.fsx):

```
let fll = ["blah";"blah";"blah"]
// val fll : string list = ["blah"; "blah"; "blah"]
let fal = [| for i in 1..3 -> 42 |]
// val fal : int [] = [|42; 42; 42|]
let fsl = seq { for i in 1..3 do yield 42.0 }
// val fsl : seq<float>
// fsl;;
// val it : seq<float> = seq [42.0; 42.0; 42.0]
```

In addition to `replicate`, F# core library for **array** collections exclusively provides the `create` and `zeroCreate` functions as shown below (Ch8_2.fsx):

```
Array.create: count:int -> value:'T -> 'T[]
Array.zeroCreate: count:int -> 'T[]
let fac = Array.create 3 "blah"
// val fac : string [] = [|"blah"; "blah"; "blah"|]
let fazc: string[] = Array.zeroCreate 3
// val fazc : string [] = [|null; null; null|]
let fazci = Array.zeroCreate<int> 3
// val fazci : int [] = [|0; 0; 0|]
```

Note that `zeroCreate`, by design, does not give any clue about the type of the target array to the F# compiler. So, in order to avoid the infamous `error FS0030: Value restriction` error message that is going to take place if the matter of the target array type is delegated to the type inference, the type annotation can be added to the value itself, such as `string[]` for `fazc`, or a type argument can be added to the function name itself, such as `<int>` for `fazci` in the preceding code.

Generating a collection of a known size – elements may have different values

What if elements of the collection need to be of different values? The F# core library comes to our help with the `init` function for each base collection type that has signatures as following:

```
List.init: length:int -> initializer:(int -> 'T) -> 'T list
Array.init : count:int -> initializer:(int -> 'T) -> 'T[]
Seq. init: count:int -> initializer:(int -> 'T) -> seq<'T>
```

Examples of this usage are given as following (`Ch8_2.fsx`):

```
let vl = List.init 4 ((*) 2)
// val vl : int list = [0; 2; 4; 6]
let va = let src = "closure" in Array.init src.Length (fun i -> src.[i])

// val va : char [] = [|'c'; 'l'; 'o'; 's'; 'u'; 'r'; 'e'|]
let vs = Seq.init 3 id
// val vs : seq<int>
// vs;;
// val it : seq<int> = seq [0; 1; 2]
```

Note that `initializer` is given the implicit index of each element that transforms it into the element value. This transformation can be very simple, such as `vs`, or quite complex, such as `va`, where it is closed around `src` and de-facto transforms a `string` to the array of `char` of its characters.

Similar to the case of the same value elements, the alternative to `init` in order to generate lists and arrays may be literals, and for all three base collection types, the alternative could be comprehension expressions. Examples follow-`vll` and `val` for literals and the rest for a comprehension expression having (`vlcy`, `vacy`, `vscy`) or not using (`vlc`, `vac`, `vsc`) of the `yield` construction as shown here (`Ch8_2.fsx`):

```
let vll = [0; 2; 4; 6]
// val vll : int list = [0; 2; 4; 6]
let vlc = [ for i in 0..3 -> i * 2 ]
// val vlc : int list = [0; 2; 4; 6]
```

```
let vlcy = [ for i in 0..3 do yield i * 2 ]
// val vlcy : int list = [0; 2; 4; 6]
let ``val`` =
    let src = "closure" in
    [| src.[0]; src.[1]; src.[2]; src.[3]; src.[4]; src.[5]; src.[6] |]
// val val : char [] = [|'c'; 'l'; 'o'; 's'; 'u'; 'r'; 'e'|]
let vac =
    let src = "closure" in
    [| for i in 1..src.Length -> src.[i - 1] |]
// val vac : char [] = [|'c'; 'l'; 'o'; 's'; 'u'; 'r'; 'e'|]
let vacy =
    let src = "closure" in
    [| for i in 1..src.Length do
        yield src.[i - 1] |> System.Char.ToUpper |]
// val vacy : char [] = [|'C'; 'L'; 'O'; 'S'; 'U'; 'R'; 'E'|]
let vsc = seq { for i in 0..2..6 -> i }
// vsc;;
// val it : seq<int> = seq [0; 2; 4; 6]
let vscy = seq { for i in 0..2..6 do yield 6 - i }
// vscy;;
// val it : seq<int> = seq [6; 4; 2; 0]
```

Note that the expression initializing the collection element value within comprehension expressions can be arbitrarily complex; for example, in the case of vacy, it takes a value from the src closure indexed by the element place and converts the corresponding char array element into uppercase.

Before further proceeding with the rest of the use cases, let me drill deeper into comprehension expressions. They are much more powerful than what has been shown so far. I've already mentioned this in Chapter 6, *Sequences – The Core of Data Processing Patterns* when talking about sequences in which sequence expressions may contain multiple occurrences of yield as well as yield!. You are free to use this feature when creating comprehension expressions for lists and arrays as well as use recursion to your taste. To prove this, let me demonstrate all these features in one quick example, building a generator for a list of pseudo-random integers in a range between lo and hi of length len as shown in the following code (Ch8_2.fsx):

```
let randoms lo hi len =
    let r = System.Random()
    let max = hi + 1
    let rec generate n = [
        if n < len then
            yield r.Next(lo, max)
            yield! generate (n + 1)
    ]
    generate 0
```

The results of smoke testing `randoms` in FSI by modeling three series of 20 throws of a dice are given in the following screenshot:

Modelling series of throwing dice with pseudo-random number generator

Generating a collection of an unknown size

From time to time, you may get into a situation where you should generate a collection with the size that is to be found along the generation. In such situations, the following F# core library function `unfold` comes to help as shown here:

```
List.unfold<'T,'State> : generator:('State -> ('T * 'State) option) ->
state:'State -> 'T list
Array.unfold<'T,'State> : generator:('State -> ('T * 'State) option) ->
state:'State -> 'T[]
Seq.unfold    : generator:('State -> ('T * 'State) option) -> state:'State
-> seq<'T>
```

I have already provided a very simple example of this function workings in Chapter 6, *Sequences – The Core of Data Processing Patterns*; here, I describe its inner workings to the full extent. The unfold function produces result collection elements one by one. For each element, the generator function takes a 'State value as an input parameter and produces the result as an **option** value. If the returned option is of the form Some('T * 'State) consisting of the current generated collection element value 'T and the 'State value for the next iteration this return value indicates that sequence unfolding will continue. Otherwise, when generator function returns None this means that the collection unfolding has been completed.

Let me offer you a loaded example for this use case: the so-called **Collatz conjecture** (https://en.wikipedia.org/wiki/Collatz_conjecture). Let us consider an integral sequence built by a simple rule of moving from an element n to the next element nn: if n is even, then nn is n divided by 2; otherwise, it is 3 * n + 1. The conjecture itself is that for any initial n, this sequence named by German mathematician Lothar Collatz eventually reaches 1. For example,

42 -> 24 -> 12 -> 6 -> 3 -> 10 -> 5 -> 16 -> 8 -> 4 -> 2 -> 1

To this day, no starting number has been found that leads to an unbound number of elements in the Collatz sequence.

For starters, I begin with an idiomatic implementation of the Collatz sequence generator collatzLib function that relies upon the unfold library function as shown here (Ch8_2.fsx):

```
let collatzLib n =
    Seq.unfold (fun n -> match n with
                         | 0L -> None
                         | 1L -> Some(1L, 0L)
                         | n when n % 2L = 0L -> Some(n, n/2L)
                         | n -> Some(n, 3L * n + 1L)) n
```

Note the trick I used in order to deliver the value 1 to the collection that, if the generation is continued beyond it, leads to the cycle . . . 1 -> 4 -> 2 -> 1. . . . For the state of 1L, I produced the Some option that has 1L as the current value and an impossible marker value, 0L. For the marker value, the generator produces None and the collection growth terminates. Another precaution is to operate in the field of int64 numbers because even some not-that-big initial numbers may bring 'State outside of the int field, which I was able to find by switching to **checked** F# arithmetic from the default **unchecked** when the generator started taking a suspiciously long time to complete.

So far, so good. I'm going to give this implementation a try shortly. But some of you may already have this question: what's the point if this can be achieved with a sequence expression? And the answer was already given in the beginning of this chapter – *performance*. To prove this statement experimentally, let me put down the custom Collatz sequence generator implementation without using the unfold library function (Ch8_2.fsx):

```
let rec collatzCustom num =
    seq {
        yield num
        match num with
        | 1L -> ()
        | x when x % 2L = 0L ->yield! collatzCustom (x/2L)
        | x ->yield! collatzCustom ((x * 3L) + 1L)
    }
```

Now let's run collatzLib and collatzCustom against each other in order to identify the difference. For this purpose, let's find out what the longest Collatz sequence collection for initial numbers between 2 and 1000 would be. This exercise is a variation of **Project Euler problem 14** (https://projecteuler.net/problem=14). Composing the performance measuring code is not that difficult as shown here (Ch8_2.fsx):

```
[2L..1000000L] |> Seq.map (collatzLib >> Seq.length) |> Seq.max
```

Let's compare the performance of the preceding code to this one (Ch8_2.fsx):

```
[2L..1000000L] |> Seq.map (collatzCustom >> Seq.length) |> Seq.max
```

by the running time. Comparison is given in the following screenshot:

```
🔲                          fsianycpu                        _  ☐  ✕
> let collatzLib n =
      Seq.unfold (fun n -> match n with
                          | 0L -> None
                          | 1L -> Some(1L, 0L)
                          | n when n % 2L = 0L -> Some(n, n/2L)
                          | n -> Some(n, 3L * n + 1L)) n

  // Collatz sequence generator
  // with sequence expression
  let rec collatzCustom num =
    seq {
      yield num
      match num with
      | 1L -> ()
      | x when x % 2L = 0L -> yield! collatzCustom (x/2L)

      | x -> yield! collatzCustom ((x * 3L) + 1L)
    };;
val collatzLib : n:int64 -> seq<int64>
val collatzCustom : num:int64 -> seq<int64>
> #time;;
--> Timing now on
> [2L..1000000L] |> Seq.map (collatzLib >> Seq.length) |> Seq.max;;
Real: 00:00:03.147, CPU: 00:00:03.125, GC gen0: 1815, gen1: 5, gen2: 1
val it : int = 525
> [2L..1000000L] |> Seq.map (collatzCustom >> Seq.length) |> Seq.max;;
Real: 00:00:05.001, CPU: 00:00:05.000, GC gen0: 3546, gen1: 5, gen2: 0
val it : int = 525
> _
<                                                                >
```

Comparing the performance of library function-based and custom implementations

The lesson to take home is that the run using library-based `collatzLib` function takes **only 63%** of the time required for the run that uses custom-implemented `collatzCustom` function.

Do not spend time re-implementing functionality that F# core library functions offer unless you are in need for speed and absolutely sure that your custom implementation would improve the performance!

Generating a collection of an infinite size

Finally, I've reached the last use case under the Generation pattern: collections of infinite size. Apparently, when we consider this case, the underlying collection type can be the only sequence as we cannot rely on infinite memory resources yet. The F# core library function signature for the purpose of generating a sequence of infinite length is as following:

```
Seq.initInfinite: initializer:(int -> 'T) -> seq<'T>
```

It does not differ from `init` that much; it just lacks the input argument setting the collection size. Side by side with the `initInfinite` library function go custom implementations of infinite size sequences with sequence expressions.

I already covered the pattern of infinite size sequences in Chapter 6, *Sequences – The Core of Data Processing Patterns* and provided some examples there as well as some advanced examples in Chapter 7, *Advanced Techniques: Functions Revisited* so I will not repeat myself here. This use case concludes the variety that Generation data transformation pattern covers.

The aggregation pattern

The aggregation pattern can be recognized by the following kind of activity when the collection is traversed to end up with a value of type `'T`, similar to the collection elements' type `'T`, which carries some cumulative impact of all traversed elements.

Generic aggregation

The generic aggregation data transformation pattern signature is conveniently similar to the pair of concrete library functions that represent aggregation: `reduce` and `reduceBack` as shown here:

```
List.reduce: reduction:('T -> 'T -> 'T) -> list:'T list -> 'T
List.reduceBack: reduction:('T -> 'T -> 'T) -> list:'T list -> 'T
Array.reduce: reduction:('T -> 'T -> 'T) -> array:'T[] -> 'T
Array.reduceBack: reduction:('T -> 'T -> 'T) -> array:'T[] -> 'T
Seq.reduce: reduction:('T -> 'T -> 'T) -> source:seq<'T> -> 'T
```

If you recall Chapter 7, *Advanced Techniques: Functions Revisited*, the preceding code is almost as generic as `folds`; the difference is that the state threaded through the collection by `fold` can be of any arbitrary type that does not necessarily coincide with the type of collection elements, while `reduce` deals with the same type. It is easy to implement `reduce` with `fold` but not the other way around.

The `reduce` function applies the `reduction` operation from the beginning to the end of the collection; if I denote the `reduction` function as r, then for the special case of `reduce` over array collection c it will be equivalent to this expression as shown here:

```
...r (r (r c.[0] c.[1]) c.[2]) c.[3]...
```

On the contrary, `reduceBack` applies the `reduction` operation from the right-hand side to the left of the collection; if I denote the `reduction` function as r again, then for the special case of `reduceBack` over array collection c of n+1 elements it will be equivalent to this expression as shown here:

```
... (r c.[n - 3] (r c.[n - 2] (r c.[n - 1] c.[n])) ...
```

It is quite easy to notice that for the **associative** (https://en.wikipedia.org/wiki/Associative_property) `reduction` operation, the results of `reduce` and `reduceBack` over the same collection would be the same, which is confirmed by simple tests as shown here (`Ch8_3.fsx`):

```
// associative operation min
List.reduce min [1;2;3;4;5]
// val it : int = 1
List.reduceBack min [1;2;3;4;5]
// val it : int = 1

// non-associative operation (-)
List.reduce (-) [1;2;3;4;5]
// val it : int = -13
List.reduceBack (-) [1;2;3;4;5]
// val it : int = 3
```

I'd like to point at the asymmetry taking place: there is no `reduceBack` for sequences in the library out of the box.

All other library aggregate functions are just specific implementations of aggregations that can be expressed by `reduce`. Before turning to their consideration, I want to point out just another pattern: performing aggregation not on the original element type `'T` but projecting each collection element to some other type `'U` and aggregating upon `'U`.

Direct aggregation

Members of this group of aggregating library functions perform aggregation directly on the type of collection elements `'T`, such as the library members that have the following signatures:

```
List.average : list:^T list -> ^T
    when ^T : (static member ( + ) : ^T * ^T -> ^T)
    and  ^T : (static member DivideByInt : ^T*int -> ^T)
    and  ^T : (static member Zero : ^T)
Array.average : array:^T[] -> ^T
    when ^T : (static member ( + ) : ^T * ^T -> ^T)
    and  ^T : (static member DivideByInt : ^T*int -> ^T)
    and  ^T : (static member Zero : ^T)
Seq.average : source:seq<(^T)> -> ^T
    when ^T : (static member ( + ) : ^T * ^T -> ^T)
    and  ^T : (static member DivideByInt : ^T*int -> ^T)
    and  ^T : (static member Zero : ^T)
List.max : list:'T list -> 'T when 'T : comparison
Array.max : array:'T[] -> 'T  when 'T : comparison
Seq.max : source:seq<'T> -> 'T when 'T : comparison
List.min : list:'T list -> 'T when 'T : comparison
Array.min : array:'T[] -> 'T  when 'T : comparison
Seq.min : source:seq<'T> -> 'T when 'T : comparison
List.sum : list:^T list -> ^T
    when ^T : (static member ( + ) : ^T * ^T -> ^T)
    and  ^T : (static member Zero : ^T)
Array.sum : array: ^T[] -> ^T
    when ^T : (static member ( + ) : ^T * ^T -> ^T)
    and  ^T : (static member Zero : ^T)
Seq.sum : source:seq<(^T)> -> ^T
    when ^T : (static member ( + ) : ^T * ^T -> ^T)
    and  ^T : (static member Zero : ^T)
```

Based on signatures, you may notice that the library's aggregate functions introduce static constraints upon the collection type `'T` for the aggregations to make sense. For example, apparently, the max aggregation cannot be performed upon type `'T` if `'T` does not support comparison.

Projected aggregation

The projected aggregation library function, instead of performing aggregations upon original collection elements, first projects them from type `'T` into some other type `'U`, and only then it performs the aggregation over `'U` values. Here go the signatures:

```
List.averageBy : projection:('T -> ^U) -> list:'T list   -> ^U
    when ^U : (static member ( + ) : ^U * ^U -> ^U)
    and  ^U : (static member DivideByInt : ^U*int -> ^U)
    and  ^U : (static member Zero : ^U)
Array.averageBy : projection:('T -> ^U) -> array:'T[] -> ^U
    when ^U : (static member ( + ) : ^U * ^U -> ^U)
    and  ^U : (static member DivideByInt : ^U*int -> ^U)
    and  ^U : (static member Zero : ^U)
Seq.averageBy : projection:('T -> ^U) -> source:seq<'T>  -> ^U
    when ^U : (static member ( + ) : ^U * ^U -> ^U)
    and  ^U : (static member DivideByInt : ^U*int -> ^U)
    and  ^U : (static member Zero : ^U)
List.maxBy : projection:('T -> 'U) -> list:'T list -> 'T
    when 'U : comparison
Array.maxBy  : projection:('T -> 'U) -> array:'T[] -> 'T
    when 'U : comparison
Seq.maxBy : projection:('T -> 'U) -> source:seq<'T> -> 'T
    when 'U : comparison
List.minBy : projection:('T -> 'U) -> list:'T list -> 'T
    when 'U : comparison
Array.minBy : projection:('T -> 'U) -> array:'T[] -> 'T
    when 'U : comparison
Seq.minBy : projection:('T -> 'U) -> source:seq<'T> -> 'T
    when 'U : comparison
List.sumBy : projection:('T -> ^U) -> list:'T list -> ^U
    when ^U : (static member ( + ) : ^U * ^U -> ^U)
    and  ^U : (static member Zero : ^U)
Array.sumBy : projection:('T -> ^U) -> array:'T[] -> ^U
    when ^U : (static member ( + ) : ^U * ^U -> ^U)
    and  ^U : (static member Zero : ^U)
Seq.sumBy : projection:('T -> ^U) -> source:seq<'T>  -> ^U
    when ^U : (static member ( + ) : ^U * ^U -> ^U)
    and  ^U : (static member Zero : ^U)
```

There is a little intricacy that should be mentioned when considering projected aggregations-while `averageBy` and `sumBy` return a result of type `'U`, `maxBy` and `minBy` return `'T`. Refer to the following code sample that highlights the mentioned detail (`Ch8_3.fsx`):

```
List.sumBy (fun x -> -x) [1;2;3]
// val it : int = -6
```

```
List.minBy (fun x -> -x) [1;2;3]
// val it : int = 3
```

Counting aggregation

The left-over two functions of aggregation data transformation pattern perform the counting of collection elements.

The first one is the good old `length` function:

```
List.length: list:'T list -> int
Array.length: array:'T[] -> int
Seq.length: source:seq<'T> -> int
```

There are no hidden surprises here. Just recognize that `Seq.length` traverses the `source` sequence and, being applied to a sequence of infinite length will eventually blow up.

The other one, `countBy`, is trickier:

```
List.countBy projection:('T -> 'Key) -> list:'T list
    -> ('Key * int) list
    when 'Key : equality
Array.countBy : projection:('T -> 'Key) -> array:'T[]
    -> ('Key * int)[]
    when 'Key : equality
Seq.countBy projection:('T -> 'Key) -> source:seq<'T>
    -> seq<'Key * int>
    when 'Key : equality
```

This higher-order function applies `projection` to each element value `'T`, converting it into a `'Key` value, counts the number of elements projected to each unique `'Key`, and in the end, delivers the distribution as a collection of tuples (`'Key`, amount). Let me make quite an interesting observation. At the beginning of this chapter, in *Generating a collection of a known size* we implemented a pseudo-random number sequence generator `randoms`. Let's look at roughly how "random" it is in emulating the throwing of a dice by building a long series of throws and then binning each score, expecting that the deviation of bin sizes is not statistically significant.

The following snippet emulates the throwing of a dice 10 million times; so, the expected number of hits of each of the six bins for outcomes should be somewhere around 1,666,000. Let's see… (`Ch8_3.fsx`):

```
randoms 1 6 10000000
|> Seq.countBy id
|> Seq.toList
```

```
|> printfn "%A"
```

The results of running the preceding code in FSI are presented in the following screenshot:

Checking the quality of a pseudo-random number generator with countBy

Based on results reflected by preceding screenshot, my gut feeling is that the underlying pseudo-random number generator is not bad for the purpose of emulating the dice. And it is pretty fast too: it took a bit more than 2 seconds to generate and bin the series of 10 million trials.

The wrapping and type conversion pattern

Library functions belonging to this data transformation pattern split into two groups as following:

- Ones that wrap the entire collection, changing its behavior
- Ones that simply transform the collection from one base type to another

The collection wrapping pattern

There are only three functions that belong to this pattern. All of them are applicable only to sequences and have the following signatures:

```
Seq.cache: source:seq<'T> -> seq<'T>
Seq.delay: generator:(unit -> seq<'T>) -> seq<'T>
Seq.readonly : source:seq<'T> -> seq<'T>
```

I have already covered the `Seq.cache` function in Chapter 6, *Sequences – The Core of Data Processing Patterns* and also used it in Chapter 7, *Advanced Techniques: Functions Revisited* in the prime number generator sample, so let me not spend any more time on it and move on to the other pair.

`Seq.delay` allows you to postpone an eager evaluation of the wrapped `generator` function. The evaluation is postponed until the wrapper gets enumerated. In the following code snippet, there is an eager list comprehension present that, if being evaluated, immediately prints `"Evaluating eagerList"` and then returns the list of `strings`. However, being wrapped into `Seq.delay`, it does not evaluate until the wrapper itself gets materialized (`Ch8_4.fsx`):

```
let eagerList = [
    printfn "Evaluating eagerList"
    yield "I"
    yield "am"
    yield "an"
    yield "eager"
    yield "list"
]
// Evaluating eagerList
// val eagerList : string list = ["I"; "am"; "an"; "eager"; "list"]
let delayedEagerList = Seq.delay(fun () -> ([ printfn "Evaluating
                                              eagerList"
                                   yield "I"
                                   yield "am"
                                   yield "an"
                                   yield "eager"
                                   yield "list"
                          ] |> Seq.ofList))
// val delayedEagerList : seq<string>

delayedEagerList |> Seq.toList
// Evaluating eagerList
// val it : string list = ["I"; "am"; "an"; "eager"; "list"]
```

The commented lines of the preceding script demonstrate that the expected behavior described earlier is actually taking place.

The `Seq.readonly` builds a wrapper sequence around the original collection, which does not allow you to rediscover and mutate it via a type cast. In the following snippet, it is possible via an upcast followed by a downcast, to create a backdoor, and mutate with its help the original mutable collection (`Ch8_4.fsx`):

```
let src = [|1;2;3|]
let srcAsSeq = src :> seq<_>
let backdoor = srcAsSeq :?> int array
backdoor.[0] <- 10
printfn "%A" src
// [|10; 2; 3|]
```

Now if `src` gets wrapped into `Seq.readonly`, an attempt to downcast the sequence back to `int []` will incur cast exception as shown in the following code (`Ch8_4.fsx`):

```
let srcAsROSeq = src |> Seq.readonly
let tryBackDoor = srcAsROSeq :?> int array
// System.InvalidCastException: Unable to cast object of type
'mkSeq@541[System.Int32]' to type 'System.Int32[]'.
```

The type conversion pattern

Library functions that belong to the type conversion pattern provide symmetric conversions between base collection types as shown here:

```
List.toSeq list:'T list -> seq<'T>
List.ofSeq: source:seq<'T> -> 'T list
List.toArray: list:'T list -> 'T[]
List.ofArray : array:'T[] -> 'T list
Array.toSeq: array:'T[] -> seq<'T>
Array.ofSeq: source:seq<'T> -> 'T[]
Array.toList: array:'T[] -> 'T list
Array.ofList: list:'T list -> 'T[]
Seq.toList: source:seq<'T> -> 'T list
Seq.ofList: source:'T list -> seq<'T>
Seq.toArray: source:seq<'T> -> 'T[]
Seq.ofArray: source:'T[] -> seq<'T>
```

These functions are very straightforward and do not require additional comments.

Apart from them stands function that converts a loosely-typed sequence from legacy pre-generic `System.Collections` namespace into a typed sequence:

```
Seq.cast: source:IEnumerable -> seq<'T>
```

This casting is often needed in interoperability scenarios between F# and legacy Microsoft systems in order to convert them into F#-friendly strongly typed sequences. As an example of this, let's take a look at the following snippet (`Ch8_4.fsx`):

```
let s = System.Collections.Stack()
s.Push(1)
s.Push('2')
s.Push("xyzzy")
s |> Seq.cast<_> |> printfn "%A"
// seq ["xyzzy"; '2'; 1]
```

Here, you can see that a `Stack` loosely typed collection was casted to a strongly typed F# sequence and printed out. The output shows the F# sequence containing elements of different types: `string`, `char`, `int`. But the sequence is strongly typed, isn't it? Can you determine the type of the preceding sequence?

The selection pattern

This kind of data transformation pattern can be recognized by segregating one or more elements from the collection based on certain characteristic(s). These traits can be very diverse: a position of element(s), an element value matching criteria, to name a few.

The genuine trait that distinguishes the selection transformation pattern from the rest of the crowd is the following: *selection result is always either a single element or a single collection carrying from zero to all elements of the original collection; the selection comes as-is, without any additional projection.*

Such a seemingly broad transformation class lays out into surprisingly few subclasses: positional selection, search, and filtering.

Position-based **selection** ties the element pick criteria with the element(s) position in the original collection; for example, take up to the first 10 elements of a collection.

Searching and **filtering** are ubiquitous data collection transformations indeed. Although these two transformations strongly resemble each other, there is a subtle difference has place between them, which is outlined below.

Filtering is usually associated with taking a source collection and copying it to the result collection element by element sifting out *all* elements that do not match given criteria.

Turning to searching, it is usually associated with a more sophisticated process. The initial state for the search is composed of the original collection, initially empty search result, and search criteria. The search process also traverses the original collection element by element applying search criteria and shaping the search result. However, searching may carry not only the matching criteria, but also a stop condition of a sort and maybe some ranking. A typical example of searching would be this: "find *any* collection element that fulfills the condition(s)".

Based on this difference, I place searching in a separate selection pattern, but consider the filtering a part of the *element group selection* pattern.

The position-based selection pattern

F# core library functions that constitute this pattern can be further broken down into two groups: single element selections and element group selections.

Single element selection

This group of functions determines the single desired element by the position it occupies in the collection. The position may be requested either explicitly via an input argument or implicitly by the associated function name. To see what I mean please compare "give me the third element" with "give me the last element". Single element selection returns either the desired element or an indication that such an element does not exist:

```
List.head: list:'T list -> 'T
Array.head: array:'T[] -> 'T
Seq.head: source:seq<'T> -> 'T

List.tryHead: list:'T list -> 'T option
Array.tryHead: array:'T[] -> 'T option
Seq.tryHead: source:seq<'T> -> 'T option

List.last: list:'T list -> 'T
Array.last: list:'T list -> 'T
Seq.last: source:seq<'T> -> 'T

List.tryLast: list:'T list -> 'T option
Array.tryLast: list:'T list -> 'T option
Seq.tryLast: source:seq<'T> -> 'T option

List.item: index:int -> list:'T list -> 'T
```

```
Array.item: index:int -> array:'T[] -> 'T
Array.get: array:'T[] -> index:int -> 'T
Seq.item: index:int -> source:seq<'T> -> 'T

List.tryItem: index:int -> list:'T list -> 'T option
Array.tryItem: index:int -> array:'T[] -> 'T option
Seq.tryItem: index:int -> source:seq<'T> -> 'T option

List.nth: list:'T list -> index:int -> 'T // obsolete
Seq.nth: index:int -> source:seq<'T> -> 'T // obsolete

List.exactlyOne: list:'T list -> 'T
Array.exactlyOne: array:'T[] -> 'T
Seq.exactlyOne: source:seq<'T> -> 'T
```

Note how members of this group differ by the manner of indicating an unsuccessful selection. Some simply throw an exception, while the others wrap the selection result into an `option`, where `None` indicates the absence of the sought-for element: (`Ch8_5.fsx`):

```
List.head<int> []
// System.ArgumentException: The input list was empty.
List.tryHead<int> []
// val it : int option = None
```

Further on functions with names that begin with `try...`: these allow to alleviate the lurking possibility of the requested element being missing and handle such unfortunate cases nicely.

Use the *imperative* forms of selection with caution. If you are not ABSOLUTELY sure that the existence of requested element is invariant, fall back to *try* forms.

Also, note that for data collections that support element indexing, often the simple use of index does the job of dedicated library function, like in the following code (`Ch8_5.fsx`):

```
let ll = [1;2;3;4]
List.head ll = ll.[0]
//val it : bool = true
```

The element group selection

This collection transformation sub-pattern arranges the procurement of a group of elements from a collection based on the whole slew of criteria: it can be an element counter, a predicate peeking at an element's value, a collection of undesired values, or an exclusion of repeated values:

```
List.take: count:int -> list:'T list -> 'T list
Array.take: count:int -> array:'T[] -> 'T[]
Seq.take: count:int -> source:seq<'T> -> seq<'T>

List.takeWhile: predicate:('T -> bool) -> list:'T list -> 'T list
Array.takeWhile: predicate:('T -> bool) -> array:'T[] -> 'T[]
Seq.takeWhile: predicate:('T -> bool) -> source:seq<'T> -> seq<'T>

List.truncate: count:int -> list:'T list -> 'T list
Array.truncate: count:int -> array:'T[] -> 'T[]
Seq.truncate: count:int -> source:seq<'T> -> seq<'T>

List.skip: count:int -> list: 'T list -> 'T list
Array.skip: count:int -> array:'T[] -> 'T[]
Seq.skip: count:int -> source:seq<'T> -> seq<'T>

List.skipWhile: predicate:('T -> bool) -> list:'T list -> 'T list
Array.skipWhile: predicate:('T -> bool) -> array:'T[] -> 'T[]
Seq.skipWhile: predicate:('T -> bool) -> source:seq<'T> -> seq<'T>

List.tail: list:'T list -> 'T list
Array.tail: array:'T[] -> 'T[]
Seq.tail: source:seq<'T> -> seq<'T>

List.filter: predicate:('T -> bool) -> list:'T list -> 'T list
Array.filter: predicate:('T -> bool) -> array:'T[] -> 'T[]
Seq.filter: predicate:('T -> bool) -> source:seq<'T> -> seq<'T>

List.except: itemsToExclude:seq<'T> -> list:'T list -> 'T list when 'T :
equality
Array.except: itemsToExclude:seq<'T> -> array:'T[] -> 'T[] when 'T :
equality
Seq.except: itemsToExclude:seq<'T> -> source:seq<'T> -> seq<'T> when 'T :
equality

List.choose: chooser:('T -> 'U option) -> list:'T list -> 'U list
Array.choose: chooser:('T -> 'U option) -> array:'T[] -> 'U[]
Seq.choose: chooser:('T -> 'U option) -> source:seq<'T> -> seq<'U>

List.where: predicate:('T -> bool) -> list:'T list -> 'T list
Array.where: predicate:('T -> bool) -> array:'T[] -> 'T[]
```

```
Seq.where: predicate:('T -> bool) -> source:seq<'T> -> seq<'T>

Array.sub: array:'T[] -> startIndex:int -> count:int -> 'T[]

List.distinct: list:'T list -> 'T list when 'T : equality
Array.distinct: array:'T[] -> 'T[] when 'T : equality
Seq.distinct: source:seq<'T> -> seq<'T> when 'T : equality

List.distinctBy: projection:('T -> 'Key) -> list:'T list -> 'T list when
'Key : equality
Array.distinctBy: projection:('T -> 'Key) -> array:'T[] -> 'T[] when 'Key :
equality
Seq.distinctBy: projection:('T -> 'Key) -> source:seq<'T> -> seq<'T> when
'Key : equality
```

Notice that the constituent of *element group selection* pattern is the ubiquitous `filter` function.

Similarly to the previous sub-pattern for collections implementing index slicing, this is an alternative way of element group selection (Ch8_5.fsx):

```
[|10;20;30;40;50;60|].[2..4]
// val it : int [] = [|30; 40; 50|]
```

You may also notice that the more generic `filter` function is accompanied by more specific filtering cases, such as `takeWhile`, `skipWhile`, or just a `where` synonym as shown here (Ch8_5.fsx):

```
let numbers = [1;2;3;4;5;6;7;8]
List.filter (fun x -> (%) x 2 = 0) numbers = List.where (fun x -> (%) x 2 =
0) numbers
// val it : bool = true
```

The searching pattern

The F# 4.0 core library offer a very normalized set of functions that constitute the **search** pattern, where the name of the function carries exhaustive characteristics of the function workings indeed.

All the functions that have `...find...` in the name perform the search for the first single element that occurs while having `...findIndex...` do the search for the same element but returning its ordinal number in the collection.

Functions that have `...Back...` in the name perform the search in the opposite direction of the natural order of elements.

Similarly to the already examined selection pattern groups, the library functions of the search pattern implement two approaches to represent the *"not found"* search outcome: those without the `try...` prefix throw an exception if the search comes back empty, while others with the `try...` prefix in this situation return the `None` option; otherwise, it returns the found element wrapped into `Some...` option as shown here:

```
List.find: predicate:('T -> bool) -> list:'T list -> 'T
Array.find: predicate:('T -> bool) -> array:'T[] -> 'T
Seq.find: predicate:('T -> bool) -> source:seq<'T> -> 'T

List.tryFind: predicate:('T -> bool) -> list:'T list -> 'T option
Array.tryFind: predicate:('T -> bool) -> array:'T[] -> 'T option
Seq.tryFind: predicate:('T -> bool) -> source:seq<'T> -> 'T option

List.findIndex: predicate:('T -> bool) -> list:'T list -> int
Array.findIndex: predicate:('T -> bool) -> array:'T[] -> int
Seq.findIndex: predicate:('T -> bool) -> source:seq<'T> -> int

List.tryFindIndex: predicate:('T -> bool) -> list:'T list -> int option
List.tryFindIndexBack: predicate:('T -> bool) -> list:'T list -> int option

List.findBack: predicate:('T -> bool) -> list:'T list -> 'T
Array.findBack: predicate:('T -> bool) -> array:'T[] -> 'T
Seq.findBack: predicate:('T -> bool) -> source:seq<'T> -> 'T

List.tryFindBack: predicate:('T -> bool) -> list:'T list -> 'T option
Array.tryFindBack: predicate:('T -> bool) -> array:'T[] -> 'T option
Seq.tryFindBack: predicate:('T -> bool) -> source:seq<'T> -> 'T option

List.findIndexBack: predicate:('T -> bool) -> list:'T list -> int
Array.findIndexBack: predicate:('T -> bool) -> array:'T[] -> int
Seq.findIndexBack: predicate:('T -> bool) -> source:seq<'T> -> int

List.pick: chooser:('T -> 'U option) -> list:'T list -> 'U
Array.pick: chooser:('T -> 'U option) -> array:'T[] -> 'U
Seq.pick: chooser:('T -> 'U option) -> source:seq<'T> -> 'U

List.tryPick: chooser:('T -> 'U option) -> list:'T list -> 'U option
Array.tryPick: chooser:('T -> 'U option) -> array:'T[] -> 'U option
```

```
Seq.tryPick: chooser:('T -> 'U option) -> source:seq<'T> -> 'U option
```

Let's demonstrate the listed above instruments in action (Ch8_5.fsx):

```
List.find (fun x -> (%) x 2 = 0) <| [1;3;5]
// System.Collections.Generic.KeyNotFoundException:
// Exception of type 'System.Collections.Generic.KeyNotFoundException' was
thrown.
List.tryFind (fun x -> (%) x 2 = 0) <| [1;3;5]
// val it : int option = None
List.find (fun x -> (%) x 2 <> 0) <| [1;3;5]
// val it : int = 1
List.tryFind (fun x -> (%) x 2 <> 0) <| [1;3;5]
// val it : int option = Some 1
List.findIndex (fun x -> (%) x 2 <> 0) <| [1;3;5]
// val it : int = 0
List.tryFindIndex (fun x -> (%) x 2 <> 0) <| [1;3;5]
// val it : int option = Some 0
List.findBack (fun x -> (%) x 2 <> 0) <| [1;3;5]
// val it : int = 5
List.tryFindBack (fun x -> (%) x 2 <> 0) <| [1;3;5]
// val it : int option = Some 5
List.findIndexBack (fun x -> (%) x 2 <> 0) <| [1;3;5]
// val it : int = 2
List.tryFindIndexBack (fun x -> (%) x 2 <> 0) <| [1;3;5]
// val it : int option = Some 2
```

Slightly apart from this very logical arrangement stands the (try)pick group of functions. Functions that belong to this group combine both search and transform functionalities together: the chooser function applies to each element of type 'T, producing None until the first element matches the search criteria somehow expressed within chooser. Then, Some is wrapped around potentially different type 'U and is returned, and the higher-order function returns the result of type 'U. If chooser does not find any suitable element, then pick throws an exception, while tryPick returns None (Ch8_5.fsx):

```
[(9,"Nine");(42,"FortyTwo");(0,"Zero")]
|> List.pick (fun (x,y) -> if x = 42 then Some y else None)
// val it : string = "FortyTwo"
[(9,"Nine");(42,"FortyTwo");(0,"Zero")]
|> List.tryPick (fun (x,y) -> if x = 42 then Some y else None)
// val it : string option = Some "FortyTwo"
[(9,"Nine");(42,"FortyTwo");(0,"Zero")]
|> List.pick (fun (x,y) -> if x = 14 then Some y else None)
// System.Collections.Generic.KeyNotFoundException:
// Exception of type 'System.Collections.Generic.KeyNotFoundException' was
thrown.
[(9,"Nine");(42,"FortyTwo");(0,"Zero")]
```

```
|> List.tryPick (fun (x,y) -> if x = 14 then Some y else None)
// val it : string option = None
```

Please pay attention how the above functions fuse together to some extent selection and transformation by applying both actions while traversing the collection only once.

The partitioning pattern

F# core library elements of **partitioning** pattern consume a single collection, usually returning more than one result collections as shown here:

```
List.chunkBySize: chunkSize:int -> list:'T list -> 'T list list
Array.chunkBySize: chunkSize:int -> array:'T[] -> 'T[][]
Seq.chunkBySize: chunkSize:int -> source:seq<'T> -> seq<'T[]>

List.groupBy : projection:('T -> 'Key) -> list:'T list -> ('Key * 'T list)
list when 'Key : equality
Array.groupBy: projection:('T -> 'Key) -> array:'T[] -> ('Key * 'T[])[]
when 'Key : equality
Seq.groupBy : projection:('T -> 'Key) -> source:seq<'T> -> seq<'Key *
seq<'T>> when 'Key : equality

List.pairwise: list:'T list -> ('T * 'T) list
Array.pairwise: array:'T[] -> ('T * 'T)[]
Seq.pairwise: source:seq<'T> -> seq<'T * 'T>

List.partition: predicate:('T -> bool) -> list:'T list -> ('T list * 'T
list)
Array.partition: predicate:('T -> bool) -> array:'T[] -> 'T[] * 'T[]

List.splitAt: index:int -> list:'T list -> ('T list * 'T list)
Array.splitAt: index:int -> array:'T[] -> ('T[] * 'T[])

List.splitInto: count:int -> list:'T list -> 'T list list
Array.splitInto: count:int -> array:'T[] -> 'T[][]
Seq.splitInto: count:int -> source:seq<'T> -> seq<'T[]>

List.windowed: windowSize:int -> list:'T list -> 'T list list
Array.windowed: windowSize:int -> array:'T[] -> 'T[][]
Seq.windowed: windowSize:int -> source:seq<'T> -> seq<'T[]>
```

Examples of simple usage of the preceding functions are as following (`Ch8_6.fsx`):

```
List.chunkBySize 2 ['a'..'g']
// val it : char list list = [['a'; 'b']; ['c'; 'd']; ['e'; 'f']; ['g']]

List.groupBy (fun n -> n / 3) [1..7]
// val it : (int * int list) list = [(0, [1; 2]); (1, [3; 4; 5]); (2, [6;
7])]

List.pairwise [1..2..10]
// val it : (int * int) list = [(1, 3); (3, 5); (5, 7); (7, 9)]

["angle";"delta";"cheese";"America"]
|> List.partition (fun (x:string) -> (System.Char.ToUpper x.[0]) = 'A')
// val it : string list * string list =
//   (["angle"; "America"], ["delta"; "cheese"])

["angle";"delta";"cheese";"America"]
|> List.splitAt 2
// val it : string list * string list =
//   (["angle"; "delta"], ["cheese"; "America"])

["angle";"delta";"cheese";"America"]
|> List.splitInto 3
// val it : string list list =
//    [["angle"; "delta"]; ["cheese"]; ["America"]]

["angle";"delta";"cheese";"America"]
|> List.windowed 2
// val it : string list list =
//    [["angle"; "delta"]; ["delta"; "cheese"]; ["cheese"; "America"]]
```

The reordering pattern

This group of F# core library functions represents the **reordering** data transformation pattern of changing the order of the elements in the collection using many forms of sorting, reversing, and permuting:

```
List.rev: list:'T list -> 'T list
Array.rev: array:'T[] -> 'T[]
Seq.rev: source:seq<'T> -> seq<'T>

List.sort: list:'T list -> 'T list when 'T : comparison
Array.sort: array:'T[] -> 'T[] when 'T : comparison
Seq.sort: source:seq<'T> -> seq<'T> when 'T : comparison
```

```
List.sortDescending: list:'T list -> 'T list when 'T : comparison
Array.sortDescending: array:'T[] -> 'T[] when 'T : comparison

List.sortBy: projection:('T -> 'Key) -> list:'T list -> 'T list when 'Key :
comparison
Array.sortBy: projection:('T -> 'Key) -> array:'T[] -> 'T[] when 'Key :
comparison
Seq.sortBy: projection:('T -> 'Key) -> source:seq<'T> -> seq<'T> when 'Key
: comparison

List.sortByDescending: projection:('T -> 'Key) -> list:'T list -> 'T list
when 'Key : comparison
Array.sortByDescending: projection:('T -> 'Key) -> array:'T[] -> 'T[] when
'Key : comparison
Seq.sortByDescending : projection:('T -> 'Key) -> source:seq<'T> -> seq<'T>
when 'Key : comparison

List.sortWith: comparer:('T -> 'T -> int) -> list:'T list -> 'T list
Array.sortWith: comparer:('T -> 'T -> int) -> array:'T[] -> 'T[]
Seq.sortWith : comparer:('T -> 'T -> int) -> source:seq<'T> -> seq<'T>

List.permute : indexMap:(int -> int) -> list:'T list -> 'T list
Array.permute : indexMap:(int -> int) -> array:'T[] -> 'T[]
Seq.permute: indexMap:(int -> int) -> source:seq<'T> -> seq<'T>

Array.sortInPlace: array:'T[] -> unit when 'T : comparison
Array.sortInPlaceBy: projection:('T -> 'Key) -> array:'T[] -> unit when
'Key : comparison
Array.sortInPlaceWith: comparer:('T -> 'T -> int) -> array:'T[] -> unit
```

Some examples of the reordering transformations are as following (Ch8_7.fsx):

```
List.sort [1;8;3;6;4;-2]
// val it : int list = [-2; 1; 3; 4; 6; 8]
List.sortDescending [1;8;3;6;4;-2]
// val it : int list = [8; 6; 4; 3; 1; -2]
List.sortBy (fun x -> x.GetHashCode()) ["Fourteen";"Zero";"Forty Two"]
// val it : string list = ["Zero"; "Forty Two"; "Fourteen"]
```

Take into account that some functions perform the reordering by mutating the input collection. These are limited to Arraysort InPlace, sortInPlaceBy, and sortInPlaceWith.

The testing pattern

This is a very straightforward pattern. **Testing** library functions instead of transforming the input collection, always returning the `bool` result: `true` if certain properties have place, otherwise `false`. They may check whether the given collection contains the given element, whether an element exists with the value, turning the given predicate to `true`, whether all elements of the collection turn the given predicate to `true`, or whether the input collection is empty as their signatures reflect below:

```
List.contains: value:'T -> source:'T list -> bool when 'T : equality
Array.contains: value:'T -> array:'T[] -> bool when 'T : equality
Seq.contains: value:'T -> source:seq<'T> -> bool when 'T : equality

List.exists: predicate:('T -> bool) -> list:'T list -> bool
Array.exists: predicate:('T -> bool) -> array:'T[] -> bool
Seq.exists: predicate:('T -> bool) -> source:seq<'T> -> bool

List.exists2: predicate:('T1 -> 'T2 -> bool) -> list1:'T1 list -> list2:'T2
list -> bool
Array.exists2: predicate:('T1 -> 'T2 -> bool) -> array1:'T1[] ->
array2:'T2[] -> bool
Seq.exists2: predicate:('T1 -> 'T2 -> bool) -> source1:seq<'T1> -> <'T2> ->
bool

List.forall: predicate:('T -> bool) -> list:'T list -> bool
Array.forall: predicate:('T -> bool) -> array:'T[] -> bool
Seq.forall: predicate:('T -> bool) -> source:seq<'T> -> bool

List.forall2: predicate:('T1 -> 'T2 -> bool) -> list1:'T1 list -> list2:'T2
list -> bool
Array.forall2: predicate:('T1 -> 'T2 -> bool) -> array1:'T1[] ->
array2:'T2[] -> bool
Seq.forall2: predicate:('T1 -> 'T2 -> bool) -> source1:seq<'T1> ->
source2:seq<'T2> -> bool

List.isEmpty: list:'T list -> bool
Array.isEmpty: array:'T[] -> bool
Seq.isEmpty: source:seq<'T> -> bool

List.compareWith: comparer:('T -> 'T -> int) -> list1:'T list -> list2:'T
list -> int
Array.compareWith: comparer:('T -> 'T -> int) -> array1:'T[] -> array2:'T[]
-> int
Seq.compareWith: comparer:('T -> 'T -> int) -> source1:seq<'T> ->
source2:seq<'T> -> int
```

The functions representing this pattern have so obvious an intent that I didn't even provide the usage samples for them; the samples can be easily found in F# core library documentation.

The iterating pattern

This is another very straightforward data transformation pattern. In fact, **iterating** pattern *does not introduce any noticeable transformations*, merely denoting instead the collection traversal. Its member functions always return `unit`. On each single traversal step the operations performed upon the current element are hidden behind the `action` function.

This manner of data transformations must vividly remind us of imperative and object-oriented paradigms as `action` effectively hides what's going on and also must exploit some side effects in order to be of any practical use. Such F# programs that massively (ab) use the iterating data transformation pattern usually indicate that their authors are still captives of a non-functional way of thinking.

The signatures of functions representing iterating pattern are given below:

```
List.iter: action:('T -> unit) -> list:'T list -> unit
Array.iter: action:('T -> unit) -> array:'T[] -> unit
Seq.iter: action:('T -> unit) -> source:seq<'T> -> unit

List.iter2: action:('T1 -> 'T2 -> unit) -> list1:'T1 list -> list2:'T2 list
-> unit
Array.iter2: action:('T1 -> 'T2 -> unit) -> array1:'T1[] -> array2:'T2[] ->
unit
Seq.iter2: action:('T1 -> 'T2 -> unit) -> source1:seq<'T1> ->
source2:seq<'T2> -> unit

List.iteri: action:(int -> 'T -> unit) -> list:'T list -> unit
Array.iteri: action:(int -> 'T -> unit) -> array:'T[] -> unit
Seq.iteri: action:(int -> 'T -> unit) -> source:seq<'T> -> unit

List.iteri2: action:(int -> 'T1 -> 'T2 -> unit) -> list1:'T1 list ->
list2:'T2 list -> unit
Array.iteri2: action:(int -> 'T1 -> 'T2 -> unit) -> array1:'T1[] ->
array2:'T2[] -> unit
Seq.iteri2: action:(int -> 'T1 -> 'T2 -> unit) -> source1:seq<'T1> ->
source2:seq<'T2> -> unit
```

Note that library member functions of this pattern demonstrate a certain level of regularization. The actions may involve elements (`iter`, `iter2`), or elements and the index (`iteri`, `iteri2`), and also may involve a single collection (`iter`, `iteri`) or pair of collections (`iter2`, `iteri2`).

As with the testing pattern, finding samples of these function's use on the Internet is not a problem.

The mapping pattern

Mappings constitute the gist of data transformations, projecting one or more input elements to the single result and then applying this projection to the entire input collection(s) producing the result collection(s) as the following member function signatures indicate:

```
List.map: mapping:('T -> 'U) -> list:'T list -> 'U list
Array.map: mapping:('T -> 'U) -> array:'T[] -> 'U[]
Seq.map: mapping:('T -> 'U) -> sequence:seq<'T> -> seq<'U>

List.map2: mapping:('T1 -> 'T2 -> 'U) -> list1:'T1 list -> list2:'T2 list
-> 'U list
Array.map2: mapping:('T1 -> 'T2 -> 'U) -> array1:'T1[] -> array2:'T2[] ->
'U[]
Seq.map2: mapping:('T1 -> 'T2 -> 'U) -> source1:seq<'T1> ->
source2:seq<'T2> -> seq<'U>

List.mapi: mapping:(int -> 'T -> 'U) -> list:'T list -> 'U list
Array.mapi: mapping:(int -> 'T -> 'U) -> array:'T[] -> 'U[]
Seq.mapi: mapping:(int -> 'T -> 'U) -> source:seq<'T> -> seq<'U>

List.mapi2: mapping:(int -> 'T1 -> 'T2 -> 'U) -> list1:'T1 list ->
list2:'T2 list -> 'U list
Array.mapi2: mapping:(int -> 'T1 -> 'T2 -> 'U) -> array1:'T1[] ->
array2:'T2[] -> 'U[]
Seq.mapi2: mapping:(int -> 'T1 -> 'T2 -> 'U) -> source1:seq<'T1> ->
source2:seq<'T2> -> seq<'U>

List.map3: mapping:('T1 -> 'T2 -> 'T3 -> 'U) -> list1:'T1 list -> list2:'T2
list -> list3:'T3 list -> 'U list
Array.map3: mapping:('T1 -> 'T2 -> 'T3 -> 'U) -> array1:'T1[] ->
array2:'T2[] -> array3:'T3[] -> 'U[]
Seq.map3: mapping:('T1 -> 'T2 -> 'T3 -> 'U) -> source1:seq<'T1> ->
source2:seq<'T2> -> source3:seq<'T3> -> seq<'U>

List.collect: mapping:('T -> 'U list) -> list:'T list -> 'U list
Array.collect: mapping:('T -> 'U[]) -> array:'T[] -> 'U[]
```

```
Seq.collect: mapping:('T -> 'Collection) -> source:seq<'T> -> seq<'U>  when
'Collection :> seq<'U>

List.indexed: list:'T list -> (int * 'T) list
Array.indexed: array:'T[] -> (int * 'T)[]
Seq.indexed: source:seq<'T> -> seq<int * 'T>
```

Note that the group of functions belonging to the mapping pattern is normalized fairly well. Functions with names resembling map (map, map2, map3) project elements of a single, a pair, or a triple of input collections to the elements of the single result collection. Functions with names resembling mapi (mapi, mapi2) also add the ordinal number of element(s) as an additional input parameter to the projection.

The collect function does not fit the same approach. Instead, it projects each element of the input collection into a matching collection and then flattens all these element-matching collections into a single result collection. It's a bit complicated, so I'd better provide an example.

Let's assume we are given an array of words and we want to convert it into a list of characters constituting input words (Ch8_7.fsx):

```
"Je ne regrette rien".Split([|' '|])
|> Seq.collect (fun x -> x.ToCharArray())
|> Seq.toList
// val it : char list =
//   ['J'; 'e'; 'n'; 'e'; 'r'; 'e'; 'g';
//    'r'; 'e'; 't'; 't'; 'e'; 'r'; 'i'; 'e'; 'n']
```

The indexed function is a helper function; it converts any collection into a collection of tuples, each combining an ordinal number of the original element and the element itself (Ch8_7.fsx):

```
"Je ne regrette rien".Split([|' '|])
|> Seq.indexed
// val it : seq<int * string> =
//   seq [(0, "Je"); (1, "ne"); (2, "regrette"); (3, "rien")]
```

The folding pattern

I've already mentioned on multiple occasions the fold function as a representation of the most universal and generic data transformation pattern of functional programming. As it has already been covered fairly well, I will not get into details here and will just list the multiple variations of this extremely versatile **folding** pattern as shown by the following member function signatures:

```
List.fold<'T,'State> : folder:('State -> 'T -> 'State) -> state:'State ->
list:'T list -> 'State
Array.fold<'T,'State> : folder:('State -> 'T -> 'State) -> state:'State ->
array: 'T[] -> 'State
Seq.fold<'T,'State> : folder:('State -> 'T -> 'State) -> state:'State ->
source:seq<'T> -> 'State
List.fold2<'T1,'T2,'State> : folder:('State -> 'T1 -> 'T2 -> 'State) ->
state:'State -> list1:'T1 list -> list2:'T2 list -> 'State
Array.fold2<'T1,'T2,'State>  : folder:('State -> 'T1 -> 'T2 -> 'State) ->
state:'State -> array1:'T1[] -> array2:'T2[] -> 'State
Seq.fold2<'T1,'T2,'State> : folder:('State -> 'T1 -> 'T2 -> 'State) ->
state:'State -> source1:seq<'T1> -> source2:seq<'T2> -> 'State
List.mapFold<'T,'State,'Result> : mapping:('State -> 'T -> 'Result *
'State) -> state:'State -> list:'T list -> 'Result list * 'State
Array.mapFold<'T,'State,'Result> : mapping:('State -> 'T -> 'Result *
'State) -> state:'State -> array:'T[] -> 'Result[] * 'State
Seq.mapFold<'T,'State,'Result> : mapping:('State -> 'T -> 'Result * 'State)
-> state:'State -> source:seq<'T> -> seq<'Result> * 'State

List.foldBack<'T,'State> : folder:('T -> 'State -> 'State) -> list:'T list
-> state:'State -> 'State
Array.foldBack<'T,'State> : folder:('T -> 'State -> 'State) -> array:'T[]
-> state:'State -> 'State
Seq.foldBack<'T,'State> : folder:('T -> 'State -> 'State) -> source:seq<'T>
-> state:'State -> 'State

List.foldBack2<'T1,'T2,'State> : folder:('T1 -> 'T2 -> 'State -> 'State) ->
list1:'T1 list -> list2:'T2 list -> state:'State -> 'State
Array.foldBack2<'T1,'T2,'State> : folder:('T1 -> 'T2 -> 'State -> 'State)
-> array1:'T1[] -> array2:'T2[] -> state:'State -> 'State
Seq.foldBack2<'T1,'T2,'State> : folder:('T1 -> 'T2 -> 'State -> 'State) ->
source1:seq<'T1> -> source2:seq<'T2> -> state:'State -> 'State

List.mapFoldBack<'T,'State,'Result> : mapping:('T -> 'State -> 'Result *
'State) -> list:'T list -> state:'State -> 'Result list * 'State
Array.mapFoldBack<'T,'State,'Result> : mapping:('T -> 'State -> 'Result *
'State) -> array:'T[] -> state:'State -> 'Result[] * 'State
Seq.mapFoldBack<'T,'State,'Result> : mapping:('T -> 'State -> 'Result *
'State) -> source:seq<'T> -> state:'State -> seq<'Result> * 'State

List.scan<'T,'State>  : folder:('State -> 'T -> 'State) -> state:'State ->
list:'T list -> 'State list
Array.scan<'T,'State> : folder:('State -> 'T -> 'State) -> state:'State ->
array:'T[] -> 'State[]
Seq.scan<'T,'State> : folder:('State -> 'T -> 'State) -> state:'State ->
source:seq<'T> -> seq<'State>

List.scanBack<'T,'State> : folder:('T -> 'State -> 'State) -> list:'T list
```

```
-> state:'State -> 'State list
Array.scanBack<'T,'State> : folder:('T -> 'State -> 'State) -> array:'T[]
-> state:'State -> 'State[]
Seq.scanBack<'T,'State> : folder:('T -> 'State -> 'State) -> source:seq<'T>
-> state:'State -> seq<'State>
```

In addition to multiple `fold` usage examples sprinkled around the book and readily available on the Internet I provide a few more in the script `Ch8_8.fsx`.

The merge/split pattern

Our long journey into the world of data transformation patterns captured by F# 4.0 core library has reached the last stop. Here, functions residing with **merge/split** pattern either merge some collections into one, or perform the opposite by splitting one collection into many:

```
List.append: list1:'T list -> list2:'T list -> 'T list
Array.append: array1:'T[] -> array2:'T[] -> 'T[]
Seq.append: source1:seq<'T>  -> source2:seq<'T> -> seq<'T>

List.concat: lists:seq<'T list> -> 'T list
Array.concat: arrays:seq<'T[]> -> 'T[]
Seq.concat: sources:seq<'Collection> -> seq<'T> when 'Collection :> seq<'T>

List.zip: list1:'T1 list -> list2:'T2 list -> ('T1 * 'T2) list
Array.zip: array1:'T1[] -> array2:'T2[] -> ('T1 * 'T2)[]
Seq.zip: source1:seq<'T1> -> source2:seq<'T2> -> seq<'T1 * 'T2>

List.zip3: list1:'T1 list -> list2:'T2 list -> list3:'T3 list -> ('T1 * 'T2
* 'T3) list
Array.zip3: array1:'T1[] -> array2:'T2[] -> array3:'T3[] -> ('T1 * 'T2 *
'T3)[]
Seq.zip3: source1:seq<'T1> -> source2:seq<'T2> -> source3:seq<'T3> ->
seq<'T1 * 'T2 * 'T3>

List.unzip: list:('T1 * 'T2) list -> ('T1 list * 'T2 list)
Array.unzip: array:('T1 * 'T2)[] -> ('T1[] * 'T2[])

List.unzip3 list:('T1 * 'T2 * 'T3) list -> ('T1 list * 'T2 list * 'T3 list)
Array.unzip3 array:('T1 * 'T2 * 'T3)[] -> ('T1[] * 'T2[] * 'T3[])
```

The `append` function is the simplest form of merge pattern as it combines a pair of collections into the single one. Elements of the second argument collection just follow the elements of the first argument collection in the result collection.

The `concat` function is the generalization of `append` to any number of input collections just wrapped into a sequence.

Finally, zippers (`zip`, `zip3`) take two or three collections and turn them into a single collection of corresponding tuples. Unzippers (`unzip`, `unzip3`) do the opposite, taking a collection of tuples and turning it into the tuple of collections. Note that the library does not provide unzippers for `seq`.

Summary

This was a long chapter, but it was an essential step into the universal patterns of data transformations and their reflection in the F# 4.0 core library. The knowledge you acquired will support the process of idiomatic blueprinting of an arbitrary data transformation by prompting you to build your F# code around the handful of retained reference points. When you mentally dissect your task at hand into a composition of functions along the patterns covered here, the high-quality library functions are always available for you to quickly compose from them an error-free and adequately performant solution.

The next chapter will continue with the data transformation theme, looking into F# data queries and the subject of data parsing.

9
More Data Crunching

Up until this point, all F# data transformation patterns covered were dealing with in-memory collections. That is, important data crunching use cases, such as querying data, already persisted within the enterprise, and ingesting data from outside of the enterprise have not been considered yet.

This chapter covers these data transformation scenarios and related coding patterns:

- Querying the external data. I'll begin with querying the data using F# query expressions. We are going to see how the same transformation patterns we distilled in `Chapter 8`, *Data Crunching – Data Transformation Patterns*, in relation to core library function members are fully applicable to querying the external data presented in a data base or a web service. It also would be interesting to push the limits of composition in query expressions.
- Parsing data from the external sources. We already spent a fair amount of time considering pattern matching amplified by active patterns. However, I do not feel an imperative need for using some advanced techniques, such as parser combinators. I'll show some from-the-trenches examples of production quality data parsing achieved with just a bit of custom coding.

Data querying

So far in the book, the sources of data collections were either collection generators or the file system. Let me move toward more realistic enterprise data sources, where data are persisted in databases. To access and transform such data, F# provides **query expressions** (h ttps://msdn.microsoft.com/visualfsharpdocs/conceptual/query-expressions-%5bf sharp%5d).

Query expressions represent a concrete type of **computation expressions** that is embedded into the language. They allow to bring data into memory by querying external sources and transforming incoming data to the desired shape.

The F# query expressions are akin to sequence expressions: both produce data sequences. However, before the final data projection shaping the produced data sequence a query expression may apply to data a wide variety of data transformations that are similar to what we used to see in **LINQ** (https://en.wikipedia.org/wiki/Language_Integrated_Query). Query expressions can be considered LINQ support in F#.

F# and LINQ before query expressions

Chronologically, query expressions were introduced in F# 3.0. Prior to that, F# allowed you to access the LINQ machinery via **.NET 3.5 Enumerable extension methods** (https://msdn.microsoft.com/en-us/library/system.linq.enumerable_methods(v=vs.110).aspx). Let's look at the following script, which finds out the last vowel in the sequence of lexicographically ordered letters of the English alphabet (Ch9_1_1.fsx):

```
let isVowel = function
            | 'A' | 'a' | 'E' | 'e' | 'I' | 'i'
            | 'O' | 'o' | 'U' | 'u' -> true
            | _ -> false

let alphabet = seq { 'A' .. 'Z' }

alphabet |> Seq.filter isVowel |> Seq.sortDescending |> Seq.head
// val it : char = 'U'
```

If we recollect that the F# sequence `alphabet` is `IEnumerable`, then the task can be achieved with LINQ extension methods (Ch9_1_2.fsx):

```
open System.Linq
let isVowel = function
            | 'A' | 'a' | 'E' | 'e' | 'I' | 'i'
            | 'O' | 'o' | 'U' | 'u' -> true
            | _ -> false
let alphabet = seq { 'A' .. 'Z' }
alphabet.Where(isVowel).OrderByDescending(fun x -> x).First()
// val it : char = 'U'
```

Using the *fluent interface* of LINQ extension methods as a rough substitute for the F# pipe operator, |>, we have achieved almost one-to-one correspondence between the definitions. The same result has been achieved by combining the Seq library functions, filter-sortDescending-head, and by combining the LINQ extension methods, Where-OrderByDescending-First.

Introducing F# query expressions

You may ask why I pay so much attention to the above similarity? That is because query expressions are nothing more than *syntactic sugar* similar to the one we observed with sequence expressions in Chapter 6, *Sequences – The Core of Data Processing Patterns*. Query expressions use F# computation expressions magic to express chain of function applications as a linear sequence of SQL-like operations within built-in computation expression builder query { ... }. This approach is similar to seq { ... } workings for generating F# sequences. The script Ch9_1_2.fsx given in the previous section may be present using a query expression as (Ch9_1_3.fsx):

```
let isVowel = function
              | 'A' | 'a' | 'E' | 'e' | 'I' | 'i'
              | 'O' | 'o' | 'U' | 'u' -> true
              | _ -> false

let alphabet = seq { 'A' .. 'Z' }

query {
    for letter in alphabet do
    where (isVowel letter)
    sortByDescending letter
    select letter // may be omitted
    head
}
// val it : char = 'U'
```

When dissecting the preceding query expression you may spot the already familiar **ETL** data transformation process considered in Chapter 8, *Data Crunching – Data Transformation Patterns*: given a collection, perform one or more modifications on its members, eventually projecting the query result. As a computation expression query provides that magic glue between adjacent lines. It makes the data flowing from one query operator to another in the manner similar to functions chained with the >> combinator.

Query operators

Although the number of **query operators** (`https://msdn.microsoft.com/en-us/visualfs harpdocs/conceptual/query-expressions-%5Bfsharp%5D`) is substantially less than the number of F# core library functions for collections – only around 40 – the query operators fit nicely into, where applicable, the hierarchy of data transformation patterns (another similar *classification* I managed to discover is the following one (`https://weblogs.asp.net/dixin /understanding-linq-to-objects-2-query-methods-and-query-expressions`). The mapping accompanied by the similar category names from the preceding classification provided in round brackets is given as following:

- **The aggregation pattern** (*aggregation*): This includes functions such as `count`, `averageBy`, `averageByNullable`, `minBy`, `maxBy`, `minByNullable`, `maxByNullable`, `sumBy`, and `sumByNullable`
- **The searching pattern**: This includes the `find` function
- **The selection pattern** (*restriction*): This contains `last`, `lastOrDefault`, `head`, `headOrDefault`, `nth`, `exactlyOne`, `exactlyOneOrDefault`, `take`, `takeWhile`, `skip`, `skipWhile`, `distinct`, and `where`
- **The partitioning pattern** (*grouping*): This contains `groupBy` and `groupValBy`
- **The reordering pattern** (*ordering*): This contains `sortBy`, `sortByDescending`, `sortByNullable`, `sortByNullableDescending`, `thenBy`, `thenByDescending`, `thenByNullable`, and `thenByNullableDescending`
- **The testing pattern** (*quantifier*): This contains `exists` and `all`
- **The mapping pattern** (*projection*): This contains `select`
- **The merge/split pattern** (*convolution*): This contains `zip`, `join`, `groupJoin`, and `leftOuterJoin`

Nice! However, so far, the consideration was rotating around in-memory collections. Then how do we encompass querying out-of-memory data? F# provides considerable flexibility in this matter; so, let's approach it gradually in order to explore the richness and variety of the available schemes.

The role of a LINQ provider

The important detail in using LINQ that often gets missed by occasional users is that the query mechanism is agnostic to the nature of the data collection. There is a layer that may be involved that abstracts the details of the concrete data source behind the **IQueryable<'T>** (`https://msdn.microsoft.com/en-us/library/bb351562(v=vs.110).aspx`) interface that we did not touch yet. Without involving this layer, you are on your own with our familiar

`IEnumerable<'T>` interface.

Both interfaces ensure deferred execution. However, `IEnumerable<'T>` just brings into memory the data collection that matches a query expressed with relevant external means, subject to further **LINQ-to-Object** in-memory manipulations.

By comparison, `IQueryable<'T>` allows **LINQ-to-Something (LINQ-to-SQL, LINQ-to-OData, LINQ-to-WMI,** to name a few) workings by the virtue of the component named **LINQ provider**. It ensures hidden translation of a LINQ query to terms that the concrete substitute of *Something* part understands, followed by the translated query execution by *Something*, bringing just the matching data collection back into the memory. Those of you interested in what entity may play the role of *Something*, I refer to the representative-although slightly outdated – **LINQ-to-Everywhere – List of LINQ Providers** (`https://blogs.msdn.microsoft.com/knom/2009/04/27/linq-to-everywhere-list-of-linq-providers/`).

There are two key moments in the previous paragraph that must be understood properly. Firstly, *the LINQ provider fully abstracts the details of query translation and execution*. For the intuitively clear case of **LINQ-to-SQL**, such translation is quite straightforward. The translated SQL query is to be executed on the side of the engaged database engine, sending back over the wire only the results of the server-side query execution. For something like, for example, **LINQ-to-CRM** (`http://linqtocrm.codeplex.com/`), some further digging would be required in order to find out what exactly this particular LINQ provider does.

Secondly, the to-be-translated LINQ query should not contain elements that cannot be expressed in terms of the translated query execution engine. Such violations may take place through selectiveness of features in the provider implementation, or unintentional capturing of unrelated elements from the context. This means that if the provider implementation, for example, does not support the sorting operation, the LINQ query that has the sorting piece will be rejected by the underlying provider. Also, sometimes, the translated query execution engines may have varying abilities and the same LINQ-to-SQL query may be successfully executed by the Microsoft SQL engine but fail miserably on a MySQL engine.

With the role of LINQ provider in mind, let's first turn to the case of LINQ provider-free F# querying.

External data querying via IEnumerable<'T>

For this use case, let me take something that can be easily reproduced by you. Being on the Microsoft platform myself, I will be using the traditional test database Microsoft supplies to developers, namely **Adventureworks 2014** (https://msftdbprodsamples.codeplex.com/releases/view/125550). It has been installed under the **localdb** Microsoft SQL engine that comes with Visual Studio 2013.

There is a [Person].[Person] table in this database that carries, among other things, names of people. Let me perform a simple analytical task on it by performing the following query:

```
select count(distinct [FirstName]) from
[Adventureworks2014].[Person].[Person]
```

This allows me to find out that the database carries 1018 distinct personal first names. Let's find out how these names are distributed by the first letter in the English alphabet.

To access the database, I will be using the simple Reader object of native .NET System.Data.SqlClient library. The first (and rather simplistic) approach would be to just provide the complete list of distinct first names over the wire to the memory on demand. The following script implements this approach (Ch9_1_4.fsx):

```
open System.Data
open System.Data.SqlClient

let alphabet = seq { 'A' .. 'Z' }

let connStr = @"Data Source=(localdb)projectsv12;Initial
Catalog=Adventureworks2014;Integrated Security=true;"
let dbConnection = new SqlConnection(connStr)
dbConnection.Open()

let dbCommand = new SqlCommand("select FirstName from
[Person].[Person]",dbConnection)
let names = seq {
                printfn "reading from db"
                use reader =
dbCommand.ExecuteReader(CommandBehavior.Default)
                while reader.Read() do yield reader.GetString(0) }
let distribution =
    query {
        for letter in alphabet do
            let howMuch =
                query {
                    for name in names do
```

```
                    where (name.StartsWith(string letter))
                    distinct
                    select name
               } |> Seq.length
          sortBy howMuch
          select (letter, howMuch)
     }

  distribution |> Seq.toList |> printfn "%A"
```

There are two query expressions here: the first goes over each `letter` of the `alphabet`, delegating the trip to the database for the complete set of data to the nested second query, and then filtering out everything in memory except names starting with the current `letter` value, throwing away duplicates and finding the resulting number of names. The outer query puts this number into its place according to the found frequency and returns the sought-for projection (`letter`, `howMuch`) as the `distribution` sequence. Materializing it in FSI, I can observe the target name distribution. The timed results of running the script `Ch9_1_4.fsx` are presented in the following screenshot, where FSI just takes source script code from the given file path:

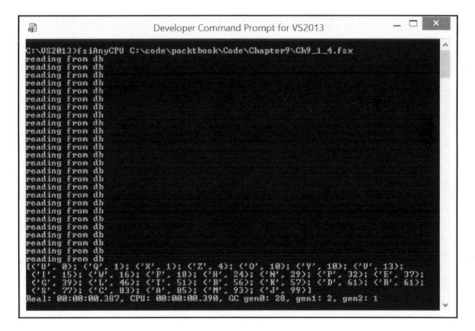

External SQL Querying: version 1

You may notice that while running, the script performed a complete reading of the list of first names from the [Person][Person] database table for 26 times, which is an apparent overkill, and the approach can be improved significantly.

For example, we may parameterize our SQL command and get back not all names, but just the distinct names for each specific letter, which will dramatically decrease the traffic over the wire with the database. The script being refactored to reflect this improvement approach is given in the following code (Ch9_1_5.fsx):

```
open System.Data
open System.Data.SqlClient

let alphabet = seq { 'A' .. 'Z' }

let connStr = @"Data Source=(localdb)projectsv12;Initial
Catalog=Adventureworks2014;Integrated Security=true;"
let dbConnection = new SqlConnection(connStr)
dbConnection.Open()
```

```
let dbCommandR l =
    new SqlCommand(
        (sprintf "%s%s%s" "select distinct FirstName from [Person].[Person]
where FirstName like '" l
        "%'"), dbConnection)

let names l = seq {
                printfn "reading from db"
                use reader = (dbCommandR
l).ExecuteReader(CommandBehavior.Default)
                while reader.Read() do yield reader.GetString(0) }

let distribution =
    query {
        for letter in alphabet do
            let howMuch = names (string letter) |> Seq.length
            sortBy howMuch
            select (letter, howMuch)
    }
#time "on"
distribution |> Seq.toList |> printfn "%A"
```

You may notice that there is no need for the nested query {...} groups now, as a significant amount of work is delegated to the SQL engine over the wire. The timed results of running the refactored script are given in the following screenshot:

External SQL Querying – version 2

You may observe an almost four-fold improvement in performance due to significant decrease of network traffic volume in the second version.

Pushing this trend of minimizing traffic to the extreme and giving as much work to the SQL server as possible, I may make all work get pushed on the side of SQL server, leaving just a rudimentary task of getting remote data for the F# query, such as in the third version of the script shown here (Ch9_1_6.fsx):

```
open System.Data
open System.Data.SqlClient

let connStr = @"Data Source=(localdb)projectsv12;Initial
Catalog=Adventureworks2014;Integrated Security=true;"
let dbConnection = new SqlConnection(connStr)
dbConnection.Open()

let dbCommandF =
    new SqlCommand("select SUBSTRING(FirstName, 1, 1),count(distinct
FirstName) as "count"
                    from [Adventureworks2014].[Person].[Person]
```

```
                    group by SUBSTRING(FirstName, 1, 1)
                    order by count",dbConnection)

let frequences = seq {
                printfn "reading from db"
                use reader =
dbCommandF.ExecuteReader(CommandBehavior.Default)
                while reader.Read() do yield (reader.GetString(0),
reader.GetInt32(1)) }

let distribution =
    query {
        for freq in frequences do
        select freq
    }
#time "on"
distribution |> Seq.toList |> printfn "%A"
```

Note that now all the dirty work is done by the SQL server, which is perfectly fine as
Microsoft SQL Server is a masterpiece of software dedicated to data storing and crunching,
and it does its work really well (if you do not detrimentally interfere, of course). The results
of running the final script refactoring are presented in the following screenshot. Do not miss
there the evidence that the whole data exchange over the wire took just a single round trip:

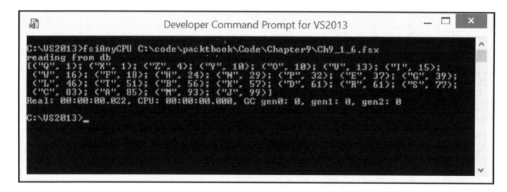

External SQL querying: version 3

Wow, this optimization is the bomb! Version 3, in comparison with version 1, has roughly
17.6 times better performance. Now your take-home lesson is hard to forget.

Enterprise development demands that the underlying technology ensures the ample ability of distributing remote load. Such ability can be granted by F# `query` as well as by other means.

External data querying via IQuerable<'T>

I hope that after the bold performance results achieved in the previous section there is no need to convince you just how important the ability of relaying LINQ query execution to the remote party is. However, do not expect to take this for granted. This direction may have a steep learning curve, which we will notice shortly.

Let's take as a use case the 100% real task I was recently addressing on the job at **Jet.com Inc.** (`https://jet.com/about-us`). I will be building a backend for a dashboard, showing some *top-paid partners of Jet.com* in real time (merchants with the largest amounts of reimbursement for fulfilled orders that they have shipped to Jet.com customers).

I will be accessing a limited amount of data from the Jet.com Quality Assurance environment, so the numbers will not be that indicative of real top-paid partners.

The data required for the dashboard backend are split between two databases: `SQL.Colossus` carries the data on payments in the `Payments` table, while `SQL.IronmanData` carries the data on partners in the `Partner` table.

If the case is that the data is located at the same SQL engine that supports cross-DB queries, then the T-SQL script that brings me the sought-for data would be something along the following lines (`Ch9_2.fsx`, commented section at the top):

```
select top (10) min(r.DisplayName) as Name, sum(p.[Amount]) as Total
from [sql.colossus].[dbo].[Payments] p
join [sql.ironmandata].[dbo].[Partner] r on r.MerchantId = p.MerchantId
where p.[IsDeposited] = 1
group by p.[MerchantId]
order by total desc
```

After being executed against the target environment in SQL Server Management Studio, this yields the results reflected in the following screenshot:

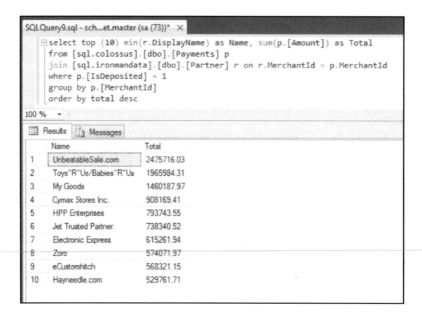

```sql
select top (10) min(r.DisplayName) as Name, sum(p.[Amount]) as Total
from [sql.colossus].[dbo].[Payments] p
join [sql.ironmandata].[dbo].[Partner] r on r.MerchantId = p.MerchantId
where p.[IsDeposited] = 1
group by p.[MerchantId]
order by total desc
```

	Name	Total
1	UnbeatableSale.com	2475716.03
2	Toys"R"Us/Babies"R"Us	1965984.31
3	My Goods	1460187.97
4	Cymax Stores Inc.	908169.41
5	HPP Enterprises	793743.55
6	Jet Trusted Partner.	738340.52
7	Electronic Express	615261.94
8	Zoro	574071.97
9	eCustomhitch	568321.15
10	Hayneedle.com	529761.71

SQL Query to feed the top-paid Jet.com Partners dashboard

Let me make the first attempt in expressing the similar T-SQL query using the F# query expression query{...}. In order to get access to LINQ-to-SQL, I will be using a more advanced F# mechanism to get strongly typed access to the data than **ADO.NET**, which I was using in the previous section. This mechanism is known as the F# **type provider**. Specifically, I will be using the **SQLDataConnection (LINQ to SQL) type provider** (http ://fsharp.org/guides/data-access/#sql-data-access), which is a part of the standard F# distribution that has been targeting Microsoft Windows since F# v3.0.

 Those of you who are totally unfamiliar with the matter can follow this **MSDN walkthrough** (https://msdn.microsoft.com/visualfsharpdocs /conceptual/walkthrough-accessing-a-sql-database-by-using-type -providers-%5bfsharp%5d) in order to better understand the contents of this section.

The F# script that can be put into the core of the dashboard backend is as follows (Ch9_2.fsx):

```
#r "FSharp.Data.TypeProviders"
#r "System.Data"
```

```fsharp
#r "System.Data.Linq"

open Microsoft.FSharp.Data.TypeProviders
open System.Linq

[<Literal>]
let compileTimeCsusCS = @"Data Source=(localdb)projectsv12;Initial
Catalog=Colossus.DB;Integrated Security=SSPI"
let runTimeCsusCS = @"Data Source=***;Initial Catalog=SQL.Colossus;User
ID=***;Password=***"
[<Literal>]
let compileTimeImCS = @"Data Source=(localdb)projectsv12;Initial
Catalog=SQL.Ironman;Integrated Security=SSPI"
let runTimeImCS = @"Data Source=***;Initial Catalog=SQL.IronmanData;User
ID=***;Password=***"

type Colossus = SqlDataConnection<compileTimeCsusCS>
type IronManData = SqlDataConnection<compileTimeImCS>

let pmtContext = Colossus.GetDataContext(runTimeCsusCS)
let imContext = IronManData.GetDataContext(runTimeImCS)

let mostPaid =
    fun x -> query {
                for payment in pmtContext.Payments do
                where (payment.IsDeposited.HasValue &&
payment.IsDeposited.Value)
                groupBy payment.MerchantId into p
                let total = query { for payment in p do sumBy
payment.Amount}
                sortByDescending total
                select (p.Key,total)
                take x
            }

let active = (mostPaid 10)
let activeIds = active |> Seq.map fst

let mostActiveNames =
    query {
        for merchant in imContext.Partner do
        where (activeIds.Contains(merchant.MerchantId))
        select (merchant.MerchantId,merchant.DisplayName)
    } |> dict

active
|> Seq.map (fun (id, total) -> (mostActiveNames.[id],total))
|> Seq.iter (fun x -> printfn "%s: %.2f" (fst x) (snd x))
```

Take into account that in order to adhere with the security requirements, I do not reveal any parameters of the Jet.com infrastructure except some (not necessarily coinciding with real ones) names of databases and tables.

When it comes to the type provider, it is important to realize that the provider itself works at compile-time, providing typed access to the fields of the involved SQL tables. In order to do this, it requires access to the SQL schema information at compile-time. This access to the structural information in the preceding script is given via the `compileTimeCsusCS` and `compileTimeImCS` connection strings for `Colossus.DB` and `SQL.Ironman` databases, respectively.

Note that compile-time access to the local SQL engine from the type provider has nothing to do with application data. It just retrieves system data about SQL schemas. These schemas are structurally similar to ones carrying application data on production SQL data engine. So, the provided `Colossus` and `IronManData` types are built off the `localdb` SQL engine, while the `pmtContext` and `imContext` runtime data contexts are built off the production server(s) with the help of `runTimeCsusCS` and `runTimeImCS` runtime connection strings.

The `mostPaid` function represents the query used to find any given number of top-paid partners along with their aggregate deposited payments. As we may expect, the signature of this function is `mostPaid : x:int -> System.Linq.IQueryable<string * decimal>`, and it is to be translated by the LINQ-to-SQL provider into plain T-SQL, to be executed on the SQL server side.

Another interesting moment is that in Jet.com's Microsoft Azure production environment, cross-database queries such as the one from Figure *SQL Query to feed the top-paid Jet.com Partners dashboard* do not work, so I split the access into three phases:

- At the first phase, `active` represents a collection of tuples `(merchantId, paymentAmount)` of which the list of pertinent partner IDs, `activeIds`, can be easily projected
- At the second phase, another query, `mostActiveNames`, retrieves only those partner display names that belong only to the top-paid partners and packages them into a dictionary
- Finally, `active` experiences a transformation where the ID is substituted by `mostActiveNames.[id]`, yielding the final data shape required for the dashboard.

The results of running the previous script with FSI are presented in the following screenshot; as expected, they are identical to previous ones:

```
C:\VS2013>fsiAnyCPU C:\code\packtbook\Code\Chapter9\Ch9_2.fsx
UnbeatableSale.com: 2475716.03
Toys"R"Us/Babies"R"Us: 1965984.31
My Goods: 1460187.97
Cymax Stores Inc.: 908169.41
HPP Enterprises: 793743.55
Jet Trusted Partner.: 738340.52
Electronic Express: 615261.94
Zoro: 574071.97
eCustomhitch: 568321.15
Hayneedle.com: 529761.71

C:\VS2013>
```

F# Query via IQueryable<'T> in action

Composable queries

Wouldn't it be great to compose smaller F# subqueries into bigger queries? Put differently, it would mean composing multiple queryables into a single LINQ query translated into SQL and executed on the database engine side.

This sounds promising, and it has attracted the attention of some individual developers and groups.

The most sizeable effort was taken by a group at the University of Edinburgh, UK, governed by functional programming authorities such as Philip Wadler. Their results can be found at the **FSharpComposableQuery** (`http://fsprojects.github.io/FSharp.Lin q.ComposableQuery/index.html`) project home page, offering a NuGet package, source code, tutorial, and even some theoretical papers on the subject. An introductory video presentation given by Philip Wader is available on the SkillsMatter website: **A practical theory of language-integrated query** (`https://skillsmatter.com/skillscasts/4486-a-pra ctical-theory-of-language-integrated-query`).

Also, a few years ago, an alternative and more lightweight approach to composable queries was suggested in this **blog post** (http://fpish.net/blog/loic.denuziere/id /3508/2013924-f-query-expressions-and-composability) by **Loïc Denuzière** (http://f pish.net/profile/loic.denuziere). It is based on splicing partial F# query expressions together in order to build more complex ones. I will make a foray into composable LINQ queries based on the latter approach.

Just before we start writing the code, I must point out a big limitation of F# querying based on LINQ-to-SQL: it is not possible to perform cross-database and cross-engine queries, as *all subqueries must share the same LINQ context!* This factor might be a show-stopper for enterprises that have a multitude of **OLTP** and **OLAP** databases.

In order to refactor to a composable query a T-SQL query from the script Ch9_2.fsx that was covered above in the dashboard use case discussion, I have moved a copy of the Partner table to the SQL.Colossus database. It can now share the same LINQ context with the Payments table.

The composition method is based on introducing a special PartialQueryBuilder class that:

- Subclasses standard Linq.QueryBuilder introducing extra method Run
- Augmenting Linq.QueryBuilder with method Source

All these measures allow you writing subqueries with the alternative expression builder pquery that gets wrapped into quotations instead of being evaluated . These quotations are embedded into ordinary queries and get evaluated uniformly.

In the following script, which relies on these features, I've omitted the separation of compile-time and run-time connections for brevity (Ch9_3.fsx):

```
#r "FSharp.Data.TypeProviders"
#r "System.Data"
#r "System.Data.Linq"

open Microsoft.FSharp.Data.TypeProviders
open System.Linq

[<Literal>]
let runTimeCsusCS = @"Data Source=***;Initial Catalog=SQL.Colossus;User
ID=***;Password=***"

type Colossus = SqlDataConnection<runTimeCsusCS>

let pmtContext = Colossus.GetDataContext(runTimeCsusCS)
```

Then goes the utility part defining `pquery`:

```
type PartialQueryBuilder() =
    inherit Linq.QueryBuilder()
    member __.Run(e:  Quotations .Expr<Linq.QuerySource<'T,IQueryable>>) =
e

let pquery = PartialQueryBuilder()

type Linq.QueryBuilder with
    [<ReflectedDefinition>]
    member __.Source(qs: Linq.QuerySource<'T,_>) = qs
```

Finally, the composed queries are as follows:

```
let mostPaid = pquery {
                for payment in pmtContext.Payments do
                where (payment.IsDeposited.HasValue &&
                        payment.IsDeposited.Value)
                groupBy payment.MerchantId into p
                let total = pquery { for payment in p do sumBy
                                        payment.Amount}
                sortByDescending total
                select (p.Key,total)
                take 10
                        }

let dashboard = pquery {
                for merchant in pmtContext.Partner do
                    for (id,total) in %mostPaid do
                    where (merchant.MerchantId = id )
                    select (merchant.DisplayName, total)
                    }

query { for m in %dashboard do
        select m } |> Seq.iter (fun x -> printfn "%s: %.2f" (fst x) (snd
x))
```

Note how `mostPaid` is spliced into the `dashboard`, creating a seamless composition, and in turn, `dashboard` is spliced into the final query.

Running the script in FSI yields the results shown here:

Getting dashboard data with the composed query

You may wonder whether there is a way to check out that the query composition really took place. Fortunately, that is not that hard to do. All it takes is adding the following property to the LINQ context, as shown here:

```
pmtContext.Payments.Context.Log <- new System.IO.StreamWriter(
    @"C:usersgenedownloadspmtlinq.log", AutoFlush = true)
```

After running the preceding script again, the LINQ log file now contains the SQL code executed by the SQL engine:

```
SELECT [t0].[DisplayName] AS [Item1], [t3].[value] AS [Item2]
FROM [dbo].[Partner] AS [t0]
CROSS JOIN (
    SELECT TOP (10) [t2].[MerchantId], [t2].[value]
    FROM (
        SELECT SUM([t1].[Amount]) AS [value], [t1].[MerchantId]
        FROM [dbo].[Payments] AS [t1]
        WHERE (([t1].[IsDeposited] IS NOT NULL) AND ((([t1].[IsDeposited]) =
1)
        GROUP BY [t1].[MerchantId]
        ) AS [t2]
    ORDER BY [t2].[value] DESC
    ) AS [t3]
WHERE [t0].[MerchantId] = [t3].[MerchantId]
ORDER BY [t3].[value] DESC
-- Context: SqlProvider(Sql2008) Model: AttributedMetaModel Build:
4.0.30319.33440
```

Note how all `IQueryable` bits and pieces from the script F# queries get molded into the single SQL statement.

Data parsing

The parsing of data is absolutely essential for the enterprise. As an enterprise F# developer at Jet.com, I come across this data transformation pattern on a daily basis. Every case of **LOB** applications' integration with a third-party system - **ERP**, **Bank**, or **Carrier** – involves data parsing on the ingesting edges. Despite a plethora of integration technologies around that promise great data quality, timeliness, integrity, you name it...time and again, I am forced by my contractors to deal with flat fixed format files, CSV files, and Excel files. This is the boring reality of today.

On this battlefield, the weaponry varies from case-by-case hand-coded solutions based on **Regex** and F# active patterns to fairly generic solutions targeting whole classes of incoming data with F# type providers. Some typical examples of semi-generic solutions are invoices in the form of CSV files and Excel files that are to be persisted in the SQL server for further processing, reconciliation, and future audit. I'll show how the high-quality parsing of incoming data can be achieved for the use case of digesting the carrier invoices ingested as an Excel file into the SQL server.

The use case – LaserShip invoicing

LaserShip is one of the "last mile" delivery companies usually engaged by e-commerce for same-day expedited deliveries. Jet.com uses LaserShip services along with other carriers.

LaserShip delivers its invoicing information packaged as Excel files. For the purposes of reconciliation and auditing, it is desirable to load LaserShip invoices into the SQL server.

Approaching the parsing task

When resembling ETL tasks pop up, I usually approach them with the following pattern:

1. Define the schema of the SQL table that will carry the loaded data. Add to the data that come from the carrier extra field(s) allowing you to reference any chunk of data back to the carrier's file it originated from. Also, add the synthetic and/or natural key field(s) and reasonable constraints. The sample SQL table schema has been provided in the form of T-SQL script `SCHEMA_LaserShip.sql`.

2. Ingest the file with the help of **Excel Provider** (http://fsprojects.github.io/E xcelProvider/). Adjust the type provider settings to suppress the default field type interpretation and force the delivery of fields as strings. The Excel file template distributed by LaserShip to their customers has been provided as Excel file Lasership Invoice Format.xlsx.

3. For the fields that may be omitted in the source represented the such as **nullable** values. Omitted values are to be filled with System.DBNull.Value singleton. Create or reuse a set of parsing functions for each field type returning a boxed parsed value or System.DBNull.Value.

4. Parse the contents of the file into the System.Data.DataTable instance matching column names with database fields and unboxing values parsed with generic parsing functions. The example invoice containing an excerpt of a real invoice with personal data wiped out has been provided as Excel file LaserShip20160701.xlsx.

5. Load the filled DataTable instance into the SQL server using the ADO.NET**SqlBulkCopy** (https://msdn.microsoft.com/en-us/library/syste m.data.sqlclient.sqlbulkcopy(v=vs.110).aspx).

LaserShip parser implementation

The approach outlined earlier is implemented by the script Ch9_4.fsx. As the script length does not fit well with the book format it will not be given here in its entirety. Instead, I'll reproduce in this section only the most important excerpts from the script with my comments:

```
#r @"C:...packagesExcelProvider.0.8.0libExcelProvider.dll"
```

The line above ensures that NuGet package **Excel Provider 0.8.0** (https://www.nuget.org /packages/ExcelProvider) is accessible from the script:

```
type LaserShip = ExcelFile< @"C:codePacktBookCodeChapter11lasership invoice
format.xlsx", HasHeaders=true, ForceString=true>
```

The line above is extremely important. It gets processed *in compile-time* by the referred F# Excel type provider. The type provider using the given file path gets to the Excel file lasership invoice format.xlsx that represents the data template. We adjust type provider settings by defining HasHeaders and ForceString static bool parameters. The type provider produces on the fly the provided type LaserShip that will allow to access any cell of the invoice row by its name:

```
let asNullableString =
```

```
function
| null -> box System.DBNull.Value
| (s: string) -> s.Trim()
                    |> function
                        | "" -> box System.DBNull.Value
                        | 1 -> box 1
```

The preceding definition of `asNullableString` function implements the idiomatic typed transition from the Excel data cell that we know is of type `string` to its `obj` representation suitable to be placed into not statically typed `System.Data.DataTable` in-memory data table. If data in Excel are omitted for the cell the function is given as argument, the returned value would be boxed `System.DBNull.Value` value suitable to be placed into the database field of type, described in T-SQL as `NVARCHAR(...) NULL`. The script defines functions similar to `asNullableString` for each type of the Excel file where strong type checking is required: `asNullableDate, asString, asNullableMoney,` and others:

```
let headers = ["invno";"JobNumber";"TDate";...;"SourceId";"RowKey";]
```

The preceding binding would be necessary for associating columns of in-memory data table with the database table columns for `SQLBulkCopy`:

```
let loadLaserShip excelPath =
    (new LaserShip(excelPath)).Data
```

This function definition is very important as it performs ingestion of invoice data from the Excel file specified by the given `excelPath` argument to the in-memory placeholder `Data` procured by the provided type `LaserShip`:

```
let fillDataTable sourceId (rows: IEnumerable<LaserShip.Row>) =
    let dt = new DataTable()
    do headers |> Seq.iter(fun h-> dt.Columns.Add(new DataColumn(h)))
    for row in rows do
        let dr = dt.NewRow()
        dr.Item(0) <- unbox (row.invno |> asString "invno")
            .   .   .   .   .
        dr.Item(36) <- unbox (row.PickupDate |> asNullableString)
        dr.Item(37) <- sourceId
        dt.Rows.Add(dr)
    printfn "loaded %d rows" dt.Rows.Count
    dt
```

The preceding definition of the `fillDataTable` function is the gist of the script. You may notice the interesting type of argument it has: `rows: IEnumerable<LaserShip.Row>`. In other words `rows` is a sequence of another provided type `LaserShip.Row` representing a single row of invoice spreadsheet. Within the function a new instance of `DataTabledt` is created and supplied by column names taken from `headers`. Then each row of the ingested Excel file is parsed into the `dt`, taking care of data validity. In the end the loaded data table `dt` is returned.

A small, but very important detail: the `sourceId` argument above just references another table that keeps track of of the processed invoices. It has been written into the each row of in-memory data table, so after the data upload the reference will be available in the persisted to SQL server data to the metadata describing the data originating source. Further details are beyond the scope here.

Finally, another important function `loadIntoSQL` makes the bulk data upload into SQL server. Its definition is as follows:

```
let loadIntoSQL tableName connStr (dataTable: DataTable) =
    use con = new SqlConnection(connStr)
    con.Open()
    use bulkCopy = new SqlBulkCopy(con, DestinationTableName = tableName)
    bulkCopy.WriteToServer(dataTable)
    printfn "Finished write to server"
```

There a connection `con` to the database gets opened using the provided connection string `connStr` value. Using the created connection and given SQL table name the instance of `SqlBulkCopy` is created and used for persisting in-memory `dataTable` to the associated SQL server table.

The preceding script can be further generalized to the degree where the only variable part will be the data related to the concrete file type. This variable part can be made pluggable into the universal Excel file parser. And this can be achieved in fewer than a hundred lines of code.

Summary

This chapter wraps up the topic of data transformation patterns. Most of it is devoted to querying persisted data with the help of F# query expressions. You should be able to grasp the nuances of query work distribution between in-memory collections and the network-located data engine.

We also touched the important issue of data parsing, demonstrating the handful of simple patterns that allow you to ingest arbitrary Excel files with the helping hand of F# type providers, which will be further covered in Chapter 11, *F# Expert Techniques.*

In the next chapter, I will concentrate on dual patterns of type specialization (augmentation) and type generalization in F#.

10

Type Augmentation and Generic Computations

To this point in the book, it was easy to notice the direct link between the use pattern and the correspondent language feature. For example, `Chapter 5`, *Algebraic Data Types*, clearly showed that the native F# algebraic types are substitutes for custom classes. Increased quality and speed of implementations based on algebraic data types reflect the payoff for the feature use.

In this chapter, I will consider a certain language features that do not make the payoff from their use obvious. Nevertheless, these features are ubiquitous in F#. I mean the ambivalent pair of code generalization against the code specialization.

We are going to cover the following topics:

- Code generalization techniques, or making the same functional code applicable to multiple function argument types
- Code specialization techniques, or making the functional code more specific than usually may be achieved by using standard features

Each of the preceding patterns carries promises of certain benefits: improved performance, more succinctness, and better static type control. The goal of this chapter is to show you how to recognize the situations when these patterns are applicable and apply them, achieving the expected benefits.

Code generalization

Let me begin by stating that F# **automatically generalizes** (`https://msdn.microsoft.com` `/visualfsharpdocs/conceptual/automatic-generalization-%5bfsharp%5d`) arguments of functions where it is possible to deal with the multiplicity of types.

So far, we have mostly been dealing with the generalization of data collections. That is, a sequence is agnostic to the type of its elements. That's why we were able to write functions that operate on sequences of arbitrary generic type. And F# type inference spots and carries this property on.

Suppose that we proudly implement our own function of reversing a list as follows (`Ch10_1.fsx`):

```
let reverse ls =
    let rec rev acc = function
    | h::t -> rev (h::acc) t
    | []   -> acc
    rev [] ls
```

Then, we may notice that the F# compiler infers the `reverse : ls:'a list -> 'alist` signature for it, where `'a` indicates that the function can be applied to any type of list elements. And if we decide to check out how exactly our `reverse` function would behave with different argument types, we may observe its behavior is consistent for the following arguments (`Ch10_1.fsx`):

```
reverse [1;2;3]
// val it : int list = [3; 2; 1]
reverse ["1";"2";"3"]
// val it : string list = ["3"; "2"; "1"]
```

And even if we try to slightly abuse type system and mix different boxed types (`Ch10_1.fsx`):

```
reverse [box 1.0; box 2.0M; box 3I]
//val it : obj list = [3 {IsEven = false;
//                        IsOne = false;
//                        IsPowerOfTwo = false;
//                        IsZero = false;
//                        Sign = 1;}; 2.0M; 1.0]
```

The `reverse` function behaves as genuinely generic with regard to the type of argument list elements.

Fine, now let's do something seemingly similar and also utterly simple, such as shifting the argument to the left by a single bit (Ch10_1.fsx):

```
let twice x  = x <<< 1
```

All of a sudden, the F# compiler infers the very specific twice : x:int -> int function signature. What's going on? Apparently, there are some types that allow this geeky way of making the value twice as big, for example, int64. Interestingly, let's look at what happens when we follow the function definition by the usage, as following (Ch10_1.fsx):

```
let twice x = x <<< 1
twice 10L
//val twice : x:int64 -> int64
//val it : int64 = 20L
```

Now the F# compiler has seemingly changed its mind about the signature of the twice function, this time inferring the argument and result types as int64. This action is irreversible, which means that trying to follow the preceding evaluation with twice 10 will be now rejected with this diagnostics: *this expression was expected to have type* int64 *but it has type* int *here.*

What's going on? Why does the generalization seemingly fail?

Statically resolved type parameters

As we just noticed, the F# compiler inferred a monomorphic type for the (<<<) operator. A step toward polymorphism would assume the ability to express it somehow – while staying within the .NET type system that only such types are fine to be twice argument that work with the operator (<<<). In other words, the compiler should deal with a **type constraint**.

The problem is that this kind of constraint cannot be expressed within the F# compilation target language **MSIL**. That is, the latest **.NET CLI standard** (http://www.ecma-international.org/publications/files/ECMA-ST/ECMA-335.pdf) in the *II.10.1.7 Generic Parameters* section constraints a type either by being a **value type** or a **reference type** for a concrete reference type that has the **default constructor**. This is the problem of the .NET type system rather than the F# language or compiler.

F# 4.0 Language Specification (`http://fsharp.org/specs/language-spec/4.0/FSharpSpec-4.0-latest.pdf`) hints at the observed compiler behavior in section 5.2.3:

> *Uses of overloaded operators do not result in generalized code unless definitions are marked as inline. For example, take a look at the function as shown here:*
> ```
> let f x = x + x
> ```
> *It results in an f function, which can be used only to add one type of value, such as int or float. The exact type is determined by later constraints.*

Fortunately, the F# compiler may enforce these (and some other) type of constraints at compile-time using the mechanism of **statically resolved type parameters**. This type parameter for our (<<<) operator will have the special "hat" prefix ^a, assuming that the type is statically known at the point of compilation (compared to 'a, assuming that the type can be anything). As this kind of statically polymorphic function would require a specific manner of compilation depending on the concrete statically resolved type that is aligned with constraints, the F# compiler achieves this goal with the help of **inlining**, as the language specification has hinted.

Function inlining

Let me apply the inlining mechanism to this failing `twice` function as shown here (`Ch10_1.fsx`):

```
let inline twice' x = x <<< 1
// val inline twice' :
//     x: ^a ->  ^a when
//          ^a : (static member ( <<< ) :   ^a * int32 ->   ^a)
```

Note how the automatically inferred signature of the inlined `twice'` function carries the **hat** type ^a along with the sought-for constraint regarding the type parameter statically resolved at compile-time: type ^a must have an operator (<<<) with the ^a * int32 -> ^a signature.

Great, now `twice'` begins to look like a polymorphic function, allowing, for example, the following evaluations (`Ch10_1.fsx`):

```
twice' 5     // int32 argument
twice' 5u    // uint32 argument
twice' 5L    // int64 argument
twice' 5UL   // uint64 argument
twice' 5y    // sbyte argument
twice' 5uy   // byte argument
twice' 5s    // int16 argument
```

```
twice' 5us  // uint16 argument
twice' 5I   // biginteger argument
twice' 5n   // nativeint argument
```

At the same time, it disallows the following evaluations (Ch10_1.fsx):

```
twice' 5m //The type 'decimal' does not support the operator '<<<'
twice' 5.0 // The type 'float' does not support the operator '<<<'
twice' "5"// The type 'string' does not support the operator '<<<'
twice' '5' // The type 'char' does not support the operator '<<<'
```

The compiler has provided all the above niceties after we merely added the `inline` qualifier to the function definition. But you should realize that the compiler literally injects the inlined function implementation into MSIL adjusting it for argument(s) having statically resolved concrete types. Inlining is the compilation method that allows to alleviate .NET CLR limitations.

Static constraints

As it was inferred by the F# compiler for the `twice'` function earlier, the argument x can be any type ^a as long as ^a : (static member (<<<) : ^a * int32 -> ^a). This condition, either inferred by the F# compiler or, perhaps, intentionally imposed by the programmer is named a **static constraint** (https://msdn.microsoft.com/en-us/visualfs harpdocs/conceptual/constraints-%5Bfsharp%5D). There are about a dozen of argument type constraint kinds. You may check the **documentation** (https://docs.microsoft.com /en-us/dotnet/articles/fsharp/language-reference/generics/constraints) for their complete list.

Constraints can be combined together with the help of the and construction, as shown in the following code snippet (Ch10_2.fsx):

```
let inline constrained (param: ^a
     when ^a: equality and ^a: comparison) = ()

type Good = Good

[<NoEquality; NoComparison>]type Bad = Bad

Good |> constrained
// Compiles just fine
Bad |> constrained
// Error: type Bad does not support comparison constraint
```

We have two discriminated unions here: Good, which is **equitable** and **comparable** by default, and Bad, which is also normally equitable and comparable, but here it is decorated with [<NoEquality; NoComparison>] attributes. As the constrained function requires its generic param argument to be of both equitable and comparable types, constrained Good gets compiled, while constrained Bad does not.

Explicit or inferred constraining?

A few years ago, I was tinkering with creating F# generic code. At that time, my thinking was along these lines: if I need to create a generic function that can deal with a restricted handful of argument types, the right approach would be to appropriately and explicitly constrain the latter. I even asked on **StackOverflow** (http://stackoverflow.com/q/16737675/917053) what the idiomatic approach would be. **One of the answers** (http://stackoverflow.com/a/16738811/917053) I want to quote here:

> *Explicit constraints are a way of stating what you want to do. What could be better than doing it and having the compiler statically prove that the argument is valid for the operations?*

Enlightening observation, isn't it?

Nevertheless, what if you still want to explicitly limit the list of generic functions' valid argument types based on some external considerations? Then, you may use the following approach I was hinted at in **the other answer** (http://stackoverflow.com/a/16739483/917053) to my StackOverflow question, which is based on overloading static methods of the auxiliary type (Ch10_2.fsx):

```
[<AutoOpen>]
module Restrict =
    let inline private impl restricted =
        printfn "%s type is OK" (restricted.GetType().FullName)

    type Restricting = Restrict with
        static member ($) (Restrict, value: byte) = impl value
        static member ($) (Restrict, value: sbyte) = impl value
        static member ($) (Restrict, value: int) = impl value
        static member ($) (Restrict, value: uint32) = impl value
        static member ($) (Restrict, value: bigint) = impl value

    let inline doit restricted = Restrict $ restricted
```

There are three components in the preceding snippet:

- The **private** function, impl, which performs a required action on a generic restricted argument of type 'a; in other words, upon an argument that's not constrained whatsoever
- The auxiliary type Restricting, which has a single discriminated union case, Restrict, augmented by the overloaded static member $ upon the required set of types (byte, sbyte, int, uint32, bigint picked just for the sake of illustration)
- The user-facing function doit, whose restricted argument has been statically constrained by the other two pieces

Let's look at the workings of the preceding in the following script (Ch10_2.fsx):

```
doit 1uy
doit 1y
doit 1
doit 1u
doit 1I
doit 1L // does not compile
doit 1.0 // does not compile
doit 1.0m // does not compile
doit '1' // does not compile
```

The first five use cases matching the restricted types compile just fine; the last four do not compile with the same diagnostics as expected:

no overloads match the op_Dollar" *method*

The successful execution of the first five use cases is presented in the following screenshot:

Executing explicitly constrained generic code

Inlining scope

Inlining in F# is not limited to just module-level functions. It is perfectly fine to use inlining for static and instance methods of F# types. For example, in the following snippet, where we have type `Bar` with a static method `doIt` and `type Foo` on any generic type `^T` that has static member `doIt` with the matching signature and the `inline` member `Invoke` calling the `doIt` method of `^T` as shown here (`Ch10_2.fsx`):

```
type Bar() =
  static member doIt() = 42

type Foo< ^T when ^T: (static member doIt: unit -> int)>(data: ^T []) =
  member inline this.Invoke () = (^T : (static member doIt : unit -> int)
())

let result = (Foo([|Bar()|]).Invoke())
// val result : int = 42
```

An intricate matter that the preceding sample illustrates is accessing static or instance `inline` methods from outside of F# using, for example, a plain C# -> F# interoperability scenario. Remember that normal MSIL cannot support such constraints.

To address this subtlety the compiled MSIL for `Invoke` method implementation above that C# may access just throws an exception. The actual inlined body of the function is kept accessible only from F# in its assembly's metadata.

Inline optimizations

The relationship between inlining and code optimization is quite subtle. Usually, it is difficult to predict what consequences of generalization via inlining would be.

However, sometimes, it is possible to achieve tremendous performance improvements via inlining. A notorious example is the F# handling of the `System.DateTime` equality, where the compilation of the `datetime1 = datetime2` expression involves boxing. Take a look at the following snippet (`Ch10_2.fsx`):

```
open System
#time "on"
let x, y = DateTime.MinValue, DateTime.MaxValue
for i = 0 to 10000000 do x = y |> ignore
//Real: 00:00:00.421, CPU: 00:00:00.406, GC gen0: 115, gen1: 2, gen2: 1
```

Here, using just the = operator, we observe a certain garbage collection activity.

However, suppose we just inline the redefined equality operator, ==, as shown in the following snippet (Ch10_2.fsx):

```
open System
#time "on"
let inline eq<'a when 'a :> IEquatable<'a>> (x:'a) (y:'a) = x.Equals y
let inline (==) x y = eq x y
for i = 0 to 10000000 do x == y |> ignore
//Real: 00:00:00.022, CPU: 00:00:00.015, GC gen0: 0, gen1: 0, gen2: 0
```

Then, we achieve no garbage collection activity whatsoever and an impressive *19(!)* times better performance.

Writing generic code

I would like to wrap up the theme of writing generic code with just another example of a non-trivial generic function that I have implemented as a **sample for a "functional programming" interview** (https://infsharpmajor.wordpress.com/2013/05/03/if-goog le-would-be-looking-to-hire-f-programmers-part-4/): given an arbitrary positive number, find a next higher number consisting of the same digits. If that does not exist, then return the original number.

We will approach the solution as a generic function, allowing the argument to be of any integral type, or anything consisting of just digits, be it byte, BigInteger, or nativeint.

The base line approach would be to split the number into a list of digits, making the list of all digit permutations, assembling digits back into numbers, sorting the list of numbers, and finally, picking the element next to the given argument. Apparently, the time and space complexities of this "solution" are awful, so let's improve it:

- The first useful observation of the optimized solution would be that the solution exists if a pair of adjacent digits exists in the given number, where the left-hand side is strictly less than the right-hand side.
- The next useful observation would be that if we scan the list of digits of the given number from right to left by a sliding window of width 2, then the first pair that matches the first observation would be the place of change. Everything to the left of it (if any exists) must stay intact.
- The final useful observation is to take the pair that matches the second observation. The sublist to the right including the right element of the pair is sorted from right to left. The digit that must substitute the left element of the pair must be the minimally greater digit from the sublist. The left element that we just substituted should be placed some place to the right, preserving the sublist order.

Now, if we concatenate (if nonempty) the sublist to the left of the changing digit, followed by the substituting digit, followed by the reversed sublist after accommodating the changing digit and convert the resulting digit list to the number, this would yield the solution with a surprisingly good time complexity of O(n) and a space complexity of O(n), where n is the number of digits in the original number. The solution snippet is as follows (Ch10_3.fsx):

```
let inline nextHigher number =
    let g0 = LanguagePrimitives.GenericZero<'a>
    let g1 = LanguagePrimitives.GenericOne<'a>
    let g10 = (g1 <<< 3) + (g1 <<< 1)

    let toDigits n =
        let rec toDigitList digits n =
            if n = g0 then digits
            else toDigitList ((n % g10) :: digits) (n / g10)
        toDigitList [] n

    let fromDigits digits =
        let rec fromDigitList n = function
            | [] -> n
            | h::t -> fromDigitList (n * g10 + h) t
        fromDigitList g0 digits

    let make p ll  =
        ll |> List.rev |> List.partition ((<) p)
        |> fun (x,y) -> (x.Head::y) @ (p::(x.Tail))

    let rec scan (changing: 'a list) source =
        match source with
        | [] -> changing
        | h::t -> if h >= changing.Head then
                    scan (h::changing) t
                  else
                    (List.rev t) @ (make h changing)

    number |> toDigits
           |> List.rev |> fun x -> scan [(x.Head)] (x.Tail)
           |> fromDigits
```

Let's see this in action by running some usage cases via FSI as shown in the following screenshot:

```
fsianycpu                                                    _ □ ✕

> let inline nextHigher number =
    let g0 = LanguagePrimitives.GenericZero<'a>
    let g1 = LanguagePrimitives.GenericOne<'a>
    let g10 = (g1 <<< 3) + (g1 <<< 1)

    let toDigits n =
        let rec toDigitList digits n =
            if n = g0 then digits
            else toDigitList ((n % g10) :: digits) (n / g10)
        toDigitList [] n

    let fromDigits digits =
        let rec fromDigitList n = function
            | [] -> n
            | h::t -> fromDigitList (n * g10 + h) t
        fromDigitList g0 digits

    let make p ll =
        ll |> List.rev |> List.partition ((<) p)
        |> fun (x,y) -> (x.Head::y) @ (p::(x.Tail))

    let rec scan (changing: 'a list) source =
        match source with
        | [] -> changing
        | h::t -> if h >= changing.Head then
                      scan (h::changing) t
                  else
                      (List.rev t) @ (make h changing)

    number |> toDigits |> List.rev
    |> fun x -> scan [(x.Head)] (x.Tail) |> fromDigits;;

val inline nextHigher :
    number: ^a -> ^a
      when  ^a : (static member get_Zero : -> ^a) and
            ^a : (static member get_One : -> ^a) and
            ^a : (static member ( + ) :  ^a *  ^a ->  ^a0) and
            ^a : (static member ( <<< ) :  ^a * int32 ->  ^a) and
          ( ^a or  ^a0) : (static member ( % ) :  ^a *  ^a0 ->  ^a) and
          ( ^a or  ^a0) : (static member ( / ) :  ^a *  ^a0 ->  ^a) and
          ( ^a or  ^a0) : (static member ( * ) :  ^a *  ^a0 ->  ^b) and
            ^a : comparison and
          ( ^b or  ^a) : (static member ( + ) :  ^b *  ^a ->  ^a)

> nextHigher 1987654321;;
val it : int = 2113456789
> nextHigher 321543321L;;
val it : int64 = 32211345L
> nextHigher 136442n;;
val it : nativeint = 142346n
>
```

Generic implementation of non-trivial function

Take into account the complexity of the static constraint expression that the F# compiler has inferred for `nextHigher`, as shown in the preceding screenshot. It would be really challenging to come up with an expression that complicated from the top of your head. Let the compiler do its job indeed.

Type augmentation

The opposite of generalization is specialization, and it is associated with **type augmentation** in F#. It is worth noting that the official **F# 4.0 Language Specification** (`http://fsharp.org /specs/language-spec/4.0/FSharpSpec-4.0-latest.pdf`) does not introduce this terminology using **type extension** instead. Nevertheless, the *type augmentation* expression is de-facto ubiquitous and used interchangeably with *type extension*. Personally, I believe that *augmentation* is free of the undesired connotation that *extension* carries as something that's *added* to an existing matter. Augmentation is a better synonym for the *specialization* of an existing matter by adding, customizing, or even removing features. So we will stick to it here.

The following figure shows two flavors of type augmentation available in F#. Both use the same syntax but represent different use cases. Intrinsic augmentation customizes your own code, while optional augmentation may customize types outside of your code:

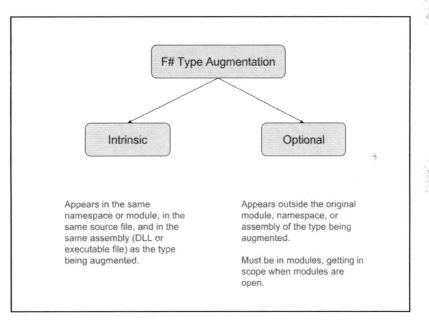

F# flavors of type augmentation

But why would you need to customize your own code in the first place? This is where certain F#-specific patterns of usage kick in. They can be spotted time and again both inside the F# core libraries and outside in third-party extensions. They explain how a bare type gets created first and then acquires an associated module that carries some helper functions and finally, how the type gets extended by some static methods. We can consider the **definition of complex type** (`https://github.com/fsprojects/powerpack-archive/blob /master/src/FSharp.PowerPack/math/complex.fs`) as a manifestation of this pattern:

- On `complex.fs` **source line 13** (`https://github.com/fsprojects/powerpack-a rchive/blob/master/src/FSharp.PowerPack/math/complex.fs#L13`), the bare type `Complex` is defined as having custom `equality` and `comparison` properties and being the value type
- On `complex.fs` **source line 39** (`https://github.com/fsprojects/powerpack-a rchive/blob/master/src/FSharp.PowerPack/math/complex.fs#L39`), the module `Complex` is defined as carrying the entire slew of helper functions covering, in particular, all math operations in complex numbers
- Finally, on `complex.fs` **source line 99** (`https://github.com/fsprojects/powe rpack-archive/blob/master/src/FSharp.PowerPack/math/complex.fs#L99`), type `Complex` is supplied by static operators for complex math numbers expressed via previously defined helper functions

The preceding definition may be considered as a very neat template of idiomatic intrinsic augmentation.

Let me walk you through some typical use cases of augmenting types.

Augment by removing

At first glance, augment by removing may sound like an oxymoron. However, it is not; just bear with me. Take a look at the following code snippet (`Ch10_4.fsx`):

```
type Outcome =
| Success
| Failure
with
    member x.IsFailure =
        match x with
        | Failure -> true
        | _ -> false
    member x.IsSuccess = not x.IsFailure
```

Here, my intent was to hide the pattern matching behind properties of the discriminated union type `Outcome`. However, suddenly, this seemingly innocuous piece of code does not compile, as the following screenshot shows:

```
type Outcome =
| Success
| Failure
with
    member x.IsFailure =
        match x w
        | Failure          The member 'IsFailure' can not be defined because the name 'IsFailure' clashes with the default augmentation of the union case 'Failure' in this type or module
        | _ -> false
    member x.IsSuccess = not x.IsFailure
```

F# DU implementation detail leaks out

The F# compiler accompanies the red squiggle line under the `IsFailure` property name with a surprise message (refer to the preceding screenshot), prompting that the compiler also augments each `<Name>` use case of discriminated unions with the `Is<Name>` private property by default, and by defining the identically named property, we made this detail leak out.

Can we effectively remove default compiler-generated augmentation from the `Outcome` definition? It so happens that we can do that using the .NET attribute especially designated for this purpose: **DefaultAugmentation** (`https://msdn.microsoft.com/visualfsharpdoc s/conceptual/core.defaultaugmentationattribute-class-%5bfsharp%5d`).

If we just decorate the `Outcome` type definition with the `[<DefaultAugmentation(false)>]` attribute, then everything gets back to the intuitively expected behavior, and the property name clash shown above vanishes.

Augment by adding

Now let me do quite the opposite and augment types by adding features. I'm going to use a real (simplified, of course) case from Jet.com technology practices.

Imagine that Jet's e-commerce platform supports the following transaction kinds (`Ch10_4.fsx`):

```
type Sale =
    | DirectSale of decimal
    | ManualSale of decimal

type Refund =
    | Refund of decimal
```

When we aggregate these transactions for payment or analytics purposes, it is highly desired that you operate upon collections that represent any mix of valid transactions. But we cannot mix different types in a typed collection, can we?

The naive brute-force approach might be exploiting the fact that any .NET type is a subtype of `System.Object`. So, the following collection might be perfectly OK (`Ch10_4.fsx`):

```
let ll: obj list = [box (DirectSale 10.00M); box (Refund -3.99M)]
```

However, this approach wipes out one of the major benefits of F#, namely static type safety, which means that unfortunately, having the following collection is also perfectly OK from the standpoint of the F# compiler:

```
let ll': obj list = [box (Refund -3.99M); box 1; box "Anything"]
```

A hardcore OOP developer would continue to lean on inheritance, introducing something like the `Transaction` superclass as shown here (`Ch10_4.fsx`):

```
type Transaction =
    | Sale of Sale
    | Refund of Refund

let ll: Transaction list = [Sale (DirectSale 5.00M); Sale (ManualSale
5.00M); Refund (Refund.Refund -1.00M)]
```

This is an acceptable approach, but it's not flexible from the standpoint of potential future extensions. Also it is awkward overall.

Any other ideas? Yes, type augmentation comes to the rescue! Well, in a sense.

Let me define a dummy **marker interface** `ITransaction`, as following:

```
type ITransaction = interface end
```

Now, unfortunately, F# does not allow you to add an interface to an already defined type later. But we can still define our transactions, augmenting the standard DU as following (`Ch10_4.fsx`):

```
type Sale =
    | DirectSale of decimal
    | ManualSale of decimal
    interface ITransaction

type Refund =
    | Refund of decimal
    interface ITransaction
```

Furthermore, we can use the idiomatic trick with F# supporting function contravariant arguments:

```
let mixer (x: ITransaction) = x
```

Now we can represent the sought-for collection as following:

```
let ll: list<_> = [mixer(DirectSale 10.00M); mixer(Refund -3.99M)]
```

So far, so good. Now `ll` is strongly typed `ITransaction` list, but it can carry any current (and future, if required) transaction kinds. Having the latter mixed together is not a big deal if a disassembly back to concrete transactions is needed, as following (`Ch10_4.fsx`):

```
#nowarn "25"

let disassemble (x: ITransaction) =
    match x with
    | :? Sale as sale -> (function DirectSale amount -> (sprintf
"%s%.2f" "Direct sale: " amount, amount)
      | ManualSale amount -> (sprintf "%s%.2f" "Manual sale: " amount,
amount)) sale
    | :? Refund as refund -> (function Refund amount -> (sprintf
"%s%.2f" "Refund: " amount, amount)) refund
```

(The cryptic turning off the compiler warning "25" in the beginning of the above script addresses the manner the matching by type works. The F# compiler assumes that it may be more types "implementing" `ITransaction` than are included into preceding `match` expression. I know that I covered all cases there, so the warning would be just a noise.)

Equipped with this machinery, it is easy to perform, for example, an aggregation of a list of concrete transactions in a single payment (`Ch10_4.fsx`):

```
[mixer(DirectSale 4.12M);mixer(Refund -0.10M);mixer(ManualSale 3.62M)]
|> List.fold (fun (details, total) transaction ->
    let message, amount = disassemble transaction in
    (message::details, total + amount))
    ([],0.00M)
|> fun (details,total) ->
    (sprintf "%s%.2f" "Total: " total) :: details
|> List.iter (printfn "%s")
```

Running the preceding script in FSI will produce the results shown in the following screenshot:

```
> type ITransaction = interface end

type Sale =
    | DirectSale of decimal
    | ManualSale of decimal
    interface ITransaction

type Refund =
    | Refund of decimal
    interface ITransaction
let mixer (x: ITransaction) = x
#nowarn "25"
let disassemble (x: ITransaction) =
    match x with
    | :? Sale as sale -> (function DirectSale amount -> (sprintf "%s%.2f" "Dir
ect sale: " amount, amount)
                                  | ManualSale amount -> (sprintf "%s%.2f" "M
anual sale: " amount, amount)) sale
    | :? Refund as refund -> (function Refund amount -> (sprintf "%s%.2f" "Ref
und: " amount, amount)) refund
;;

type ITransaction
type Sale =
    | DirectSale of decimal
    | ManualSale of decimal
    with
        interface ITransaction
    end
type Refund =
    | Refund of decimal
    with
        interface ITransaction
    end
val mixer : x:ITransaction -> ITransaction

val disassemble : x:ITransaction -> string * decimal

> [mixer(DirectSale 4.12M);mixer(Refund -0.10M);mixer(ManualSale 3.62M)]
  |> List.fold (fun (details, total) transaction ->
                  let message, amount = disassemble transaction in
                      (message::details, total + amount))
                  ([],0.00M)
  |> fun (details,total) ->
         (sprintf "%s%.2f" "Total: " total) :: details
  |> List.iter (printfn "%s");;
Total: 7.64
Manual sale: 3.62
Refund: -0.10
Direct sale: 4.12
val it : unit = ()
```

Augmenting DU with the marker interface

Summary

This chapter demonstrated how to approach matters of code generalization and/or specialization in situations when such adjustments are appropriate.

In the next chapter, we will just scratch the surface of the advanced F# patterns, as their detailed coverage may require another book.

11

F# Expert Techniques

So far in the book, we've dealt mostly with customary F# facilities that constitute the core of successful F# idiomatic use in diverse application fields. The common sign of (almost) all of the related usage patterns is that they are straightforward and ordinary. Their mastery is a must for any intermediate level F# practitioner.

In this chapter, I'm going to step out of the regular space where expressions always yield results, calculations take place sequentially, and code must be first written in order to be later used. I will walk you through some of expert level F# techniques, the area of exciting usage patterns that is often considered overcomplicated and error-prone in nonfunctional paradigms.

In this chapter I will cover the following topics in the context of F# idiomatic use:

- Type providers
- Concurrent programming
- Reactive programming
- Metaprogramming

I will approach each of these subjects by giving a brief overview accompanied with a concise usage sample taken from the enterprise trenches. I will attempt to show that these features are not really mind-bending and usually offer developers a strong safety net. However, please do not expect any sort of deep dive into these subjects. Consider the contents of this chapter more a roadmap to become skillful in these F# use patterns, as stimuli and practical application teasers.

A note on custom computation expressions

I've decided not to cover arbitrary **F# Computation Expressions** (https://docs.microsoft
.com/en-us/dotnet/articles/fsharp/language-reference/computation-expressions)
in this book despite F# itself having this mechanism baked in under the hood of significant
language features, such as *sequence expressions* (covered in Chapter 6, *Sequences – The Core of
Data Processing Patterns*), *query expressions* (covered in Chapter 9, *More Data Crunching*), and
asynchronous expressions (to be addressed in this chapter). Although custom computation
expressions allow crafting very elegant code in some cases, I feel that covering this feature
here may divert us from the practicality path we are pursuing.

Those of you interested in a solid understanding and mastery of the F#
computation expressions may turn to this excellent detailed reading on the
subject by Scott Wlaschin: **The "Computation Expressions" series** (https
://fsharpforfunandprofit.com/series/computation-expressions.ht
ml).

Exploring type providers

Frankly, I consider **type providers** as one of the most exciting, powerful, and pragmatic F#
features. Ability to apply type providers is, in my opinion, among the strongest arguments
for the usage of F# in enterprise software development.

The feature review

Type providers in F# represent a pretty unique *practical* pattern of manipulating various
data sources in a strongly typed manner. This manipulation is accomplished via types,
methods, and properties that were derived from the data source features and built at
compile-time in a fully automated fashion. The developer is not required to author and/or
maintain these automatically *provided* data manipulation means.

The idea of automatic code generation itself is as old as pyramids, but what makes the
difference is versatility, ease of usage, and a painless experience. Those who've ever
wrestled with **SqlMetal** (https://msdn.microsoft.com/en-us/library/bb386987(v=vs.
110).aspx) or **WSDLTool** (https://msdn.microsoft.com/en-us/library/7h3ystb6(v=vs
.100).aspx) would appreciate the way of type providers a lot.

It is also true that *creating* a useful type provider of production quality may require a lot of skill and effort. Nevertheless, once created, the type provider component can be used without any limits, so the usage benefits overweigh the construction pains by many times.

It is also worth mentioning that since the introduction of type providers in F# 3.0, many valuable data source kinds have already been covered. Since the initial wave of type provider construction mentioned in **Twelve F# type providers in action** (`https://blogs.m sdn.microsoft.com/dsyme/2013/01/30/twelve-f-type-providers-in-action/`), the available providers have gotten significantly more mature, providing a slick and smooth usage experience.

Enough talking; let's first take a look at the big picture of F# type provider workings. This is shown in the following figure:

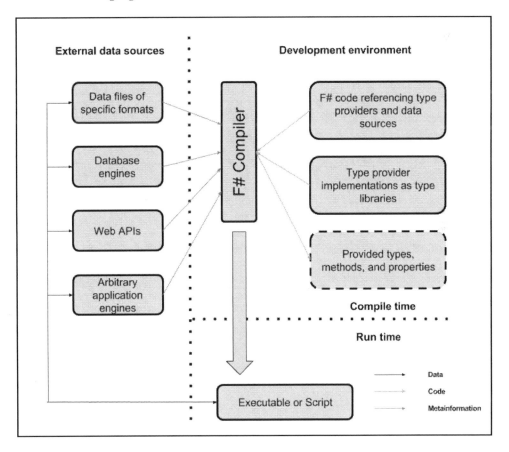

F# type provider workings

Without pretending to cover all potential external data sources, I am mentioning the following ones here:

- Files of many specific formats (Excel, comma-separated, JSON, and so on) frequently utilized in enterprise development
- Database engines (Microsoft SQL Server, Oracle, MySQL, and so on)
- A variety of web APIs implementing different protocols and data presentation formats
- A variety of application engines (Python, R, MatLab, and so on) that can be remotely controlled in order to implement the desired processing and yielding results being given input data

The magic begins at compile-time, when the developer references code type(s) that are expected to be provided from the given data source(s) within the F# application: results of a given query against a database, tabular data from some Excel file, clustering results of certain data; you name it. The F# compiler needs the corresponding type provider(s) to be available in the form of library packages. Reaching out to given data sources for the required metadata at compile-time, the type provider in concert with the F# compiler builds provided types, methods, and properties that allow you to treat external data on the fly in a strongly typed manner.

For example, **SQLClient type provider** (`http://fsprojects.github.io/FSharp.Data.Sql Client`) takes compile-time connection strings, connects *during compilation* to the given data engine instance, and having the text of the given query in T-SQL on hand uses certain system stored procedures in order to find types associated with the columns of the to-be-returned result set. This type information translates into a built-on-the-fly type associated with the query. As a result, if we are compiling under Visual Studio, we are getting Intellisense with regard to the fields associated with the result set that is present as the F# sequence of the compiler-provided type.

If at run-time we shoot the same query against *some other* data engine that has data with table schemas similar to the table(s) participating in the compiled query, the provided data access type will still be good for data transformations.

It is important to understand that the correspondence between database schemas and the query associated with the provided type is kept under static typing scrutiny; if any part of this equation (either the query expression or the involved schemas) changes, the code simply does not compile.

This is simultaneously a fault and a blessing as it reliably protects from potential mishaps between the application code and the data layer. However, the necessity of having access to the SQL data engine at compile-time complicates arrangements such as builds, continuous integration, and so on.

Personally, I am a big fan of the aforementioned type provider and found it interesting that often, people do not realize the delineation that exists between compile-time and run-time and effectively confining the possibilities.

Some developers ask from time to time whether the query associated with the provided type can be changed at run-time. Apparently, the answer is a big *no* as that would require you to change the already generated type-specific code. At the same time, it is just fine (and expected) to change the connection string at run-time in order to access the target data engine where the data to be processed resides. Usually, the latter may be achieved with the provided type constructor having the run-time connection string as an argument.

I'm going to use this type provider for demo purposes later in this chapter, so you will have a chance to check your understanding.

The demo problem

When picking a demo problem for type provider subject, I was initially doubtful whether it's feasible to delve into the type provider creation process or whether this book's format limits me to using only the existing type providers. I even solicited an opinion from a group of colleagues on whether it's possible to implement a practically sound type provider not exceeding 20 lines of F# code. The answer turned out to be affirmative, thanks to one of the authors of the aforementioned SQLClient type provider, who pointed out the interesting side problem this provider brought to light: the relationship between SQL code and the F# code.

From the separation of concerns standpoint, it is not an impeccable proposition to have T-SQL queries belonging to an application embedded into the F# code as literals. Ideally, it would be great to keep these queries separately from the F# code in a separate SQL script directory, having designated `.sql` file per each query. But how can such an arrangement be possible if we need the contents of these files to be represented as string literals in the application code at compile-time?

Eureka! The way out would be using just another type provider!

An internal "file reader" type provider may associate a corresponding *provided* type with the SQL query text stored there as a literal field with each SQL query file at compile-time. The literal field does not anyhow differ from the literal string constant in the text. Such an elegant approach indeed!

Taking into account an apparent didactic value behind this clear delineation between compile-time and run-time considerations, I decided to come up with something similar.

Imagine that we want to protect the execution of an application with a secret key but do not want to have the key value present anywhere in the source code. Instead, the secret may be kept in a key vault of some sort and be associated with the application only during the build. The deficiency of such protection is apparent as the secret value would be still present somewhere in the compiled application assembly. But that is not the point of the exercise. The requirement is this: there should be no secret key value in the source code.

The demo solution

Our solution would be to create a type provider that, given a reference to the external repository that contains the secret key, would provide a type with the `string` secret value extracted from the repository and stored as a literal field. This means that such a field can be used as a case value in the `match...with` F# expression without revealing the underlying value in any manner. Also, you would acquire a firm understanding of the inner type provider workings as well as a sticky pattern to recall each time when in doubt about what activity happens when in type providing scenarios.

I'm ready to jump upon the implementation. Writing a type provider in 2016 is a breeze compared to how it was in 2012, when the feature was first delivered to the masses. Thanks to the open source effort of the amazing F# community for assembling together and packaging a sort of SDK in the form of the NuGet package for the creation of F# type providers, namely **FSharp.TypeProviders.StarterPack** (`https://www.nuget.org/packages /FSharp.TypeProviders.StarterPack`). Bear with me. Just perform the following steps:

1. Shoot out a new Visual Studio project to create the F# library named **KeyTypeProvider**.
2. Get rid of the two generated files with the `.fs` and `.fsx` extensions.

3. Using **Package Manager Console**, add the Type Provider Starter Pack NuGet package to the just created project, issuing the `Install-Package FSharp.TypeProviders.StarterPack` command and observing a bunch of source code files added to the project (`ProvidedTypes.fsi`, `ProvidedTypes.fs`, and `DebugProvidedTypes.fs`).

4. Add a new F# source code file named `KeyTypeProvider.fs` and place it *below* the last of injected files listed in the previous bullet (remember that the order in which the F# source code files are introduced to the compiler matters a lot).

That's it; we are ready to craft the type provider code into the latter file. I am placing the snippet with the corresponding code as follows (`KeyTypeProvider.fs`):

```
namespace FSharp.IO.DesignTime

#nowarn "0025"

open System.Reflection
open System.IO
open Microsoft.FSharp.Core.CompilerServices
open ProviderImplementation.ProvidedTypes

[<TypeProvider>]
type public KeyStringProvider(config : TypeProviderConfig) as this =
    inherit TypeProviderForNamespaces()

    let nameSpace = "FSharp.IO"
    let assembly = Assembly.LoadFrom(config.RuntimeAssembly)
    let providerType = ProvidedTypeDefinition(assembly, nameSpace,
        "SecretKey", baseType = None, HideObjectMethods = true)

    do
        providerType.DefineStaticParameters(
            parameters = [ ProvidedStaticParameter("Path",
                typeof<string>) ],
            instantiationFunction = fun typeName [| :? string as path
              |] ->
                let t = ProvidedTypeDefinition(assembly, nameSpace,
                  typeName, baseType = Some typeof<obj>,
                  HideObjectMethods = true)
                let fullPath = if Path.IsPathRooted(path) then path
                  else Path.Combine(config.ResolutionFolder, path)
                let content = File.ReadAllText(fullPath)
                t.AddMember <| ProvidedLiteralField("Key",
                    typeof<string>, content)
                t
        )
```

```
            this.AddNamespace(nameSpace, [ providerType ])

    [<assembly:TypeProviderAssembly()>]
    do()
```

That's not exactly 20 lines of code, but it's quite close. I will just outline the purpose of the bits and pieces in the preceding snippet.

 Those of you willing to tinker with the code of such sort may walk through **Tutorial: Creating a Type Provider** (https://docs.microsoft.c om/en-us/dotnet/articles/fsharp/tutorials/type-providers/creat ing-a-type-provider) as a supplementary helper.

After referring the pertinent libraries, the definition of our KeyStringProvider *type provider type* (yes, type provider has its own type, sure thing) follows decorated with the [<TypeProvider>] attribute and inherited from the TypeProviderForNamespaces type, which is defined elsewhere in these auto-inserted code files.

The next three lines of code define the name and location of the provided type: FSharp.IO.SecretKey and the run-time assembly.

The body of the following do expression is the meat of the implementation. It defines that the provided type will have a single Path static parameter of type string, and most importantly, upon instantiation, the provider will read the text contained in the file referred by the Path and make the ingested string the value of the provided type's literal static field named Key. Right, I agree that the local text file is not the most reliable of key vaults, but this design choice is taken for brevity; the way the secret is kept is completely irrelevant to the subject. This part may be implemented in principle in any other manner.

The final do() expression decorated with the [<assembly:TypeProviderAssembly()>] attribute is just a type provider-specific assembly marker for the .NET assembly-loading machinery.

We are done. Building our project should produce KeyTypeProvider.dll in the target bin directory. Our type provider is ready to be put to work.

I've created the following short F# script for this purpose (Ch11_2.fsx):

```
#r @"C:\code\packtbook\KeyTypeProvider\bin\Debug\KeyTypeProvider.dll"
open FSharp.IO
open System

type Vault = SecretKey< @".\Secret.txt">

let unlock = function
| Vault.Key -> true
| _ -> false

while Console.ReadLine() |> unlock |> not do
    printfn "Go away, Hacker!"

printfn "Please proceed, Master!"
```

In order for this script to compile, it is required that you put the Secret.txt file referred in the type declaration of Vault using our demo provided type, FSharp.IO.SecretKey, into the project directory side by side with the preceding script in the file system. As soon as we do this, Intellisense in Visual Studio begins working, which is reflected in the following figure:

Local file contents packaged as a type's static field literal value

Note that the type provider revealed the contents of the secret (the ABigSecret string line) at compile-time via Intellisense. Nevertheless, the secret is not present in the source code whatsoever. Also, having the secret referred to as a Vault.Key case of the function expression without any objections from the F# compiler clearly indicates that the compiler fully buys into it being a genuine literal string!

Now, it is time to see how all this plays outside of the type provider development environment, within a separate FSI session. The results are presented in the following screenshot and are fully aligned with the expectations. Just recollect the workings of this fun F# type provider application every time you feel any confusion about the type provider pattern applicability and abilities it should help you sort things out.

```
> #r @"C:\code\packtbook\KeyTypeProvider\bin\Debug\KeyTypeProvider.dll"
- open FSharp.IO
- open System

- type Vault = SecretKey< @".\Secret.txt">

- let unlock = function
- | Vault.Key -> true
- | _ -> false

- while Console.ReadLine() |> unlock |> not do
-     printfn "Go away, Hacker!"

- printfn "Please proceed, Master!"
- ;;

--> Referenced 'C:\code\packtbook\KeyTypeProvider\bin\Debug\KeyTypeProvider.dll'
(file may be locked by F# Interactive process)

sesame open
Go away, Hacker!
Ab3acadab3a
Go away, Hacker!
ABigSecret
Please proceed, Master!

type Vault = FSharp.IO.SecretKey<...>
val unlock : _arg1:string -> bool
val it : unit = ()

>
```

Using the SecretKey type provider from the FSI script

Wrapping up, F# type providers represent a rather unique idiomatic feature of automatic types generation that may deliver significant boosts in productivity and code quality.

Exploring concurrent computations

To a great extent, the reinvigorated industrial attention on functional programming after many years of increased academic interest stems from the achieved capacities of electronics. On the one hand, the capabilities of contemporary computers make computer science findings considered more of a pure science savor thirty years ago quite practical today owing to an enormous increase in the speed and capacity of calculations. On the other hand, at the silicon level, the science has hit the physical limit for the further speeding-up of a single processor core operation. So the practical computation speed-up is happening along the lines of splitting a given amount of calculations between a group of processors working in a close concert.

The feature review

The thing is that the brave new world of cheap multicore processors cannot afford expensive, error-prone, mentally onerous methods of programming. It is demanding the concurrency taming abstractions of a much higher level than the programming primitives for it that were developed by computer science in the era of the extensive growth of computing power.

These primitives have played their role in exposing the major problem behind concurrent calculations – such calculations are much less deterministic than we are accustomed to by dealing with sequential calculations. If the indeterminism in sequential calculations is usually associated with the imperfections of ambient physical environment materializing the former, the lack of determinism in concurrent calculations is intrinsic. This means that error-prone manipulation of programming primitives for synchronization between multiple co-executed calculations offers plenty of ways to shoot yourself in the foot.

The most prominent example of self-imposed indeterminism is **deadlock** (`https://en.wiki pedia.org/wiki/Deadlock`) when concurrent program parts lacking proper synchronization over shared resources may, under some conditions, mutually lock each other.

Much trickier (and potentially much more dangerous) are cases where the concurrent code may misbehave only under extremely rare conditions. This may be really dangerous because such conditions may not introduce themselves during quality assurance and user acceptance testing. Then, the defective code basically carrying a "bomb" gets released into production, and in full accordance with Murphy's Law, blows up at the most inappropriate obstacles.

The functional programming promise for better quality concurrent programs is so dear to the industry today that many mainstream programming languages are getting supplied with add-on functional features.

Before we look deeper into what F# offers to tame concurrency indeterminism, let's take a look at the distinctive facets under the common concurrency umbrella that are important to recognize:

- **Synchronous and asynchronous**: The first one, given a few expressions to evaluate, does not start the evaluation of the next expression before the previous one has been evaluated. The second one allows you to move between some half-evaluated expressions.
- **Concurrent and parallel**: Parallelism assumes simultaneous evaluation of more than one expression using multiple processing units, while concurrency may be asynchronous partial evaluation of a few expressions by a single processing unit.
- **Interactive and reactive**: The former drives the external environment, while the latter responds to external environment demands.

F# offers usage patterns taming concurrency using a uniform mechanism of **asynchronous expressions/workflows** (https://docs.microsoft.com/en-us/dotnet/articles/fsharp /language-reference/asynchronous-workflows). Concisely, an asynchronous expression, which is a particular specific form of the computation expression mentioned earlier, is written in this form:

```
async { expression }
```

It has the generic type of `Async<'T>`. In turn, the `Async` class has a bunch of functions that trigger actual asynchronous evaluation of the preceding expression following a few scenarios.

This is a very elegant and straightforward mechanism indeed. It allows you to conceal the fact that evaluation is going to be concurrent behind familiar forms of function composition. For example, take into account this innocuous code snippet:

```
[ for i in 91..100 -> async { return i * i }] // Async<int> list
|> Async.Parallel // Async<int []>
|> Async.RunSynchronously // int []
```

It performs a rather loaded function composition with intermediary types presented as line comments, where the first line using a list comprehension expression yields a `list` of `Async<int>`, which then with the help of the `Async.Parallel` combinator fans out into `Async<int []>` parallel calculations that, in turn, with another `Async.RunSynchronously` combinator, join their asynchronously calculated expressions into the `int []` array of results, yielding 10 numbers:

```
val it : int [] =
  [|8281; 8464; 8649; 8836; 9025; 9216; 9409; 9604; 9801;
    10000|]
```

I will not attempt to prove to you that the preceding snippet will allow you to demonstrate performance gains from calculation parallelization. The preceding evaluation is so simple that the parallel snippet must in fact be *slower* than just sequential calculation analog:

```
[for i in 91..100 -> i * i]
```

This is because the parallel CPU asynchronous arrangement should introduce an overhead in comparison with a straightforward sequential list comprehension evaluation.

However, it all changes when we step into territory that is dear to enterprise development, namely begin dealing with parallel I/O. Performance gains from the I/O parallelization are going to be the subject of the following demo problem illustrating the design pattern enabled by F# asynchronous calculations.

The demo problem

Let me build an I/O-bound application that would allow the demonstration of a really overwhelming speedup when F# parallel I/O async pattern is applied. A good use case for this would be SQL Server with its scaling capabilities allowing you to reach persuasive improvements in comparison with multiple demos of concurrent web requests that F# authors and bloggers usually provide.

As an asynchronous concurrency vehicle, I'll be using the feature of the `FSharp.Data.SqlClient` type provider's **SQLCommandProvider** (https://github.com /fsprojects/FSharp.Data.SqlClient/blob/master/src/SqlClient/SqlCommandProvid er.fs), which allows asynchronous querying with the help of the `AsyncExecute()` method.

I will create synchronous and asynchronous implementations of the same task of extracting data from SQL Server and then carrying out a performance comparison to detect and measure gains secured by F# asynchronous I/O usage pattern application.

The demo solution

For the sake of conciseness, the SQL-related part is going to be extremely simple. Executing the following T-SQL script against the instance of the `(localdb)\ProjectsV12` database engine accompanying the installation of Visual Studio 2013 or any other Microsoft SQL Server installation available to you, given it fulfills the type provider **system requirements** (http://fsprojects.github.io/FSharp.Data.SqlClient/), will create the necessary database components from scratch (`Ch11_1.sql`):

```
CREATE DATABASE demo  --(1)
GO

Use demo
GO

SET ANSI_NULLS ON
GO

SET QUOTED_IDENTIFIER ON
GO

CREATE PROCEDURE dbo.MockQuery  --(2)
AS
BEGIN
  SET NOCOUNT ON;
  WAITFOR DELAY '00:00:01'
  SELECT 1
END
GO
```

Here, the part marked (1) creates and prepares for use the instance of the demo database, and the part marked (2) puts the dbo.MockQuery stored procedure into this database. This stored procedure, which lacks input arguments, implements an extremely simple query. Specifically, first, it introduces a time delay of 1 second, mocking some data search activity and then it returns a single data row with the integer 1 as the execution result.

Now, I turn to commenting the F# script for the demo solution (Ch11_1.fsx):

```
#I __SOURCE_DIRECTORY__
#r
@"../packages/FSharp.Data.SqlClient.1.8.1/lib/net40/FSharp.Data.SqlClient.d
ll"
open FSharp.Data
open System.Diagnostics

[<Literal>]
let connStr = @"Data Source=(localdb)\ProjectsV12;Initial
Catalog=demo;Integrated Security=True"

type Mock = SqlCommandProvider<"exec MockQuery", connStr>

let querySync nReq =
    use cmd = new Mock()
    seq {
        for i in 1..nReq do
            yield (cmd.Execute() |> Seq.head)
    } |> Seq.sum

let query _ =
    use cmd = new Mock()
    async {
        let! resp = cmd.AsyncExecute()
        return (resp |> Seq.head)
    }

let queryAsync nReq =
    [| for i in 1..nReq -> i |]
    |> Array.map query
    |> Async.Parallel
    |> Async.RunSynchronously
    |> Array.sum

let timing header f args =
    let watch = Stopwatch.StartNew()
    f args |> printfn "%s %s %d" header "result ="
    let elapsed = watch.ElapsedMilliseconds
    watch.Stop()
```

```
    printfn "%s: %d %s %d %s" header elapsed "ms. for" args
"requests"
```

Consider that the preceding F# code taken literally will not compile because of a few line wraps introduced by typesetting. Instead, use the code part accompanying the book as the source of working F# code.

After loading the type provider package and opening the required libraries, the `connStr` value decorated with the `[<Literal>]` attribute signifies both design-time and execution-time SQL server connection strings. This line might require modifications if you are using some other version of database engine.

The next line delivers the type provider magic by introducing the `SqlCommandProvider` provided type `Mock` ensuring statically typed access to the results of the wrapped query that is represented by the stored procedure call, `exec MockQuery`, over our `connStr` connection string.

The following `querySync` function ensures sequential execution of the `cmd` command represented by the instance of the provided `Mock` type given the number of times `nReq` yields a sequence of query results (each is just 1 from the single row of the result set) and then aggregates this sequence with `Seq.sum`. If we evaluate the `querySync 10` expression, we may expect a bit above a 10 second delay in getting back a single number, `10`.

So far, so good. The following `query` function takes any argument and returns an asynchronous computation of type `Async<int>`. I put this function within the combined expression wrapped into the `queryAsync` function, effectively representing the concurrent variant of `querySync`. Specifically, the array of `nReq` numbers is mapped into an `Async<int>` array of the same size, and then they are all fanned out by `Async.Parallel`, joined back after completion with `Async.RunSynchronously` and eventually aggregated by `Array.sum` into a single number.

The last piece is an instrumentation higher-order `timing` function that just measures and outputs the evaluation of the `f args` computation duration in milliseconds.

Alright; now, it is time to take our script for a spin. I put the code into FSI and measure the duration of executing `querySync` and `queryAsync` 100 times. You can see the measurement results in the following screenshot:

Measuring synchronous versus asynchronous SQL querying

Are you as impressed as I am? Results show that I/O parallelization in the case of SQL queries allowed improved performance approximately 100-fold!

This demo is quite persuasive and I strongly recommend that you master and use this and other F# idiomatic concurrency patterns in your practical work.

Exploring reactive computations

Reactive computations are the part of concurrent computations' scope. They just stress a slightly different matter, namely the processing of general events. The processing of events may be genuinely concurrent, when one or more of simultaneously occurring events are processed without any sort of serialization or genuinely sequential if a new event is not processed until the processing of the previous one has finished.

The feature review

Usually, the event processing view akin to concurrency takes roots at the development of the systems that have **user interface (UI)** component(s) when sluggish processing of data coming from input devices and/or data reflecting the visual state of graphic UI components is simply unacceptable as it creates a terrible **user experience (UX)**.

This is all good and true, but let's concentrate on an aspect not directly related to UI/UX, namely the conceptual consideration of **event processing** taking place. As this consideration is tied to F#, I will limit the review with .NET boundaries.

Historically, the development of interactive operating systems such as Windows coined the concept of **callback** (https://en.wikipedia.org/wiki/Callback_(computer_programming)), which brought to consideration **events** and **event handlers**. This is the lowest conceptual level of reactive programming, where the developer's responsibility is to provide the handlers for each event class.

The next abstraction level in reactive computations came with object-oriented programming and is manifested by the **Observer design pattern** (https://en.wikipedia.org/wiki/Observer_pattern). Now, the developer may think of a specific event type processing flow as an interaction between the event type (in other words, **subject**) source named **Observable** and zero or more parties interested in the processing of this subject event named **Observers**. Observers manifest their interest in the subject by dynamically **registering** and **unregistering** with the corresponding Observable. As soon as the next event belonging to the subject comes into existence, all Observers registered at the moment with the corresponding Observer get notified about the chance of processing the event and then continue waiting for the next one.

Finally, the conceptual quintessence for reactive computations took place with the seminal work of a group headed by computer scientist **Erik Meijer** (https://en.wikipedia.org/wiki/Erik_Meijer_(computer_scientist)), who created **Reactive Extensions (Rx) for .NET** (https://msdn.microsoft.com/en-us/library/hh242985(v=vs.103).aspx).

The key idea behind Rx is concentrating on **pushing** versus **pulling** data sequences by introducing a fundamental `IObservable` interface that is a reversal of `IEnumerable` in the way it exposes the event data stream. This is similar to how "normal" data sequences, after being enumerated, can be pulled–composed by higher-order functions and queried using LINQ–and observable event sequences (event streams) may be received–composed with higher-order functions and processed by LINQ.

F# supports all three of the preceding abstractions, throwing in some improvements in comparison with other programming languages of the .NET platform.

This subject matter is very well documented and I refer you to related F#-specific documentation on the `Microsoft.FSharp.Control` namespace pieces and `Reactive Extensions (Rx)` for details:

Event module (`https://msdn.microsoft.com/visualfsharpdocs/conceptual/control.event-module-%5bfsharp%5d`).

Observable module (`https://msdn.microsoft.com/visualfsharpdocs/conceptual/control.observable-module-%5bfsharp%5d`).

Reactive Extensions (`https://msdn.microsoft.com/en-us/data/gg577609.aspx`).

Instead of retelling the preceding documentation, I will take F# reactive computation features for a spin, implementing a relevant practical task. I will try to make the implementation self-contained.

The demo problem

Let's consider the following **integration pattern** (`http://www.enterpriseintegrationpatterns.com/patterns/messaging/`) that is quite typical for the enterprise: document message exchange over two point-to-point channels. We are a client of an external service that communicates with us using a pair of dedicated channels. If we need to send a document message, we just push it into the outbound channel and the remote service somehow consumes it. If the service sends a message(s) back to us, they are delivered into the inbound channel. As soon as we pull a document message from the inbound channel, it gets removed from there. The following figure illustrates this interaction.

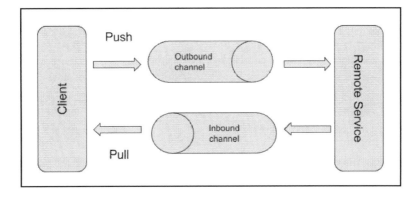

Enterprise two-way document exchange

Those of you who get involved in Enterprise LOB development have perhaps already recognized a typical case of peer-to-peer **Electronic Data Interchange (EDI)** (https://en.w ikipedia.org/wiki/Electronic_data_interchange#Peer-to-Peer). Often, providers are quite conservative in choosing specific transfer protocols and prefer sticking to "old but gold" technologies such as **SSH File Transfer Protocol (SFTP)** (https://en.wikipedia.or g/wiki/SSH_File_Transfer_Protocol) for a reasonably inexpensive way of integration when data security is a requirement. As an enterprise may be involved into EDI with multiple remote service providers, the amount of such arrangements may be quite significant.

Nevertheless, I'm not going to concentrate on building a configurable library that allows the addition of a new EDI provider with a few lines of code. Instead, I will address the semantics layer that usually stands outside of architectural considerations, namely relations that may need to be enforced between bidirectional document message exchanges that, for SFTP transfer, translate into pushing and pulling formatted files to/from the service provider.

To be a bit more specific, I offer to your attention a real case from the **Jet.com** (https://jet .com/) Finance realm, where I at the moment write F# code for a living. Let's consider the payment system as a client and the bank as a service provider. The service gist is to execute payment advices and deliver remittances to the bank accounts of legal and physical entities with whom Jet.com gets into temporary "I owe you" relations: suppliers and vendors, merchants of the marketplace, employees with outstanding reimbursable business expenses and the like.

Now, let's assume that we have built our communication code around SFTP, which pushes remittances to the bank, gets back statements, originations and the like, all retries are in place, and all wheels are rotating smoothly. Are we doing fine?

Turns out the answer is "not really". We silently assume at this point that the bank's implementation is free of problems based on a whole slew of fallacies, such as "it's about finance", "the bank would not survive if it had bugs", "it is too big to allow failures" and similar. However, the bank's software is just software and is susceptible to all kinds of human errors. We may expect its reliability to be overall higher than in a random start-up minimal viable product code constituting a web application implementing a hot business idea and written in a garage during few hackathons. On the other hand, each bank's software release carries the next "last bug" in it, doesn't it?

It so happened one day that Jet's bank client software did not provision for the following scenario: what if the bank correctly accepts and executes each payment advice, but once in a while it does not communicate the deferred final payment status back to us? The payment recipients are all happy with remittance cash hitting their accounts and no communication errors taking place. If we take the successful outcome of our deliverable payment advices for granted, this bug may stay there forever! This is a low probability scenario but not absolutely improbable. In fact, a similar defect went unnoticed in Jet's payment arrangement for a short time until marketplace reports started showing a growing amount of deferred payments. That was embarrassing!

Can we fix this by being proactive with our "pull" data transfer part? Keep reading for the outline of the potential solution.

The demo solution

One of the (overly simplified) potential solutions would be to mix the flow of "heartbeat" events with the flow of guarded events. As the generalization of guarding a single event of a certain type to any number events of a similar type is not challenging, let me consider a single guarded event of a type for brevity.

Within this guarded event flow mix, we establish a threshold upon how many heartbeats are considered healthy between the start of guarding the event and the actual occurrence of the guarded event. For example (the specific numbers do not anyhow coincide with real ones), we may say that if the ACH payment is being sent and after following three heartbeat events, ACHOrigination event is still not received, this should be the indication of a problem and the responsible personnel must be alerted of the deviation.

Now let me implement the preceding using Reactive Extensions (Ch11_3.fsx):

```
#I __SOURCE_DIRECTORY__
#r
"../packages/FSharp.Control.Reactive.3.4.1/lib/net45/FSharp.Control.Reactiv
e.dll"
#r "../packages/Rx-Core.2.2.5/lib/net45/System.Reactive.Core.dll"
#r "../packages/Rx-
Interfaces.2.2.5/lib/net45/System.Reactive.Interfaces.dll"
#r "../packages/Rx-Linq.2.2.5/lib/net45/System.Reactive.Linq.dll"

open System.Reactive.Subjects

type PaymentFlowEvent =
| HeartBeat
| ACHOrigination
```

```
    | GuardOn

type GuardACHOrigination(flow: Subject<PaymentFlowEvent>, alerter:
Subject<string>) =
    let threshold = 3
    let mutable beats = 0
    let mutable guardOn = false

    member x.Guard() =
        beats <- 0
        guardOn <- false
        flow.Subscribe(function
            | HeartBeat -> if guardOn then beats <- beats + 1;
                printfn "Heartbeat processed";
                if beats > threshold && guardOn
                    then alerter.OnNext "No timely ACHOrigination"
            | ACHOrigination -> beats <- 0;
                guardOn <- false
                printfn "ACHOrigination processed"
            | GuardOn -> beats <- 0; guardOn <- true;
                printfn "ACHOrigination is guarded")

let paymentFlow = new Subject<PaymentFlowEvent>()
let alerter = new Subject<string>()
let notifier = alerter.Subscribe(fun x -> printfn "Logged error %s" x)

ignore <| GuardACHOrigination(paymentFlow,alerter).Guard()
```

After loading a slew of required components from the corresponding NuGet libraries, I introduce the `PaymentFlowEvent` type reflecting the mix of the previously mentioned three events.

Next, the `GuardACHOrigination` class combines the stream of `PaymentFlowEvent` events set by argument `flow`, which is also known as `Subject`, `alerter` for the carrying out of notifications, and business logic combining all these parts together. **Subject** (`https://msdn.microsoft.com/en-us/library/hh242970(v=vs.103).aspx`) is a combination of the observable sequence and Observer, and it plays the central role in the preceding implementation.

The `Guard()` method takes `flow`, and with the help of its `Subscribe` method, sets a simple state machine tracking of what is going on upon the arrival of each instance of flowing through events of type `PaymentFlowEvents`. Given that the abnormality is recognized, the diagnostics notification is pushed into `alerter`.

Now, I create the required bits and pieces: `paymentFlow` representing the event stream of interest, `alerter` to receive notifications within `Guard()`, `notifier` to act upon notification events from `alerter`, and finally, fireup everything to life with `GuardACHOrigination(paymentFlow,alerter).Guard()`.

Great; now it's time to push a stream of events into the built arrangement and observe the reactive behavior in FSI. The following screenshot reflects that the code behavior is completely aligned with the expected: timely guarded events pass smoothly, overdue guarded events trigger alerts, and unguarded events get disregarded:

Guarding the event flow with the F# reactive code

The demonstrated pattern of applying F# in a reactive manner is an important tool belt skill that should be mastered by enterprise practitioners.

Exploring quotations and metaprogramming

The last feature I want to cover among the advanced patterns of F# use is **Code Quotations** (`https://docs.microsoft.com/en-us/dotnet/articles/fsharp/language-reference/code-quotations`). This feature is quite mind-bending, allowing you to work with the program code as if it is data, and evaluate these "program as data" pieces when needed and in the needed manner.

The feature review

Looking at this feature from the more operational angle, a program piece may be represented as an expression tree representing the code but without running the code generation off this representation. This allows for arbitrary execution behavior when the expression tree is to be evaluated. It can be evaluated as F# code or as source to generate JavaScript code or even as GPU-executed code or in any other feasible manner.

The cool thing about quoted expressions is that they are typed, they can be spliced together from parts, or they can be decomposed into parts using active patterns, among other features. Without delving into too much detail, I want to demonstrate that if required, F# offers this extra layer of flexibility by allowing you to tweak the program code and evaluate the tweaked code programmatically. For this purpose, I will be using **F# Quotations Evaluator** (`http://fsprojects.github.io/FSharp.Quotations.Evaluator/index.html`).

A very brief demonstration of the feature abilities is as follows (`Ch11_4.fsx`):

- Get the required library support:

```
#I __SOURCE_DIRECTORY__
#r
 "../packages/FSharp.Quotations.Evaluator.1.0.7/lib
 /net40/FSharp.Quotations.Evaluator.dll"
open FSharp.Quotations.Evaluator
```

- Create a `mutable` quoted `divider` value:

```
let mutable divider = Quotations.Expr.Value (5)
```

- Create and compile a function with `divider` spliced into this:

```
let is5Divisor = <@ fun x -> x % %%divider = 0 @>
    |> QuotationEvaluator.Evaluate
```

- Apply the compiled `is5Divisor` function to a few arguments:

```
is5Divisor 14 // false
is5Divisor 15 // true
```

- Change the spliced `divider` value:

```
divider <- Quotations.Expr.Value (7)
```

- Note that `is5Divisor` workings did not change:

```
is5Divisor 14 // false
```

- Recompile the spliced `divider` value into another function:

```
let is7Divisor = <@ fun x -> x % %%divider = 0 @>
    |> QuotationEvaluator.Evaluate
```

- Apply the newly compiled `is7divisor` function:

```
is7Divisor 14 // true
```

Equipped with some understanding of how quotations work, let me now apply the feature to a sizable demo problem.

The demo problem

While looking for a demo problem, I turn to the finance space again. Let's look at the matter of invoice total adjustment based on the timeliness of payment. Paying an outstanding invoice early may bring some savings, while being late on it may impose penalties. When a vendor or supplier establishes payment terms, any combination of premiums and/or penalties may be set: neither premium nor penalty, just a premium, just a penalty, and both premium and penalty. It would be great to have an arrangement that would allow you to easily and naturally handle this variety. In other words, an adjustment is sought – for that, when applied to the invoice total and the payment date, finds out what the actual payment amount aligned with the payment terms would be.

The demo solution

Here is the script implementing the sought adjustment object (Ch11_4.fsx):

```
#I __SOURCE_DIRECTORY__
#r "../packages/FSharp
Quotations.Evaluator.1.0.7/lib/net40/FSharp.Quotations.Evaluator.dll"
open FSharp.Quotations.Evaluator
open System.Collections.Generic
open System

type Adjustment =
| Absent
| Premium of TimeSpan * decimal
| Penalty of TimeSpan * decimal

type Terms(?premium: Adjustment, ?penalty: Adjustment) =
    let penalty = defaultArg penalty Absent
    let premium = defaultArg premium Absent
    member x.Adjust() =
        match premium,penalty with
        | Absent,Absent -> None
        | Absent,Penalty (d,m) -> Some(<@ fun ((date:DateTime),amount) ->
if DateTime.UtcNow.Date - date.Date > d then Decimal.Round(amount * (1M +
m),2) else amount @> |> QuotationEvaluator.Evaluate)
        | Premium(d,m),Absent -> Some(<@ fun ((date:DateTime),amount) -> if
DateTime.UtcNow.Date - date.Date < d then Decimal.Round(amount * (1M -
m),2) else amount @> |> QuotationEvaluator.Evaluate)
        | Premium(d',m'),Penalty (d,m) -> Some(<@ fun
((date:DateTime),amount) ->
            if DateTime.UtcNow.Date - date.Date > d then
Decimal.Round(amount * (1M + m),2)
            elif DateTime.UtcNow.Date - date.Date < d' then
Decimal.Round(amount * (1M - m'),2)
            else amount @> |> QuotationEvaluator.Evaluate)
        | _,_ -> None
```

The first thing to note is that the the necessary library is loaded.

Then the `Adjustment` type is defined, which is either `Absent` or `Premium`/`Penalty` with the structure of the `System.TimeSpan*decimal` tuple, where the `TimeSpan` part defines the amount of time between invoice issuance and payment dates and `decimal` sets the adjustment multiplier. For `Premium`, the tuple is interpreted as "if the number of days between the invoice issuance and payment is less or equal to `TimeSpan`, then the amount of payment should be decreased by the `decimal` multiplier". For `Penalty`, it is "if the number of days between the invoice issuance and payment is greater or equal to `TimeSpan`, then the amount of payment should be increased by the `decimal` multiplier".

The `Terms` type captures the adjustment terms within the `Adjust` method. Using F# quotations, it defines payment adjustment functions for each potential combination of terms, and then it either implements the prescribed adjustment or it doesn't.

Now, in order to see how it would work, we need a test bed. Let's define a record representing invoice:

```
type Invoice = { total:decimal ; date:System.DateTime; }
```

Let's also define test list of invoices:

```
let invoices = [
    { total=1005.20M; date=System.DateTime.Today.AddDays(-3.0) }
    { total=5027.78M; date=System.DateTime.Today.AddDays(-29.0) }
    { total=51400.49M; date=System.DateTime.Today.AddDays(-36.0) }
]
```

The function deriving the amount of payment due is now based on terms, and the invoice may look like the following:

```
let payment (terms: Terms) invoice = let adjust = terms.Adjust() in if
adjust.IsSome then (adjust.Value) (invoice.date, invoice.total) else
invoice.total
```

Now, it is time to define a full variety of the possible terms:

```
let terms = Terms(penalty=Penalty(TimeSpan.FromDays(31.),0.015M),
  premium=Premium(TimeSpan.FromDays(5.),0.02M))
let termsA = Terms()
let termsB = Terms(Premium(TimeSpan.FromDays(4.),0.02M))
let termsC = Terms(penalty=Penalty(TimeSpan.FromDays(30.),0.02M))
```

And finally, we can observe in the following screenshot how all this plays together after being applied to test invoices by applying each payment term to the same invoice group:

```
                 Developer Command Prompt for VS2015 - fsianycpu        – □ ✕
> let invoices = [
      { total=1005.20M; date=System.DateTime.Today.AddDays(-3.0) }
      { total=5027.78M; date=System.DateTime.Today.AddDays(-29.0) }
      { total=51400.49M; date=System.DateTime.Today.AddDays(-36.0) }
  ];;

val invoices : Invoice list =
  [{total = 1005.20M;
    date = 10/28/2016 12:00:00 AM;}; {total = 5027.78M;
                                      date = 10/2/2016 12:00:00 AM;};
   {total = 51400.49M;
    date = 9/25/2016 12:00:00 AM;}]

> let terms = Terms(penalty=Penalty(TimeSpan.FromDays(31.),0.015M),premium=Premi
- um(TimeSpan.FromDays(5.),0.02M))
- let termsA = Terms()
- let termsB = Terms(Premium(TimeSpan.FromDays(4.),0.02M))
- let termsC = Terms(penalty=Penalty(TimeSpan.FromDays(30.),0.02M));;

val terms : Terms
val termsA : Terms
val termsB : Terms
val termsC : Terms

> List.map (payment terms) invoices;;
val it : decimal list = [985.10M; 5027.78M; 52171.50M]
> List.map (payment termsA) invoices;;
val it : decimal list = [1005.20M; 5027.78M; 51400.49M]
> List.map (payment termsB) invoices;;
val it : decimal list = [985.10M; 5027.78M; 51400.49M]
> List.map (payment termsC) invoices;;
val it : decimal list = [1005.20M; 5027.78M; 52428.50M]
```

Using F# quotations

Summary

In this chapter, we assayed a few features of advanced F# usage category. I hope I was able to demonstrate that even for the advanced features, F# continues to keep the promise of "solving complex problems with simple code".

Now is a good time to pay further attention to the subject constituting this book's title. The content so far did not in any way cross the traditional view of design patterns usually associated with the contents of **Gang of Four Book** (https://en.wikipedia.org/wiki/Design_Patterns). In the next chapter, I will justify the taken approach by observing the "classic" design patterns and principles from a functional-first view point.

12

F# and OOP Principles/Design Patterns

Previous chapters were aimed at developing and honing your taste for the usage patterns of functional programming, paying very occasional attention to comparison with OOP arrangements. This chapter caters to those of you who have an OOP background and may be anxiously expecting for the book to begin meticulously porting each and every one of the of **23 original Gang of Four object-oriented design patterns** (https://en.wikipedia.org/wiki/Design_Patterns), one by one into F#.

I may disappoint you, as all topics covered so far indicate that staying with the functional-first facet of F# promoted by the book may make some of these patterns just irrelevant, intrinsic, or ubiquitous. In other words, the original patterns may morph into something much less fundamental compared to their role in the OOP world.

A similar transformation applies to OOP principles, collectively known as **SOLID** (https://en.wikipedia.org/wiki/SOLID_(object-oriented_design)). That is, from a functional programming standpoint, these principles may become either granted, irrelevant, or just respected, without much extra effort required from developers.

The goal of this chapter is to briefly demonstrate some cases of the morphing outlined in the preceding paragraphs. In this chapter, we will take a look at the following topics:

- How OOP SOLID principles get morphed within the functional-first paradigm, and what exactly happens to each of these five pillars
- How some of the specific design patterns (Command, Template, Strategy) diminish in role, or just become simply equivalent to bits and pieces of the functional-first paradigm

I will not attempt to lay out an exhaustive, thorough review. In the end, this book aims to develop skills and techniques of the functional-first paradigm, not any other paradigms supported by F#.

Morphing SOLID principles

Let's consider how the functional programming paradigm morphs the five basic principles of the object-oriented design known under this bold acronym of **SOLID**.

Single Responsibility Principle

The gist of **Single Responsibility Principle** (https://en.wikipedia.org/wiki/Single_re
sponsibility_principle) **(SRP)**, standing for the letter "S" in **SOLID**, in OOP terms is:

> *"There should never be more than one reason for a class to change"*

In other words, if a class implementation is to be changed in response to two or more independent modifications to a functionality, this is an evidence of the **Single Responsibility Principle (SRP)** violation in its design. Following this principle in the OOP world entails designs consisting of many lean classes in lieu of fewer but bulkier classes.

If we consider a function as a degenerate case of class free of encapsulated data and having only the single method, then this is nothing but a quintessence of SRP applied. The following figure illustrates this transformation:

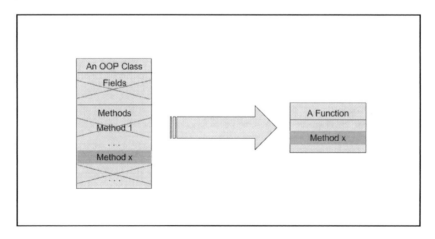

Honoring Single Responsibility Principle in functional programming

When we program in idiomatic F#, we compose the functions of a single purpose together. In other words, SRP is naturally promoted and enforced in F#.

Open/Closed Principle

Open/Closed Principle (`https://en.wikipedia.org/wiki/Open/closed_principle`) (OCP), representing the letter "O" in SOLID, states that:

> *"software entities (classes, modules, functions, etc.) should be open for extension, but closed for modification"*

In the pure OOP realm, such a property is granted by **inheritance**, both by direct **implementation inheritance** (that is, substituting a superclass with its subclass) and by **polymorphic implementation** (that is, just another implementation of a given interface that keeps itself closed to a modification but is open to additionally implementing other interfaces). Both of these forms of OCP are near, clear, and dear to the OOP facet of F#; however, they are not idiomatic to any extent. The functional-first mechanisms of extension in idiomatic F# are type augmentation and composition. The following figure serves as a cheat sheet here, as we have devoted a fair amount of attention in the book to these extension methods:

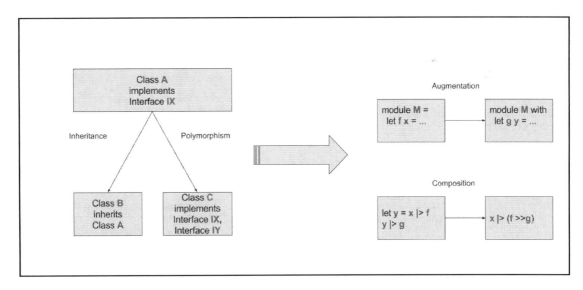

Honoring Open/Closed Principle in functional programming

The figure above shows in a very compelling manner how simple, succinct, and to the point the extensibility mechanics is within the functional-first idioms.

Liskov Substitution Principle

The letter "L" in **SOLID** comes from **Liskov Substitution Principle** (`https://en.wikipedia.org/wiki/Liskov_substitution_principle`) (**LSP**) that states:

> *"objects in a program should be replaceable with instances of their subtypes without altering the correctness of that program"*

As formulated **LSP** is concerned purely with OOP inheritance, it does not seem related to idiomatic F#. Nevertheless, I would mention at least the following three F# functional-first idioms that strongly enforce this principle:

- **Referential transparency**: If a function is pure and produces a certain result given an argument of type `T`, then given the corresponding instance of type `S` that is a subtype of `T` as an argument, it must produce the identical result indeed

- **F# function argument type substitution**: Based on what has been discussed in the preceding bullet point, if we have a type `'S` that derives from type `'T`, then an instance of `'S` can be used as a substitute for the corresponding instance of `'T`; so for the following function f: `'T -> 'R`, expression `f('S())` *does not require any coercion* of the argument, as the following snippet demonstrates (`Ch12_1.fsx`):

  ```
  type T = interface end // base
  type S() = interface T // an implementation
  let f (x: T) = () // a function upon base
  f(S()) // application does not require coercion!
  ```

- **Immutability**: If we have built a valid immutable instance of `'S`, it cannot anyhow be invalidated by using it as a substitute for the instance of `'T` by the virtue of its immutability

Interface Segregation Principle

Standing for the letter "I" in **SOLID**, **Interface Segregation Principle** (`https://en.wikipedia.org/wiki/Interface_segregation_principle`) (**ISP**) claims that:

> *"many client-specific interfaces are better than one general-purpose interface"*

In other words, an interface that a client is linked with should not introduce dependencies that are not used by the client. The **ISP** is just SRP being applied to interfaces. Idiomatic F# fully supports ISP by statelessness and naturally segregated functions representing interfaces that contain exactly one method.

Dependency Inversion Principle

The letter "**D**" in **SOLID** stands for **Dependency Inversion Principle** (https://en.wikiped ia.org/wiki/Dependency_inversion_principle) (**DIP**) stating:

"depend upon abstractions, do not depend upon concretions"

The following figure shows how **DIP** is achieved in OOP: if an instance of class A refers the instance of class B, this is a direct dependency violating DIP. This problem may be fixed by making an instance of class A dependent on the interface IB. So far, so good, but something must implement IB, right? Let it be the instance of class B, which is now a dependent of IB, so the inversion of dependency takes place.

It is easy to notice that in idiomatic F#, the role of dependency inversion plays a vanilla higher-order function: for example, function f has a parameter function, g which is used in defining f. When f is called, any of the argument functions a, b, or c may play the role of g as long as their signatures conform to g:

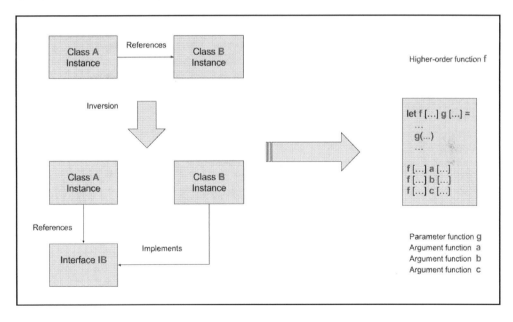

Honoring Dependency Inversion Principle in functional programming

Diminishing patterns

Similarly to **SOLID** principles, many OOP design patterns in the context of idiomatic functional-first F# either diminish (sometimes to the extent of disappearing) or significantly morph. Let's take a quick look at some instances of such transformation. I will be using samples taken from the code base I authored, implementing payment applications for Jet.com. Samples are somewhat simplified to align with the book format.

The Command design pattern

The **Command Design Pattern** (https://en.wikipedia.org/wiki/Command_pattern) in OOP stands for a behavioral design pattern where all the information required to perform an action at a later time is encapsulated in an object. But wait a minute; doesn't this exactly coincide with what a function is? That's right; almost any idiomatic F# pattern of dealing with a higher-order function to traverse a data structure while applying a lower-order function to each element can be considered an occurrence of the Command pattern. Mapping, folding, you name it – all fit into this category. Doing what the Command pattern prescribes is an ubiquitous idiom in functional-first F#.

Let's consider an example: an order flow of a merchant participating in an e-commerce marketplace consists of transactions, each representing either **sale** or **refund**. By taking any continuous sequence of elements of the order flow, its running balance can be found. Now, the factor that makes things more interesting is that some orders may be nullified during an established period of time since their introduction being canceled. We are charged with tracking a running total for the marketplace finance department.

The functional-first aspect of F# allows for a very clean, idiomatic solution. I begin with two core domain objects, representing order types and customer transactions, combining the order type and its cost of goods (Ch12_2.fsx):

```
type OrderType = Sale | Refund
type Transaction = Transaction of OrderType * decimal
```

I continue with two core functions accounting for the total based on the order type:

```
let sale total cost = total + cost
let refund total cost = total - cost
```

Equipped with this, it is time to define our **commands** in the pattern's sense. Both `Order` and `Cancellation` will take a running total and a transaction and return a new running total adjusted accordingly (note that `Cancellation` mirrors `Order` in terms of the total):

```
let Order total = function
| Transaction(OrderType.Sale, cost) -> sale total cost
| Transaction(OrderType.Refund, cost) -> refund total cost
let Cancellation total = function
| Transaction(OrderType.Sale, cost) -> refund total cost
| Transaction(OrderType.Refund, cost) -> sale total cost
```

I'm done! Let me just demonstrate the built code in action by applying it to a sample order flow in FSI. The results are presented in the following screenshot, where a sequence of some `orderFlow` transactions is run through orders yielding `totalForward` of $271.86 and then through cancelation, eventually yielding the expected running total `totalBackward` of $0.00:

Command pattern as idiomatic F# folding

The Template design pattern

The **Template design pattern** (https://en.wikipedia.org/wiki/Template_method_pattern) in OOP defines a common skeleton of an algorithm or a program, of which components can be overwritten but the general structure stays unchanged. Again, achieving this effect following the route that has functions as first class objects is trivial. For example, passing functions as parameters will work nicely, so the pattern diminishes to non-existing.

Idiomatic F# is even richer than this approach, allowing functions to cohesively keep participating in an interface and providing any of the concrete implementations in the form of an object expression.

Let's turn to a corresponding code sample taken from the enterprise codebase of Jet.com payment applications. The process of paying a partner participating in the Jet.com marketplace consists of three consecutive steps:

1. Obtaining payment requisites and the amount due based on the merchant ID.
2. Formatting a payment for the use of a specific payment method.
3. Submitting payment advice to the bank for execution.

The template keeps the preceding parts together, allowing you to change each of the pieces to the case at the same time. As shown in the previous example, I begin with defining a few core domain entities (Ch12_3.fsx):

```
open System
type PayBy = ACH | Check | Wire
            override x.ToString() =
                match x with
                | ACH -> "By ACH"
                | Check -> "By Check"
                | Wire -> "By Wire"
type Payment = string
type BankReqs = { ABA: string; Account: string}
type Merchant = { MerchantId: Guid; Requisites: BankReqs }
```

Here, PayBy represents a specific payment instrument (Check/ACH/Wire), formatted Payment is just a type abbreviation, BankReqs represents a merchant's bank requisites for the account to accept the deposited payment, and Merchant wires together the merchant ID and bank requisites.

Now I define the template as an interface that reflects parts of the payment process being cohesive (Ch12_3.fsx):

```
type ITemplate =
    abstract GetPaymentDue: Guid -> Merchant*decimal
    abstract FormatPayment: Merchant*decimal -> Payment
    abstract SubmitPayment: Payment ->bool
```

This piece is quite straightforward; GetPaymentDue retrieves the given merchant's requisites and payment amount due from the relevant persisted store, FormatPayment performs the required payment advice formatting, and SubmitPayment takes care of delivering the advice to Jet's bank. Note that I intentionally didn't specify the payment format here as this detail may be delayed for the implementation.

Then, here, I provide a specific (mock) implementation for ITemplate. Still, you can see that this arrangement allows plenty of flexibility; in particular, I made a specific payment instrument a parameter of the implementation (Ch12_3.fsx):

```
let Template  payBy =
    { new ITemplate with
        member ___.GetPaymentDuemerchantId =
          printfn "Getting payment due of %s"
          (merchantId.ToString())
        (* mock access to ERP getting Accounts payable due for
           merchantId *)
        ({ MerchantId = merchantId;
          Requisites = {ABA="021000021";
          Account="123456789009"} }, 25366.76M)
        member ___.FormatPayment (m,t)   =
          printfn "Formatting payment of %s"
          (m.MerchantId.ToString())
        sprintf "%s:%s:%s:%s:%.2f" "Payment to" m.Requisites.ABA
          m.Requisites.Account (payBy.ToString()) t
        member ___.SubmitPayment p =
          printfn "Submitting %s..." p
          true
    }
```

Finally, I wrap everything together into the function using the template (Ch12_3.fsx):

```
let makePaymentmerchantIdpayBy   =
    let template = Template payBy in
template.GetPaymentDuemerchantId
    |>template.FormatPayment
    |>template.SubmitPayment
```

As usual, in order to see this code in action, I turn to FSI, presenting the results of running some mock payments in the following screenshot. I've omitted the complete script source from here for the sake of fitting the figure within a single book page:

Template pattern disappearing in idiomatic F#

The Strategy pattern

The **Strategy pattern** (`https://en.wikipedia.org/wiki/Strategy_pattern`) is simply about adjusting the algorithm behavior in runtime by implementing a family of algorithms and using them interchangeably. Once again, what could suit this purpose better than a functional-first setting with functions as first-class language citizens?

To illustrate the use of the Strategy pattern, I will use just another use case from Jet.com's Payment system. In its shipping operations, Jet.com uses multiple carriers, and due to the significant volume of shipments, it processes carrier invoices electronically. The gist of this processing is the loading of invoices from each carrier into a staging data table, and then merging the contents of this data table with corresponding persistent stores in the **upsert** (h `ttps://en.wikipedia.org/wiki/Merge_(SQL)`) manner.

I approach the implementation of this **EDI** (https://en.wikipedia.org/wiki/Electronic
_data_interchange) by outlining the implementation of the core behavior first
(Ch12_4.fsx):

```
open System
open System.Data
type InvoiceFormat =
| Excel
| Csv
let load (format: InvoiceFormat) (path: String) =
    let dt = new DataTable() in
    (* IMPLEMENTATION GOES HERE *)
dt
let merge (target: string) (dt: DataTable) =
    (* IMPLEMENTATION GOES HERE *)
    ()
```

The preceding snippet indicates that the supported invoice formats are either Excel or CSV,
and there are two generic functions available to load invoices, somehow delivered to a
location in any acceptable format, into a data table, and to merge the filled data table with
the existing contents of the corresponding persistent store.

So far, so good; these two functions may be made accessible via an interface whose
implementation is to be specific for each of the supported carriers (Ch12_4.fsx):

```
type ILoadVendorInvoices =
    abstract LoadInvoices: String ->DataTable
    abstract member MergeInvoices: DataTable -> unit
```

Now, I provide specific implementations of the preceding interface for two of the carriers
Jet.com engages into order shipments, namely FedEX and LaserShip (Ch12_4.fsx):

```
let LoadFedex =
    { new ILoadVendorInvoices with
        member __.LoadInvoices path = load Csv path
        member __.MergeInvoicesdataTable =
            merge "Fedex" dataTable
    }
let LoadLasership =
    { new ILoadVendorInvoices with
        member __.LoadInvoices path = load Excel path
        member __.MergeInvoicesdataTable =
            merge "Lasership" dataTable
    }
```

Now stay with me; we have two objects of the `ILoadVendorInvoices` type, each encapsulating its own carrier specifics. However, we can use them uniformly for EDI, as shown in the following function (`Ch12_4.fsx`):

```
let importEDIData (loader: ILoadVendorInvoices) path =
    loader.LoadInvoices path |>loader.MergeInvoices
```

Just beautiful; now we can use instances of `LoadFedex` and `LoadLasership` to switch the behavior of EDI processing exactly in a manner the Strategy pattern prescribes. Let's turn to FSI for the demonstration. The following screenshot shows the results:

Strategy pattern expressed using F# idioms

Summary

This chapter highlighted that the functional-first approach does not blindly contradicts principles and patterns of object-oriented programming. Sometimes it also supports and amplifies them.

I'm going to devote the final chapter of this book to the subject of troubleshooting functional-first code, as it has certain specifics.

13
Troubleshooting Functional Code

In this chapter, I touch on an important aspect of the functional-first programming approach that kicks in when the F# code is in the process of being developed. It so happens that the troubleshooting of the functional-first code differs from the troubleshooting of, say, imperative code. The goal of this chapter is to share with you some of my observations collected while authoring idiomatic F# code. It should leave you equipped with some considerations and a few techniques for effective bug squashing.

In this chapter, we will look into the following topics:

- Understanding reasons for idiomatic F# having a low defect rate
- Using REPL and explorative programming style
- Addressing some compile-time problems
- Addressing run-time problems

Why idiomatic F# admits less defects

Without going back to the side-by-side comparison of functional-first and other paradigms available for F# programmer to employ, I will reiterate the (mostly anecdotal) point that an idiomatic F# code admits fewer defects than equivalent implementations based on object-oriented or imperative paradigms.

The previous twelve chapters have contributed significantly to this judgment. But let me briefly revisit some considerations in order to conclude that:

- This decrease in the defect rate is not something taken for granted. This artifact is what you gain in exchange for the pain of mind-bending while acquiring functional thinking habits and the following rigor in applying them
- The use of F# by itself is not a remedy from the defects; there is still enough space for bugs to sneak into the code, although in significantly lower amounts
- Typical F# bugs are quite specific and often may be anticipated and avoided

Reduced bug rate

This observation is very important and stems from a few factors:

- The language's succinctness contributes to the reduced bug rate literally: fewer lines of code carry fewer chances for bugs to sneak in and stay unnoticed
- Strict static typing and type inference simply do not allow oversights that are typical for dynamic languages, when the misplacement of types may lead to bugs that are hard to detect and eliminate later on
- Raised level of abstraction, library higher-order functions, and immutability. All of these contribute to eliminating many bugs that come from the unpredictable execution order of stateful code, more "moving parts" involved, and needless re-implementation of core library facilities

Prevalence of F# compile-time errors over run-time bugs

The syntactic correctness of a program written using a conventional programming language usually does not prompt any assumptions about the outcome of its execution. Generally speaking, these two factors are not correlated.

It seems that this is not the case for the implementations following the F# functional-first approach. There is plenty of anecdotal evidence on the Internet in F# and non-F# functional programming context stating that

"if it compiles it works"

For example, this **Haskell wiki post** (https://wiki.haskell.org/Why_Haskell_just_wor ks) states a similar observation in relation to programs written in the allied Haskell programming language.

Actually, strict static typing and type inference may catch many random defects at compile-time, shielding programmers from the costly process of observing a problem at run-time and then often performing lengthy and skill-demanding activities known as *debugging* in order to nail down the genuine cause of the problem at the source code level.

Another extremely important factor is to implement the algorithm by sticking to a handful of idiomatic patterns supported by core libraries instead of manipulating lower-level language constructs. To give you a better idea of what I'm talking about here, try to answer this question: Which approach carries more chances for implementation mistakes, folding a sequence with `Seq.fold` or materializing the sequence into the array and traversing elements using indexing while aggregating the result in a mutable value? The right answer easily translates into what has been mentioned on many occasions throughout the book: the positive effect of "minimizing the amount of moving parts" in a functional paradigm.

Still, your fold should be the rightly one for the overall correctness of the implementation from an algorithmic standpoint. And F# offers just another bug-squashing facility. This facility allows the developer to perform fast, easy, and frequent quick checks along the course of implementation with the help of so-called **REPL** covered in the next section.

Using REPL and the explorative programming style

REPL stands for **Read-Evaluate-Print Loop** (https://en.wikipedia.org/wiki/Read%E 2%80%93eval%E2%80%93print_loop) and represents a manner of program development that quite deviates from what old-style C# programmers were used to, namely *edit source code – build the compiled program version – run and debug loop*. From its very early days, F# has introduced **interactive development manner** (https://docs.microsoft.com/en-us/dotne t/articles/fsharp/tutorials/fsharp-interactive/index). However, more broadly, it equips the F# developer with just another programming style collectively referred to as **exploratory programming** (https://en.wikipedia.org/wiki/Exploratory_programming). F# offers a tool known as **F# Interactive** (32-bit `fsi.exe` or 64-bit-capable `fsiAnyCPU.exe`) both as a standalone, or as a part of Visual Studio reachable from any F# Project. It allows you to evaluate any F# expression presented in the form of a standalone F# script or just a selected F# program fragment in a dynamically built run-time environment.

F# Interactive is a tool of immense versatility. Its use cases span a quick check of just implemented one-liner function behavior to running F#-implemented microservices in the production environment. Yes, I'm not kidding; the quality of the F# Interactive compiler is pretty much the same as that of normal build compiler. At one time, the whole Jet.com microservices architecture was implemented as a set of F# scripts, each executed by a dedicated `fsi` process.

The habit of doing quick checks while developing any F# code by evaluating this or that fragment in `fsi` may significantly help in achieving practically bug-free F# implementations. I highly recommend that you acquire and follow F# explorative programming style in your day after day practice.

Addressing some compile-time problems

Although REPL can help explore and tweak correct F# code, it keeps compiler errors intact, as evaluating a code snippet includes compilation by the F# compiler embedded into `fsi`. And I must admit that some compile-time errors may puzzle an inexperienced F# developer. Here, I will analyze several kinds of such errors and provide advice on how to get rid of them. Before I do this, you should keep in mind that because an initial defect usually gets ingested by type inference as correct code, the reported compilation error is in line with that convoluted type inference determination. That is, type inference often masks the authentic cause of an error. We will go over some occasions of this layout soon.

The if-then return value

One of the easiest-to-grasp occurrences of the similar convoluted determination takes place for the result type of F# `if...then...` expressions. Usually, it seems counterintuitive that this result cannot be anything but `unit`. Let's look at why this happens.

In the following snippet, I chose the specific (<) comparison operator within the implementation just to keep things simple (`Ch13_1.fsx`):

```
let f a b =
    if a < b then
        a
    else
        b
```

Here, the inferred signature of function f representing the result of evaluating the F# expression if-then-else is f: 'a -> 'a -> 'a (requires comparison), which makes perfect sense (it should not take much effort to recognize a generic implementation of the min function in the preceding code).

Now let's look at what happens if I omit the else part (Ch13_1.fsx):

```
let f' a b =
    if a < b then
        a
```

Now the inferred signature of f' is f': unit->unit->unit; in other words, both arguments and the result must be of type unit. What gives? The reasoning behind the seemingly counterintuitive type inference outcome is, in fact, to continue making perfect sense. Let's think what value the function f' must return when the condition a < b is false? The compiler, in the absence of explicit directions, decides that it must be unit. But wait a minute; shouldn't both branches of the if-then-else expression be of the same type? This condition can be only fulfilled if argument a is of type unit, which means argument b must be of type unit as well.

Fine; but what would happen if I try to push type inference into certain ways, for example, forcefully attempting a to be of generic type 'a (Ch13_1.fsx):

```
let f'' (a:'a) b =
    if a < b then
        a
```

Or, what if we try pushing a in the direction of being less generic by forcing it to be of a concrete type, for example, int (Ch13_1.fsx):

```
let f''' (a:int) b =
    if a < b then
        a
```

Turns out both attempts are futile, as consideration about the unit return type of the omitted else branch is still valid. In the first case, the compiler will just make a nasty warning pointing that

> *This construct causes code to be less generic than indicated by the type annotations. The type variable* 'a *has been constrained to be type* 'unit'.

In the second case, from a compiler standpoint, there's a plain and simple error

> *This expression was expected to have type unit but here has type* `int`.

So, how should we handle the `if...then...` expressions? The moral is that this short form of conditional statement may be used only in cases where a side-effect is needed. Good examples would be logging some diagnostics or changing a mutable value. For cases where a genuine non-`unit` result has to be returned, the full-blown `if-then-else` expression must be evaluated with both branches returning values of the same type.

Value restriction

This compile problem usually makes intermediate level F# developers who have grasped and proudly put to use F# features such as *partial application* and *automatic generalization* stumble. Imagine that you came out with a powerful data processing algorithm and are implementing it, enjoying the power and beauty of idiomatic F# code in the process. At some moment, you realize that you need a function that takes a list of lists and finds out whether all element lists are empty or not. Not a problem for a seasoned functional programmer like you, right? So you coin something like this (`Ch13_2.fsx`):

```
let allEmpty  = List.forall ((=) [])
```

Surprise! It does not compile with the compiler warning:

> *Value restriction. The value* `'allEmpty'` *has been inferred to have generic type*
> `val allEmpty : ('_a list list -> bool) when '_a:equality`
> *Either make the arguments to* `'allEmpty'` *explicit or, if you do not intend for it to be generic, add a type annotation.*

And you (I should admit I did this on multiple occasions in the past) first stare at this mess in disbelief as the F# compiler has accurately inferred your intent but somehow dislikes it. Then you Google "f# value restriction" and get referred to **MSDN Automatic Generalization** (`https://docs.microsoft.com/en-us/dotnet/articles/fsharp/language-reference/generics/automatic-generalization`), where you are told that:

> *The compiler performs automatic generalization only on complete function definitions that have explicit arguments, and on simple immutable values.*

This is followed by practical recipes of working around a sudden problem. You try this advice and get the problem fixed, but you are left with the aftertaste of some black magic.

For me, the eye-opener was reading through this excellent blog post: **Finer Points of F#**
Value Restriction (`https://blogs.msdn.microsoft.com/mulambda/2010/05/01/finer-po`
`ints-of-f-value-restriction/`). I will demonstrate the hidden dangers of generalization
applied to mutable values that may create a motive for you to read this blog post and
understand the rationale behind the F# compiler behavior.

Let's look at a seemingly innocuous code fragment here (`Ch13_2.fsx`):

```
let gr<'a> : 'a list ref = ref []
gr := ["a"]
let x: string list = !gr
printfn "%A" x
```

Guess what would be the printed `x` value upon this fragment execution? That would be
`["a"]`, right?

Wrong; `[]` is what happens! The cause of this is that `gr`, despite appearing as a value of
type `'a list ref`, is, in fact, a type function. Used on the left-hand side of the `:=` operator,
it just brings a fresh unbound reference instance. Used on the right-hand side of operator `!`,
it brings just another fresh reference instance that refers to an empty list, `[]`. In order to
achieve the intuitively expected behavior, we need to bind `gr` applied to the type argument
string to the concrete typed variable `cr`, and then the latter, being a normal reference, will
behave as expected (`Ch13_2.fsx`):

```
let cr = gr<string>
cr := ["a"]
let y = !cr
printfn "%A" y
```

Now the printed value is `["a"]` indeed. Imposing a value restriction error in all cases
where the situation deviates from the safest use case compiler protects developers from the
surprise code behavior of the kind demonstrated earlier. Getting back to my initial sample,
the possible remedial action can be any of the following (`Ch13_2.fsx`):

```
let allEmpty xs = List.forall ((=) []) xs // remedy 1
let allEmpty : int list list -> bool  = List.forall ((=) [])
// remedy 2
let allEmpty = fun x -> List.forall ((=) []) x // remedy 3
```

Imperfect pattern matching

Many seemingly counterintuitive F# compile-time errors and warnings belong to the field of pattern matching. For example, take a look the following naive detection of the integer argument sign:

```
let positive = function
| x when x > 0 -> true
| x when x <= 0 -> false
```

Despite seeming completeness, this produces the compiler's warning:

incomplete pattern matches on this expression

Turns out that the F# compiler, if presented with the when guards, assumes that this construction designates an incomplete match case by definition. This is why regardless of the fact that the given set of cases is semantically complete, the compiler considers the function definition incomplete. Simply removing the excessive last when guard immediately fixes the problem (Ch13_3.fsx):

```
let positive' = function
| x when x > 0 -> true
| _ -> false
```

Another common related problem is unreachable matching rules. Most of the time, unreachable matching rules get into play when the programmer mistakenly uses a variable instead of a literal in the sequence of rules, creating a premature catch-all case. In such cases, the compiler uses benign warnings, although almost always, the run-time results are messed-up. Therefore, perhaps denoting these occasions as errors would be a better design choice. A couple of years ago I wrote a **blog post** (https://infsharpmajor.wordpress.com/2011/10/13/union-matching-challenge/) on this matter, which I reproduce here as the illustration of the problem in the following snippet (Ch13_3.fsx):

```
type TickTack = Tick | Tack

let ticker x =
    match x with
    | Tick -> printfn "Tick"
    | Tock -> printfn "Tock"
    | Tack -> printfn "Tack"
ticker Tick
ticker Tack
```

This may trick you into expecting the `Tick` output followed by `Tack`, but in fact, the `Tick` output is to be followed by `Tock`!

The F# compiler issues two warnings for the preceding fragment. The first warning prompts you that typo `Tock` is taken as a variable and not a literal, like literals of type `TickTack` in two other cases:

> *Uppercase variable identifiers should not generally be used in patterns, and may indicate a misspelt pattern name*

The second warning:

> *This rule will never be matched*

directly indicates the outcome caused by the typo.

The moral here is that the F# developer should be attentive to warnings. Treating rule unreachability by the compiler as an error would be more adequate perhaps.

Addressing run-time problems

The mantra "*if it compiles, it works*" helps followers score amazingly well in time-to-market ratings for enterprise software development.

Taking Jet.com as an example of building green field e-commerce platform implementation, it has really condensed the path from zero to **minimum viable product** (**MVP**) in less than a year. Release of the platform to the production mode took place in a bit more than a year from the reception.

Does this mean following a functional-first approach is a software development silver bullet? Surely not on an absolute scale, although on a relative scale, the improvements are just great.

Why is the success not exhaustive? The thing is that the practice requires transition from gory ideas to mundane implementation issues. No matter how accurate our implementations are, there are always dark corners exist where unexpected problems may lurk.

Let me demonstrate this with a sample taken from F# enterprise development practice at Jet.com. Jet represents an innovative e-commerce platform, bringing together many business areas, such as Internet ordering, retail selling, warehousing, finance, accounting, transportation, you name it. Each of these areas usually carries its own unique metadata classifications; so, in order to run them side by side, one of the most common operations within the implementation is mapping. And the generally accepted practice of using unique non-clashing identifications is based on GUIDs or **Global Unique Identifiers** (https://en. wikipedia.org/wiki/Globally_unique_identifier).

Realistically assuming that quite frequently, enterprise software deals with dictionaries and caches using GUIDs as access keys, let's look at how good the core .NET library System.Guid implementation for the purpose would be.

Here goes a quite simplistic explorative implementation using a dictionary that has instances of the System.Guid type as keys. I created a simple dictionary based on the standard F# core library implementation having type IDictionary<Guid,int>. I populated it with the size number of pairs (Guid, int), just for the sake of simplicity. Now, I will imitate a big trials number of random accesses to the dictionary using array keys as a level of indirection and measuring the performance. The following snippet shows the composition of the required code pieces (Ch13_4.fsx):

```
open System
open System.Collections.Generic
let size = 1000
let keys = Array.zeroCreate<Guid> size
let mutable dictionary : IDictionary<Guid,int> =
    Unchecked.defaultof<IDictionary<Guid,int>>
let generate () =
    for i in 0..(size-1) do
        keys.[i] <- Guid.NewGuid()
    dictionary <- seq { for i in 0..(size-1) -> (keys.[i],i) } |> dict
generate()
let trials = 10000000
let rg = Random()
let mutable result = 0
for i in 0..trials-1 do
    result <- dictionary.Item(keys.[rg.Next(size-1)])
```

Running this snippet through FSI with timing turned on yields the performance indicators shown in the following screenshot (only the valuable output is shown for brevity):

Using native System.Guid to access a dictionary

10 million accesses for 6.445 seconds translates into a bit higher than 1.5 million accesses per second. Not too fast. Let's take it for the baseline. Also, a worrying sign is a number of garbage collections that took place: 287 per 10000 accesses is not light.

Without digging dipper into the causes of the observed code behavior here, let me just show the results of the findings performed for Jet.com in an attempt to improve the watermark. I will introduce a simple change instead of using the genuine System.Guid type that is a quite complicated Windows system data structure as a dictionary key, I will use the representation of the GUID value as a hexadecimal string that is leftover when the canonical presentation is stripped of dashes. For example, the f4d1734c-1e9e-4a25-b8d9-b7d96f48e0f GUID will be represented as a f4d1734c1e9e4a25b8d9b7d96f48e0f string. This will require minimal changes to the previous snippet (Ch13_4.fsx):

```
let keys' = Array.zeroCreate<string> size
let mutable dictionary' : IDictionary<string,int> =
    Unchecked.defaultof<IDictionary<string,int>>
let generate' () =
```

```
for i in 0..(size-1) do
    keys'.[i] <- keys.[i].ToString("N")
dictionary' <- seq { for i in 0..(size-1) -> (keys'.[i],i) } |> dict
generate'()
for i in 0..trials-1 do
    result <- dictionary'.Item(keys'.[rg.Next(size-1)])
```

Here, I will just create a new `keys'` indirection layer made from corresponding parts of `keys` via a simple data conversion. Turning to FSI with this change brings a big surprise reflected in the following screenshot:

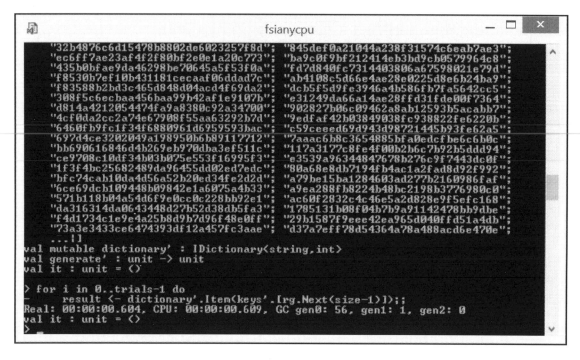

Switching from System.Guid to string in order to access a dictionary

Compared to the baseline, the new access rate constitutes 16.4 millions accesses per second almost 11 times better! Also, garbage collection experiences a five-fold improvement.

Now remember that mappings based on `System.Guid` are ubiquitous for the platform and you can imagine the amount of impact from the above simple change to the overall platform performance.

Summary

This chapter should leave you prepared for the defect type displacement taking place in the functional-first development in comparison to other development paradigms. A decreased rate of run-time errors typical to F# code shortens the time to market for developed systems and releases development resources for performance optimizations if they are deemed necessary.

We have reached the end of the book, where I equipped you with a whole slew of patterns of idiomatic F# use. The key assumption that the book makes is that such use requires from developers that come from other programming paradigms a certain shift in thinking habits, a distinct angle of seeing problems, and correspondent patterns and techniques populating the functional programmer tool belt. At this point you should be able to approach thinking through any problem by decomposing it into a handful of known building blocks and then composing the solution with appropriate functions and combinators. You also were shown the benefits of using standard F# algebraic data types over crafting custom .NET classes. Rely on patterns that you have acquired here in your functional designs; retain, recall, and reuse them in your day-to-day practices.

I hope that this book may guide you onto a path to the field of idiomatic functional programming. Good luck getting there!

Index

Made in the USA
San Bernardino, CA
23 January 2019